Egypt's
Political
Economy

Defn of Property regimes
        & power relations

Intro:

Setting up the Diss

- Eco Dev
- Property regimes (som)
- Issuing Policies (som)

Nasser (Statism)
Sadat (Infitah)
Mubarak — n-l

Nasser (Som)
Sadat
Mubarak

compared to
some general patter
of political policies
(new penalty)

Empirically strong
especially on
1990 – 2005
period –

Theoretically – weak
role of the state
1805 – 2005

Egypt's Political Economy

Power Relations in Development

Nadia Ramsis Farah

The American University in Cairo Press
Cairo • New York

First published in Egypt in 2009 by
The American University in Cairo Press
113 Sharia Kasr el Aini, Cairo, Egypt
420 Fifth Avenue, New York 10018
www.aucpress.com

Copyright © 2009 by Nadia Ramsis Farah

All rights reserved. No part of this publication may be reproduced, stored in a retrieval system, or transmitted in any form or by any means, electronic, mechanical, photocopying, recording, or otherwise, without the prior written permission of the publisher.

Dar el Kutub No. 11465/08
ISBN 978 977 416 217 6

Dar el Kutub Cataloging-in-Publication Data

Farah, Nadia Ramsis

       Egypt's Political Economy: Power Relations in Development / Nadia Ramsis Farah.—

  Cairo: The American University in Cairo Press, 2008
       p.cm.
       ISBN 977 416 217 X
       1. Economics—Egypt I. Title
       330.962

1 2 3 4 5 6 7 8 14 13 12 11 10 09

Designed by Sally Boylan
Printed in Egypt

Contents

Introduction	**1**
Power Relations	4
Power Relations in Development: A Theoretical Explanation	5
The State, Power Relations, and the Economy	6
Democracy, Power Relations, and Regime Type	8
Religion, Ideology, and Power Relations	10
Gender, the State, and Power Relations	12
1. The Role of the State in Development	**17**
The State and Development: The Theoretical Controversy	19
Historical Review of the Role of the Egyptian State in Development (1805–1952)	25
The Nasserist Experiment in State-led Development (1952–70)	30
Economic Liberalization and the Emergence of a Rentier Economy (1974–91)	37
Economic Reform and Structural Adjustment Policies (1991–2005)	41
The Neoliberals and Their Reform Agenda	48
Egypt: A Developmental State?	52
2. The State, Democracy, and Development	**53**
The Relationship between Democracy and Development	54
The Seeds of Liberalism: From Muhammad 'Ali to the British Invasion of Egypt	61
Restricted Liberalism and the Emergence of an Industrial Elite (1923–52)	65
Authoritarianism, Nationalism, and State Autonomy (1952–76)	71

v

vi   Contents

Restricted Political Liberalization, the State, and the
Emergence of a New Capitalist Class (1976–91)   77
Steps toward Democracy: The Consolidation of the
Capitalist Class and the Gradual Retreat of the State
from Its Developmental Role (1991–2005)   80
Egypt: A Hybrid Regime?   85

3. Politicized Religion, Conflict, and Development: 87
The Islamists and the State

Religion and Development: Theoretical Approaches   88
Nationalism and Islamism: The Case of Egypt   95
The Transition Crisis, the State, and the Use of
Politicized Islam as State Ideology (1970–2005)   112

4. Gender and Development: Women's Rights,   123
State, and Society

Gender Inequalities and Development   123
The Role of the State in the Determination
of Gender Inequalities   130
Gender Relations and Development in Egypt   135

Notes   **153**
Bibliography   **173**
Index   **189**

Introduction

This study deals with the unfolding of the great political and economic transformations of the modern state of Egypt, from the appointment of Muhammad 'Ali as *wali* (governor) in 1805 to the period of President Mubarak.

The aim of this study is to investigate the role of power relations in economic and political development or transformation by tracing the development of the modern state in Egypt (1805–2005), but also by focusing on the period 1990–2005. This latter period witnessed a more rigorous implementation of structural adjustment policies; the acceleration of economic privatization and liberalization; the emergence of a group of neoliberals within the ruling National Democratic Party (NDP) who favored free-market rules and the withdrawal of the state from the economy; and the consolidation of business interests and representation in both parliament and government. Structural adjustment policies were implemented largely under pressures from the International Monetary Fund and the World Bank to deepen the privatization and economic liberalization process. Hirst claims that the reforms expanded and entrenched poverty while cementing the power of the business elites.[1] This resulted in a generalized economic crisis that weakened the middle class and created an elite that was nurtured and protected by the state.

These business elites replaced the bureaucratic elites of 1956–90 as a source of vital and important support to the ruling regime, in addition to replacing "the traditional political elites, the armed forces and the security

1

2   Introduction

apparatus."[2] Alterman claims that for the first time since 1952, the government has abandoned all pretence of populism and that the configuration of power is tilted solidly toward a tiny elite.[3] In order to consolidate the hegemony of the new elites, the alliance between the state and the new business elites was promoted and strengthened by a group of neoliberals within the ruling National Democratic Party. In 2003 and 2004, the NDP's Policy Secretariat, headed by Mr. Gamal Mubarak, prepared a number of so-called reform policy papers to restructure the economic, political, and social systems.[4] This restructuring aimed at cementing the power of the new business elites by expanding their integration into the political system and by welding them to the centers of power. In 2004 a new cabinet (under Prime Minister Ahmad Nazif) was formed to carry out these changes. In 2005 the parliamentary elections brought a great number of businessmen (more than seventy-five), who ran as NDP candidates, to the legislative chamber. Another Nazif cabinet was formed after the 2005 elections to deepen the proposed reforms. The new cabinet appointed a large number of businessmen as ministers, claiming that their expertise in the private sector was particularly necessary for the successful implementation of the proposed reforms.

In addition to consolidating the power of the new business elites, the end of this period also witnessed a limited attempt at political liberalization and the introduction of some constitutional amendments. In 2005, President Hosni Mubarak amended article 76 of the constitution. The amendment introduced, for the first time in Egypt's history, the concept of presidential elections, instead of the usual referendum held every five years, where the dominant party (the President's) nominated a single candidate. The state also allowed a high degree of freedom of speech, especially in the press and to a lesser degree in radio and television.

During the 1990–2005 period, the state maintained a version of Islam as a dominant ideology. This ideology had been introduced in the 1970s by President Anwar Sadat, who was forced to abandon nationalist ideologies in order to build his own social base. The 1970s witnessed the emergence of policies of economic liberalization designed to reintegrate Egypt into the international economic system. To ease the transition from the Nasserists' so-called socialist system to a more open market economy, the state allied itself with Islamists and actively sought the establishment of Islamist groups in universities, syndicates, and factories as a counter to Nasserists and leftists. This led the state to adopt a politicized Islamic

Introduction 3

ideology in order to discredit its foes and solidify its social base. In doing so, Sadat's regime reversed a long trend of nationalist ideologies (both Egyptian and Arab) that had emerged in the second half of the nineteenth century and held sway up to the beginning of the 1970s. Each of these ideologies was pursued to achieve the following:[5]

- build a social base for the ruling elites;
- mold the elites' factions into a cohesive group;[6]
- restrict political opposition; and
- downplay class conflicts under the banner of the encompassing ideology of Nation or Islamic *umma* (nation).

The adoption of the policies of economic liberalization and limited political liberalization, and the adoption of political Islam as a dominant ideology, have all had an impact on the status of women. On the one hand, women suffered from a higher degree of marginalization in the economic and political spheres, but, on the other, women's organizations succeeded in advancing a number of legal reforms that have in theory improved the status of women in Egypt. The role of the state in the determination of gender inequalities hinges on the interplay of complex factors. For one thing, the choice of development and economic strategy influences the balance of power between the genders by maintaining, increasing, or decreasing inequalities. It is my contention, however, that gender inequalities in Egypt are rooted in a personal status law (family law) that codifies unequal power relations. Regardless of attempts to modernize and secularize Egyptian society from the beginnings of the nineteenth century, the basic principles of the family code have not changed except in the most marginal ways.

Therefore, in this study I argue that it is power relations that have been a prime cause in the unfolding of Egypt's trajectory during the last two centuries. Modernization did not lead to a complete transformation of the country's economy and society. A pattern of uneven development characterized and continues to characterize the Egyptian system. While certain economic and social sectors have on the whole been modernized, the largest sectors are still dominated by traditional forces. This path of uneven development has led to the fragmentation of social forces, including the fragmentation of the elites themselves. For an elite to impose its interests on other elites and on society as a whole, it has to succeed in forging alliances with non-elites, that is, with social forces outside the immediate ruling system. In this sense, power relations, their

4   Introduction

articulation, and the way they have managed to impose the hegemony of factions within certain elites have determined the trajectory of the modernization process in Egypt over the last two centuries.

Power Relations

Barry Hindess presents two major definitions of power: power as capacity and power as relation. Power as capacity is said to be the ability to pursue one's objectives, and it involves the concept of domination. This is because power relations are by definition unequal between those who employ power to attain their objectives and those who are subject to such power. Power as relation, on the other hand, refers to actions that affect the actions of others, rather than power as a direct form of coercion.[7] This definition of power as relation derives from the concept of power advanced by Foucault. For Foucault, power relations are not simply relations of coercion but may be productive. Power as relation does not simply refer to the power of coercion and the use of violence but is the ability to act on the actions of others. Power, then, presupposes freedom and the potential for refusal.[8] In this sense power does not necessarily result in the removal of freedom or choice. Power can be productive in the sense that it may empower others to act as autonomous and independent decision-makers.

On the other hand, C. Wright Mills claims that institutions are the locus of power. It is the institution, which grants individuals in certain positions decision-making power over the use and distribution of that institution's resources, that endows these individuals with the power they exercise over others.[9]

Power, therefore, is fragmented, among individuals holding key institutional positions in society. This applies to economic power, political power, ideological power, and so on. Accordingly, Mills claims that:

> The power elite is composed of men . . . in positions to make decisions having major consequences . . . . They are in command of the major hierarchies and organizations of modern society. They rule the big corporations. They run the machinery of the state and claim its prerogatives. They direct the military establishment. They occupy the strategic command posts of the social structure, in which are now centered the effective means of the power and the wealth and the celebrity which they enjoy."[10]

Power Relations in Development: A Theoretical Explanation   5

Mills goes further, claiming that the hierarchies of state, corporations, and armies constitute the means of power. He adds that in American society major national power resides in the economic, political, and military domains.[11]

Poulantzas rejects the institutional explanation of power. Power for Poulantzas is a structured relationship between classes. It is not an attribute of institutions and organizations.[12] However, Poulantzas, while anchoring power relations in the economic structure, recognizes that there might be dislocations between economic, political, and ideological structures. Such dislocations might lead at certain times to the domination of the political structure over the other structures of society. In the case of the domination of the political structure, political power relations determine to a large degree access to the country's economic resources and their benefits. Ideological interpellations are used by power elites to impose their domination on other elites' factions and on other classes.[13]

In this book, I adopt a structural approach to examining power relations in developing nations. I contend that it is the political structure that is the dominant structure in third world social systems and that power relations, particularly between elite factions, are responsible for the development of the economy, democracy, the ruling elite's ideology, and gender relations.

Power Relations in Development: A Theoretical Explanation

Most third world countries have gone through three major phases of development:

1. A primary product export-oriented growth phase;
2. An internally oriented industrialization phase (import-substitution strategy); and
3. A re-internalization phase, where the national economy is reintegrated into the international economic system, and where industrialization is pursued not necessarily for the satisfaction of internal demand but for promotion of exports (export-oriented strategy).

The change from one development phase to another is usually the outcome of dominant power relations, the way these relations are modified and restructured in response to changes in the international economic system, and/or changes in domestic development policies and strategies.

6   Introduction

The periodization of third world development is crucial in the demarcation of different phases.[14] The end of each phase of development is signaled by symptoms of exhaustion, that is, the inability of a certain development phase to maintain sustained economic growth. Exhaustion usually results in structural strains, destabilizing social relations and threatening the dominant power relations. In many cases periods of structural change erupt in political conflict. Conflict is a symptom of disequilibrium in the structure of dominant power relations, reflecting struggle among social groups. Resolution of the conflict lies in the ability of certain social groups to impose their interests on the society as a whole. This requires a restructuring of dominant power relations. To a large degree, the forms that such re-equilibrations of power relations take determine the characteristics of the new socioeconomic order, the type of state, the degree of political liberalization, the dominant ideology, and the place of minorities in the system, particularly women.

The state itself is a social relation that reflects the actual configuration of relative power relations.[15] As such, the state plays a determining role in economic development, the degree of political liberalization, forms of dominant political ideologies, and varying structures of social inequalities, which may derive as much from unequal power relations as from inequalities of income.

The State, Power Relations, and the Economy

The state as social relation determines to a large degree the process and the strategies of economic development. While neoliberal theory claims that the state should not intervene in the economy, a large literature of development studies demonstrates that the state, not as institution but as social relation, that is, as an actor among other social actors, usually intervenes in the development process.

State intervention might lead to rapid economic growth or to stagnation, according to the dominant power alliance determining state type. Peter Evans distinguishes three forms of state: predatory, intermediate, and developmental.[16] The predatory state is controlled by a political elite that is bent on fulfilling its own interests even at the expense of the interests of society as a whole. An inefficient state bureaucracy that helps facilitate the plunder of a country's economy by the ruling elite usually runs the state. The intermediate state has built a certain administrative capacity. Still, the structures of such a state are mostly fragmented and can be penetrated by different interest groups. The developmental state, on the other hand, has a well-developed bureau-cracy, recruited on merit, with a high capacity to perform all functions required to further economic development. While this bureaucracy is relatively autonomous from interest groups, it maintains close ties with large private corporations; that is, it is embedded in selected social net-works, particularly industrial networks.[17] However, a state can demonstrate aspects of both a developmental state and a predatory state. The two types are not mutually exclusive.

The relative autonomy of the developmental state from dominant classes and class factions is vital to the economic transformation of soci-ety.[18] State autonomy is an important requirement if the state is to cease supporting inefficient and rent-seeking industries.[19]

According to Evans, the developmental efficacy of a state is limited by the emergence of strong social groups, which, over time, penetrate the state, thus eroding its autonomy; the relative autonomy of the state is therefore time-bound.[20] The post-developmental state might retain a competent and embedded bureaucracy, but it loses its relative auton-omy in the long run. With economic growth, capital and labor are strengthened and eventually relative state autonomy weakens consider-ably. Polidano disputes that autonomy requires bureaucratic competence and the embeddedness of the bureaucracy in important social networks. If that were the case, both the United States and the United Kingdom, which have competent bureaucracies embedded in social networks would qualify as developmental states. He contends that the experience of some countries in Northern Asia demonstrates that state autonomy in post-developmental states is still an important component of state capacity, allowing it a high degree of freedom in setting growth targets, in withdrawing support from inefficient industries, and in determining consumption and therefore savings and investments.[21]

State autonomy might take the form of total autonomy from all social forces in society, a rare occurrence, or relative autonomy, where the state, while connected to some social forces, maintains a degree of autonomy from all forces. Even if the actual configuration of power relations is more amenable to the realization of the interests of some social groups, this does not mean that the state is simply the tool of these groups. To impose certain economic policies, the state has to balance societal inter-ests in order to maintain regime stability. Regime stability is an important requirement for the pursuit of long-term economic strategies. Otherwise, even in the most authoritarian states, the less dominant

8   Introduction

social forces might resort to violence to overturn a system that is inimical to its interests. Therefore, it is necessary to trace the historical development of these power relations to determine the configuration leading to growth or stagnation. These power relations also determine the degree of political liberalization.

Democracy, Power Relations, and Regime Type

While most research focuses on a simple causal relationship between democracy and economic growth, other research explains changes in regime type through a more complex analysis of stages of economic development, the maturation of social forces, and the interplay of power relations in the context of development. O'Donnell and Schmitter view transitions to democracy in less developed countries as the consequence of important divisions within the authoritarian regimes themselves, the interaction of elites, and the opposition of interests and strategies.[22]

The historical development of many third world countries demonstrates that inter-elite power conflict was the prime determining factor of the type of a country's political structure and the degree of its political liberalization. Inter-elite power relations determine to a large extent the struggle for democratization; such conflict does not stop at the level of domestic elites. In many instances, it is the conflict between national elites and foreign elites that forces national elites to form alliances with other classes in society, particularly the middle class, in order to protect their own interests against the power of foreign elites.

A number of comparative historical studies extend the O'Donnell and Schmitter thesis by analyzing regime types through changes in economic structures and concomitant changes in class differentiation and power relations. A pioneering study, which adopts the comparative historical approach, is that of Rueschemeyer et al.,[23] who contend that democracy is possible only if there is a strong institutional separation of politics from the system of inequality in society. Further, not only do power relations between state and society determine the relationship of capitalist development to democracy, but, in addition, democracy is possible only if based on significant changes in the distribution of power, specifically enlargement of the working classes, which makes it more difficult for elites to exclude them.

Accordingly, Rueschemeyer et al. advance a "Relative Class Power Model of Democratization." They argue that against the power of the dominant elites, the growth of a counter hegemony of subordinate classes, particularly the working class, is critical to the promotion of democracy. They consider classes to be shaped by the structure of capitalist economic production and its development. However, they maintain that different courses of economic development result in different class structures and that the international division of labor shapes dependent development and curtails the expansion of the working class.[24] Classes will support democracy if and only if they stand to gain from it.

This analysis by Rueschemeyer et al. seems to ground classes in the objective reality of the economic structure. However, the relationship between democracy and development, while depending on the development of the subordinate classes and especially on working class maturation and power, is conditional on the will of the classes that will benefit from democracy. But the thesis does not explain how the subordinate classes, and especially the working class, benefit from democracy, except through the act of revolution against authoritarian regimes.[25]

Evelyne Huber Stephens elaborates on the effect of dependent development on class formations and the crystallization of power relations in Latin America, using the advanced comparative historical approach.[26] Her main hypothesis is that "the nature of a country's integration into the world market (enclaves versus nationally controlled export sectors), the labor requirements of agriculture, the degree of subsidiary industrialization generated by the export sector, the process of consolidation of state power, the role of the state in shaping civil society, the class alliances to which the economic and social structures gave rise, along with the nature of political parties, strongly influence the dynamics of democratization."[27]

However, Huber Stephens does not postulate a unilinear relationship between the above-mentioned factors and democracy. "Some factors have contradictory consequences for democratization, some effects change over time, and the various factors interact over time."[28] She further argues that the way economic growth and patterns of dependence shape classes and class relations influences political change.

The historical analysis of democratic processes in South America demonstrates that where agriculture was the dominant sector in the economy, where agricultural products relying on intensive labor techniques formed a large percentage of exports, and where agriculture was dominated by domestic elites, openings for democracy were quite limited, if not unfeasible. Landowners obstructed unrestricted democracy

10   Introduction

for fear of losing control of labor, and they were successful in blocking demands for democratization by urban classes or groups.

Industrialization in South America in its import-substitution phase, while it enlarged the middle class, did not result in wide expansion of the working class; therefore, according to Rueschemeyer et al., no real pressures for democratization emerged under this pattern of industrialization. Contrary, however, to the thesis postulated by Rueschemeyer et al., the working classes did not play a major role in generating pressures for democratization in South America. The middle classes were the forces that agitated for political liberalization.

By contrast, Huber Stephens claims that enclave economies, especially in mining, facilitated the emergence of a labor force that could be organized. The alliance of this working class with the middle class opposed the owning oligarchy and provided potential for political liberalization.[29]

While this analysis has merit with respect to the relationships between types of economies, class structures, class alliances, and the potential for political liberalization, the stress on subordinate classes, especially the working class, as the main catalyst for political liberalization is overdone. Nevertheless, such a conceptual framework postulates the need for a long historical perspective focusing on power relations in society, relations between civil society and the state, and the effects of economic development and of transnational structures on internal power relations, as a means through which to understand the effects of class structure and class alliances on regime forms. The historical development of the economy, society, and polity in many developing countries demonstrates that inter-elite power struggles were the prime factor in the quest for political liberalization. In their power struggle, different elites use different ideologies to build their social bases and to weaken the opposition. One of the ideologies that the elites might use is a politicized form of religion.

Religion, Ideology, and Power Relations
Recent research attempts to establish causal relationships between religion and development. Mostly, that research tries to discover the direct impact of religion on values and attitudes that affect labor and the propensities to save and invest. Most empirical research finds that economic growth and development tend to reduce religiosity (as measured by church attendance and belief). But most importantly, the research shows that differences in composition of any one population among different religious dominations have little impact on economic growth.

However, the research neglects an important aspect of the relationship between religion and development: the politicization of religion, and its use as a tool for political domination and the imposition of the hegemony of certain elites on the socioeconomic system as a whole.

The use of politicized religion as ideology has emerged in the Middle East as a consequence of deep structural economic crises, but not every crisis triggers profound changes in the socioeconomic structure. A very special type of crisis, the so-called transition crisis, is capable of engineering deep fractures in economic paradigms, political structures, and ideological beliefs.[30] The transition crisis is symptomatic of deep structural changes in development processes and strategies, such as the move from an independent development strategy (import substitution) and a welfare state orientation to a free-market economy and an export-industrialization strategy. Development transition processes entail deep changes that affect social relations and restructure power relations.[31] Social groups may feel threatened by the process of structuration and restructuration of social and power relations entailed in these changes. If the changes threaten some social groups with loss of access to economic resources and benefits, especially if that access depends on relative power relations, violence can be expected to erupt between the competing groups. A transition crisis is not only an economic crisis: to effect the transition, dominant elites and opposition groups resort to specific ideologies to attract followers, and they combat other elites and groups by denigrating their ideologies. The use of religion as ideology gives these movements for change, whether by elites or the opposition, a religious character, and the movements calling for change can take the form of religious movements that appeal to and attract adherents on the basis of an identity shared by large segments of the population. The conflict between different social groups might erupt into violence clothed in religious rhetoric and take the form of what social scientists call religious fundamentalism.

One social group often much affected by a transition crisis is women. Women tend to be marginalized and are often used as a symbol of cultural authenticity to refashion power relations in society as a whole. Gender inequalities usually tend to increase during times of structural stresses and strains. The state, specific social groups, and civil society as a whole might use women's status as a card in political confrontations and the restructuration of power relations.

Gender, the State, and Power Relations

Gender inequalities are a symptom of unequal power relations between men and women. They permeate all societies, regardless of their stage of socioeconomic development. However, gender inequalities vary from one society to the other. A main determinant of gender inequalities is development, but gender inequalities are also, in turn, said to impact the course of development. Gender inequalities result from inequalities in access to and control of resources, inequalities in decision-making power, and unequal legal and political relations of power. These inequalities are perpetuated and sometimes accentuated by social and cultural norms, which, in turn, are shaped by families, schools, and religious and other institutions, as well as by a country's economic structure. Gender inequalities in employment and earning, especially in the context of neoliberal policies, which reduce the role of the state in promoting development and in extending social services, help perpetuate this state of affairs. The state itself, through its development strategies, economic policies, and welfare services, is partly responsible for maintaining or alleviating gender inequalities.

Many countries in the Middle East, including Egypt, have attempted to integrate women into the public sphere (education and employment) but have failed to change family laws that codify unequal power relations irrespective of their stage of development and modernization. For this reason, this study maintains that in these countries the perpetuation of gender inequalities is rooted in family laws. Most family laws or personal status laws in the region can be traced to the Islamic *fiqh* (legal) schools of the thirteenth century. Despite the attempts at modernization and secularization that began in some of the countries of the Middle East from the early nineteenth century, the basic principles of family codes did not change in any major way. Built on the concept of the complementarity of gender roles, rather than the concept of equality, the codes have enforced the perception of different gender roles within the family and have created a gender culture that is based on men's superiority and women's inferiority.

The traditional gender culture rooted in family codes is one of the major causes of the perpetuation of gender inequalities in all other spheres of society, such as inequalities in education, employment, political representation, decision-making, and so on. To achieve gender equality in the public sphere, the conceptual basis of personal status laws has to change from complementarity to equality.

The reluctance to secularize the personal status laws is due in part to the basically patriarchal culture of the elites, but it is also due to the fact that equal rights between the genders have been sacrificed to the requirements of political accommodation in periods of intense conflict between different factions of the elites. In order not to antagonize religious conservatives, the state has always left the area of family law to quasi-religious interpretations, which rely on tradition and custom and not necessarily on Islamic shari'a as such.

Caroline Moser does not view the state as an impartial or neutral agent in the constitution of gender relations within the family.[32] According to her, the state mediates relationships between men, women, and children and therefore has a critical role in liberating women from patriarchal domination. The state is also a condensation of power relations. If we define gender relations as power relations, then gender relations are part and parcel of the state. However, state policies will benefit more powerful groups at the expense of the less powerful, and the state will use different policies affecting gender relations in mediating conflicts and competing power interests. Thus, gender relations are often used by the state as a card in the wider game of power relations.

One of the major reasons behind the state's perpetuation and even reinforcement of unequal gender relations both in the public and the private spheres is the use or misuse of women's rights as a bargaining tool in power conflicts between political elites. Often, the rights of women have been jeopardized, or even threatened, as a result of a political conflict, either between national elites or between national and foreign elites, as part of a bargaining process or when the rights of women are said to be an integral part of cultural authenticity. In this case, women's rights become hostage to the relative power of competing elites to dominate the political system nationally, or to international pressures on the ruling elites. Clearly, the UN system's espousal of women's rights and the convening of international women's conferences have motivated certain countries in the third world to modify some of the laws pertaining to women's status, or to improve women's welfare in order to improve the country's status and image internationally. In Egypt, both internal and international power relations have impacted women's status but not necessarily in the same direction.

Taking the above theoretical framework as a broad guide, this book covers the following subjects. The first chapter, "The Role of the State in

Development," examines the theoretical controversy raging between the proponents of neoliberalism, who advocate the complete withdrawal of the state from the economy, and the proponents of the "developmental state," that is, a state that intervenes in underdeveloped economies to nurture a capitalist class that will later be able to carry out independently the functions of capital accumulation and development. An analysis of the economic role of the Egyptian state during the last two hundred years demonstrates that every time the state intervenes in the economy, the rate of economic growth increases rapidly. A reduction or cessation of state intervention usually results in a slower economy, high unemployment, and increasing poverty rates. Worth noting is the articulation of state intervention in the economy with periods of high state autonomy, that is, a situation in which the state is autonomous from the power of all social classes. This kind of state autonomy has occurred only twice in Egypt during the last two hundred years: under the Muhammad 'Ali state and during Nasser's time. State autonomy is not a permanent state of affairs, however, since eventually state autonomy erodes and diverse interest groups penetrate the state. In Egypt, erosion of state autonomy led ultimately to the domination of the system by special interest groups, a decline in the economic role of the state, and the deterioration of development.

The second chapter "The State, Democracy, and Development," examines the interrelationships between democracy and development. A new politicist trend in social sciences maintains that development is contingent on the existence of a prior democratic system. Traditional modernization and Marxist theories, on the other hand, have argued that a certain degree of development is a precondition to political liberalization. This study rejects these causal explanations of political liberalization. Political liberalization is, rather, the outcome of power relations between factions of elites, or between national and foreign elites. The history of parliamentarism in Egypt supports this assertion. When Khedive Isma'il attempted to resist foreign intervention in Egypt in the 1870s, he allied himself with the members of the Assembly of Delegates, established in 1866, to regain his independence from European powers. While the Assembly of Delegates had limited powers, its members refused the decree to abolish the Assembly issued by Isma'il in 1879 under pressure from the foreign creditors. On the other hand, the early 1970s witnessed intense competition between factions of the bureaucratic elites, which emerged during the 1960s within the confines of the Nasserist state. The resulting intense power conflict was resolved

Gender, the State, and Power Relations   15

through an internal coup d'état in May 1971, when Anwar Sadat eliminated the pro-Nasserist bureaucratic elites through arrests and lengthy periods of imprisonment.

The third chapter, "Politicized Religion, Conflict, and Development: The Islamists and the State," deals with the relationship between development and religion. A renewed interest in religion has spurred a spate of research that tries to establish a causal relationship between the two phenomena. In the case of Egypt, which was once ruled by the caliphate on a religious-political basis, the separation between religion and state has always been tenuous. Since the emergence of the modern state in the early nineteenth century, all political regimes in Egypt have used religion either as a dominant ideology and source for legislation or as a sub-ideology in periods when more secular regimes emerged. Egypt seems to be unable to decide which ideology and which form of state it should have. The vacillation between semi-secular and semi-religious state has been and still is a dominant characteristic of the Egyptian polity, although dominant power relations and the struggle between different factions of elites mostly determine this vacillation. The last thirty-five years have been marked by a strident religious ideology designed to justify the abolition of the Nasserist system and the reintegration of Egypt into the international economic system. The alliances between the state and Islamist political groups during the 1970s created the conditions for the disappearance of the secular nationalist trend that emerged with the 'Urabi revolt in the 1880s. During the last few years the regime has been attempting to curb the power of the Islamist groups, but still maintains religion as a political ideology in the face of mounting pressures from within and without to liberalize the political system. As long as the state is unable to steer the political ideology to secularism, the crisis between the state and the Islamists will continue, with dire consequences for the country as a whole.

The fourth and final chapter, "Gender and Development: Women's Rights, State, and Society," discusses the interrelationships between women's status and development. The classical approach asserts that higher economic growth rates tend to improve the status of women. A new approach adopted by the World Bank in the 1990s affirms that women's status affects the development process, that is, in order to accelerate economic growth, gender gaps have to be narrowed and women's status has to improve dramatically.[33] Nonetheless, a reduction of gender inequalities hinges on changes in gender power relations. The

Egyptian state, through its inability or unwillingness to change the personal status laws, based on a very conservative reading of the shari'a, has undermined the ability of women to gain equality. The perpetuation of unequal gender relations in the private sphere affects the theoretical equality of women in the public sphere. The status of women also represents a political card for successive regimes since Egypt's declaration of independence in 1922. The state has many times ignored issues relating to women's equality in order to mollify Islamist and conservative political groups, whether in confrontation or in alliance with them. In short, the amelioration of women's status does not depend on economic development alone but, more importantly, on the articulation of political power relations in society as a whole.

Finally, the examination of the role of the state in development, political liberalization, religious extremism, and gender relations in Egypt leads us to a major conclusion: that of the necessity to reshape dominant power relations in order for Egypt to solve its problems, perpetuated for the last two hundred years. Egypt has to identify once and for all its political identity, promote people-based development policies, and work hard to narrow social gaps in the socioeconomic system, especially gender gaps.

1

The Role of the State in Development

With the rise of neoliberalism in the mid-1970s, the collapse of the Soviet Union in the early 1990s, and the increasing globalization of international production and international trade, development strategies began to converge around the ideal of the free-market economy. The overwhelming new consensus (The Washington Consensus) is for the state to withdraw from the economy and to leave an unfettered market mechanism to determine production and income distribution.

The Washington Consensus threatens the survival of development theory itself. If the market is to reign supreme, there is no need for a development theory to foster economic growth in post-colonial countries. Development, in essence, requires the intervention of modernizing elites to restructure the traditional socioeconomic systems toward modernity and growth. Neoliberalism claims that both the state and development theory are dead.

The success of the newly industrialized countries tells a different story, however. East Asian, and more recently, Southern Asian, newly industrialized countries, while relying on the market mechanism, foreign direct investment, and the new international division of labor, demonstrate a strong role for the state in increasing economic growth and development. This new type of state, the developmental state, is one that creates, nurtures, and guides an efficient and capable capitalist class, which can carry the responsibility of rapid growth and development. This contrasts with the notion of the state as sole owner of the means of

18   The Role of the State in Development

production without the intermediary of a monitored and controlled capitalist class to carry out its designs.

Neoliberal theory regards the state as an institution managed by a bureaucracy that might interfere in the economy, playing havoc with the market mechanism. The proponents of the developmental state thesis, on the other hand, indicate that the state may play an important and sometimes necessary role in furthering the development process. One of the main characteristics of the developmental state is its relative autonomy from all social forces, although some instrumental explanations of the state regard the state as completely subsumed by ruling economic elites. Miliband contends that the ruling class in a capitalist society is the class that owns the means of production. By virtue of its economic power, the ruling class is able to use the state as an instrument of domination.[1] According to this view, the ruling elites tend to control the state by occupying key positions in its governmental, administrative, coercive, and other important apparatuses. Contrary to this interpretation of the state, the structuralists maintain that the state is a social relation reflecting the structure of power in society. The state is not simply the instrument of the ruling classes. Power relations between the dominant classes and other social forces are condensed, or brought together, in the state structure. In some instances, the state might obstruct the fulfillment of the immediate interests of the ruling elites in order to preserve their interests in the long run.[2] In this sense, the state's relative autonomy from the ruling classes is essential to the preservation of the capitalist system as a whole.

However, if the state is a social relation as propounded by the structuralists, it is also the site of a complex interplay of power relations. Power relations are not static. They tend to change according to the stage of a country's economic development and the maturation of social forces. This change is not automatic, however. In many instances, emerging social groups resort to violence to restructure existing power relations to weaken or even eliminate the power of hegemonic groups, whose interests, exemplified in the dominant economic structures and policies, have become an obstacle to further growth and development. During such periods, the state's autonomy increases and its ability to change economic policy and strategies is enhanced.

In Egypt, the role of the state has always been crucial in furthering the restructuration of economic and power relations required to create the conditions necessary for rapid growth and development. Two main experiments illustrate the vital role of state autonomy in furthering development: the Muhammad 'Ali (1805–49) and the Nasser (1952–70) experiments. The decline of state autonomy has usually resulted in long-term economic stagnation.

From the mid-1970s to the early 1990s, the state adopted an economic liberalization policy that did not bring about the desired developmental gains. In the early 1990s, with a staggering foreign debt, the state was forced to implement the recommended World Bank and IMF policies of economic reform and structural adjustment. The results have been far from satisfactory. Long periods of slow economic growth and high unemployment, and periods of high inflation have marred the last twenty-five years. The Egyptian capitalist class, while subsidized by the state, does not seem to be able to promote growth and development. The withdrawal of the state from the economy and the inability of the Egyptian government to play the role of a developmental state are the main reasons for the lackluster performance of Egypt's economy.

The State and Development: The Theoretical Controversy

The authors of an important World Bank Policy Research Paper contend that since the 1960s the World Average Annual Per Capita Gross Domestic Product has been declining. East Asia had witnessed the highest growth rates, followed by South Asia. On the other hand, Latin America, Sub-Saharan Africa, and the Middle East experienced their highest growth during the 1960s and the 1970s. Since then, these three regions' growth has been declining, although some countries of the Middle East and Latin America regained some momentum during the 1990s. The highest growth rates were in East and South Asia, with China the undisputed front-runner. "In Latin America, 15 out of 17 countries on the continent experienced negative growth rates in the 1980s. Chile and Columbia were the exceptions."[3]

It is remarkable that most developing economies have experienced either very low or negative growth rates during the last two decades. This might be the result of neoliberal strategies and of structural adjustment policies. Structural adjustment policies have been imposed on heavily indebted countries in the developing world in order to reduce foreign balance deficits and thereby enable these countries to repay their foreign debts. Further lending hinged on the adoption of Structural Adjustment Policies. The Bretton Woods Institutions, that is, the World Bank and the International Monetary Fund would abstain from giving the indebted

20 The Role of the State in Development

countries a clean bill of health, in other words, from declaring them to be creditworthy, if they did not restructure their economies away from protectionist policies of industrialization or import substitution industrialization. The most important aspect of structural adjustment policies is the adoption of free-market rules, but most significant of all is the withdrawal of the state from any activist role in the economy. Curbing of government expenditure, sale of public enterprises (privatization), floating of exchange rates, lifting of controls on capital movements, and liberalization of foreign trade are all aspects of structural adjustment.

Neoliberalism emerged as a response to the economic crisis of the 1970s, in turn triggered by the sharp increase in oil prices in the wake of the 1973 Arab-Israeli War. High inflation and unemployment were blamed on state intervention in the economy and the use of Keynesian policies, which aimed to achieve full employment. Neoliberal policies recommended: 1) tight monetary policies to fight inflation; 2) the reduction of government expenditures (including social welfare); and 3) the increase of interest rates to decrease fiscal deficits. Accordingly, labor markets were deregulated, public enterprises privatized, and international trade liberalized. Neoliberals claimed that their policies would lead to unprecedented economic growth and technological progress. International trade was hailed once again as the real engine of growth and neoliberals extended the application of their theory to developing countries.

This was in clear contradistinction to the main recommendations of the modernization theory that had dominated the development literature of the 1950s and 1960s. The proponents of that theory argued that less developed countries, kept behind by the dominance of the traditional economic structure, namely, that which is labor-intensive and based on subsistence rather than wealth accumulation, should pursue a modernization process that would proceed through successive stages to move their so-called traditional economies toward a fully fledged capitalist system. In the neoliberal approach, the state, led by a modernizing elite, would be responsible for reining in traditional forces and restructuring the economy away from the domination of traditional interests and into the path of modernization and fast economic growth; in other words, state intervention was imperative for the process of economic development. At the same time, the Economic Commission of Latin America, headed by Raoul Prebish, declared that for development to succeed, less developed countries needed to adopt an import substitution industrialization strategy to protect infant industries. Thus, the state had a crucial role in promoting industrialization and capital accumulation. Most developing economies adopted import-substitution industrialization during the 1960s and 1970s, achieving high levels of growth and development, with the state as the main engine of growth and development. However, the fiscal crisis of the 1970s, caused by spiraling oil prices, brought this strategy to a halt.

The neoliberals alleged that the dismal record of development in the second half of the 1970s was the outcome of import-substitution industrialization policies that gave the state a preeminent role in the economy. Developing countries should pursue export-led industrialization policies to benefit from the new globalized free economy. Restrictions on foreign direct investment should be lifted, and import-substitution policies should be abolished. Only an unfettered free-market system was capable of generating growth and development.

The neoliberals' claims rest on theoretical assumptions rather than empirical evidence. The main assumptions are: 1) Markets are self-regulating mechanisms; 2) If allowed to operate freely, the market efficiently utilizes all economic resources; and 3) Freely operating markets will lead to full employment. In the short run, the adoption of the free-market system by less developed countries might result in some disruptions. However, in the long run the market will optimize economic benefits. Therefore, developing countries should undergo what neoliberals call "shock therapy," an assault on all the institutions and practices that limit the free interplay of the market system.

In its extreme form, neoliberalism also contends that states and governments should not pursue policies designed to reduce income inequalities and/or alleviate poverty. Hayek, one of the main architects of neoliberalism, justifies this position by suggesting that social justice is meaningless.[4] Correct redistribution policies demand a knowledge of the needs, preferences, and goals of all the people, information impossible to obtain in any society. In the absence of this knowledge, government redistribution policies only succeed in circumventing the workings of the market mechanism, without achieving the goals of equity.

The dismal record of most developing economies in the last two decades is an outcome of the spread of neoliberalism as a development strategy. Contrary to the neoliberals' claims, the liberalization and globalization of markets, and especially the capital markets, did not accelerate economic growth in developing countries. On the contrary, it led to slower and more unstable growth in most regions of Latin America, Sub-Saharan

Africa, and the Middle East. The lack of a state role in furthering development and economic growth is the main problem for most developing nations. Only countries with strong developmental states have escaped the fate of economic stagnation and increased economic pauperization.

The neoliberals hailed East Asia's strong initial economic performance as an example of strong development based on the workings of the free market. By extolling the virtues of unbridled capitalism, the neoliberals disregarded the pioneering analysis by Chamlers Johnson of Japan's reconstruction and growth after the Second World War, which introduced the concept of the developmental state and its role in fomenting economic growth.[5] Amsden and Wade soon disabused free market proponents of their assertions by proving that the state in both South Korea and Taiwan played a strong interventionist role to promote industrialization and rapid development.[6] According to Evans, Skocpol, and Rueschemeyer, less developed countries lack the presence of a strong entrepreneurial class capable of restructuring the economy toward the desired goals of development and economic growth.[7] As the experience of late industrializers in Europe and the United States demonstrates, a certain degree of state intervention is necessary to promote growth and development.[8] Evans and others argue that in the case of the late developers, strong state intervention is essential to overcome the disadvantages of late development.[9] If the state simply implements the neoliberal program and waits around for an indigenous (non-existent) capitalist class to lead the development process, the result is bound to be a stunning failure.[10]

Kotz compares the experiences of Russia and China to demonstrate the crucial role of the state, especially in situations of transition from central planning to a free-market economy. The Russian state quickly implemented a broad neoliberal agenda, including immediate lifting of price controls, rapid privatization of the public sector, deep cuts in government spending, tight monetary policy, and liberalization of trade and capital. China, to the contrary, adopted a gradual and sometimes slow process for the lifting of price controls and the privatization of the state sector; it increased the money supply, raised government spending, kept tight control over foreign trade and capital movements, and kept the banking system under government control.[11] The results are well known. While Russia is still fighting to regain the economic standards that prevailed before the transition, China is one of the fastest-growing economies in recent history.

Nonetheless, not all types of state intervention in the economy lead to rapid industrialization and development. In fact, the type of state in question (see pages 6–8) determines the outcome of state intervention. It is the contention of this study that most states demonstrate a combination of the state types distinguished by Evans. Pure state types might be convenient for the theoretical demarcation of boundaries but rarely occur in reality. Alice Sindzingre goes further, claiming that the presence of cronyism or corruption in the developmental state does not necessarily lower economic growth rates if rents resulting from corruption are channeled into production.[12]

While the developmental state is embedded in selective social networks, a key aspect of such a state should be its relative autonomy from all social forces. I contend that in the case of Egypt, the autonomy of the state, whether relative or, in a very few instances, total, is the main explanatory variable of high levels of autonomous economic growth. When the state is enmeshed in external relations or embedded in the elites' social networks, it becomes relatively incapable of steering the economy and falls prey to special interests. I also contend that the role of the Egyptian state in economic development does not depend on its embeddedness in social networks. The emergence of strong special groups that penetrate the state apparatuses, whether economic or political, bend the state to their interests.

The history of modern Egypt (1805 to the present) reveals different forms of state intervention in the economy. From total control under the reign of Muhammad 'Ali, to minimal intervention between 1845 and the 1920s, to the development of an import-substitution strategy for industrialization that required state intervention to protect infant industries and which grew gradually from the 1920s and reached its peak under the Nasser regime (1957–73). Next came the economic liberalization of the 1970s, the attempts at integration into the international economic system with the adoption of structural adjustment policies in the 1990s, and then the emergence of neoliberals with their full belief in minimal state intervention and an accelerated pace of liberalization, privatization, floating exchange rates, lowering of income taxes and customs, and appointment of businessmen to positions of government and their increasing participation in parliament. And, finally, political liberalization, a trend that began in 2002 and resulted partly in the control of the state by private business interests, particularly under the second Nazif cabinet (2005).

In this long trajectory, the Egyptian economy realized rapid growth only when the state enjoyed complete autonomy under Muhammad 'Ali, and a high degree of relative autonomy under Nasser. In these two historical instances we can characterize the Egyptian state as a developmental state, but one that took upon itself the tasks of capital accumulation and development, a far cry from the experience of East Asia, where the state invited the creation of a separate capitalist class to carry out the work of development under its guidance. Under Muhammad 'Ali and Nasser, the state did not only target economic growth but aimed at a complete restructuration of the Egyptian economy and society. In both cases, the restructuration required the elimination of previous dominant elites that had shackled the economy and restrained its development; in other words it required a change of dominant power relations. The move to economic liberalization under Sadat also necessitated a change in dominant power relations, to ease the transformation from a system dominated by a state bureaucracy to a system that tried to nurture a new capitalist elite capable of leading the economy. This new capitalist elite was strengthened under the rule of President Mubarak, but did not come into its own as a social force until a few years ago. In 2003, the National Democratic Party (NDP) issued a number of policy papers purportedly aimed at reforming the socioeconomic system. The main policy changes seek to strengthen the private sector and serve the interests of the capitalist elites. Some of the reforms are an attempt to emulate the policies of the East Asian developmental states. The state in East Asia, however, has relative autonomy from big business, while big business dominated the Egyptian state cabinet in 2005. The latest cabinet includes six ministers who hail from the private sector and who have been handed portfolios that closely mirror their private-sector activities.[13]

State autonomy does not imply the relative autonomy of the state simply from internal social forces, but also from external forces and international power relations.[14]

Through the course of its modern history, the Egyptian state has tried the following strategies:[15]

1. The state replaces traditional elites and controls the economy. The Muhammad 'Ali state is a pure example of this strategy. The first years of the Nasser Regime (1952–60) also fall under this category;
2. The state actively nurtures a capitalist elite, in some case creating such an elite, and this is implemented through direct business

subsidy, the extension of cheap credit, the granting of licenses and contracts, and the blocking of competition. The import substitution policies of the liberal state in the period 1922–52 and the liberalization period 1974–91 fall into this category;

3. The state subsidizes the elites through the manipulation of state monetary and fiscal tools and by state investments in infrastructure. This model is exemplified by the period of the implementation of the Economic Reform and Structural Adjustment Policies, 1991–2005.

4. Where a substantial public sector exists, it might be used to subsidize the private sector by creating various channels for the appropriation, exploitation, and even pillage of public revenues and funds, or by selling public sector enterprises to elites at nominal prices. The pillage of the public sector began in the mid-1960s and continues to this date.

Historical Review of the Role of the Egyptian State in Development (1805–1952)
Muhammad 'Ali's Developmental State

The French, under the leadership of Napoleon Bonaparte, invaded Egypt in 1798. Ottoman forces came to Egypt in 1801 to fight the French. Muhammad 'Ali, a junior commander in the Albanian battalion of the Ottoman army, started to build alliances with the Egyptian elites of the time, especially the al-Azhar *ulama* (religious clergy), who were at the forefront of rebellion against the French troops. After the French left Egypt, a struggle for power emerged among the previous ruling elites: the Mamluks (slave warriors), who had more or less ruled Egypt since the twelfth century; the Ottoman empire, which wanted to regain hegemony over Egypt; and the Albanian battalion led by Muhammad 'Ali. Muhammad 'Ali succeeded in recruiting the support of the *ulama* for his appointment as the Ottoman viceroy of Egypt in 1805.

From 1805 to 1811, Muhammad 'Ali engaged in an all-out war against the Mamluks to strengthen his rule, a war that ended with the elimination of the leaders of the Mamluks in the famous Citadel event, when Muhammad 'Ali's forces disposed of Mamluk rule forever.[16] Becoming sole ruler of Egypt required that Muhammad 'Ali also rid himself of the *ulama* who had supported his bid for Egypt's rule, and through a mixture of intrigue, enforced exile, and imprisonment, he succeeded in quashing any would-be bid for a share of his power. To

26   The Role of the State in Development

consolidate his rule, Muhammad 'Ali opted for the building of a strong
military, capable of protecting his power and expanding it to the east
through the conquest of greater Syria and to the south by the conquest
of Sudan.

Muhammad 'Ali nationalized all agricultural land, a move aimed at
preventing the remaining Mamluks still empowered by the Ottoman
caliph to levy heavy taxes—the revenue of which was divided between
the caliph and the Mamluks themselves—from regaining their power by
rebuilding their military strength. Extensive new irrigation projects dou-
bled the amount of agricultural land. Experimentation in developing
new varieties of crops, including cotton, which later became Egypt's
main export commodity, and sugar cane, increased the variety of agricultural products. The peasants, who had usufruct rights, were obliged to
sell their products to the state commodity board at low prices. The state
then resold these products either internally or as exports at much higher
prices, and the profits were directed to the building of industries, particularly military industries.[17]

All industry was state owned. It covered a wide range, from textiles to
armaments and the building of a military navy later used for the military
invasion of Greater Syria and Sudan. The textile industry was protected
by bans on the import of cheap British textiles, while smaller industries
and guilds were crushed and workers subsequently forced to work for
state factories. All profits went to the state and were reinvested in the
expansion of agriculture and the industrial sector.

To administer the state monopolies, Muhammad 'Ali introduced a
modern education system to produce a bureaucracy capable of that
administration. And for the first time in thousands of years, Egyptians
were recruited as soldiers into the modern army built by Muhammad 'Ali.

It is possible to define Muhammad 'Ali's state as a totally autonomous
state. In due course, his habit of granting land to members of his family
and to some of his retainers led to the emergence of private property in
land, even if this represented a small proportion of state-owned land and
the owners were mostly of Turkish-Circassian and Albanian origin.[18] The
modern education system resulted in the formation of a state bureaucracy, the fate of which hinged on its complete allegiance to the state
represented by Muhammad 'Ali himself.

Muhammad 'Ali also used his modern army to expand his state beyond
the Egyptian borders, through his expeditions into Sudan, Palestine,
Syria, and Lebanon at the expense of the Ottoman Empire.

The great powers of the day, especially England and France, and even Prussia and Russia, felt threatened by Muhammad 'Ali's attempts to forge a modern state at the expense of the Ottoman Empire, the so-called sick man of Europe. England in particular regarded Ali's industry building as a threat to its own industrialization process. To defeat Muhammad 'Ali's army, Britain, France, Russia, and Prussia combined their forces with those of the Ottomans and waged war on Egypt. They succeeded in forcing Muhammad 'Ali to withdraw from his newly acquired territories and to revert to ruling Egypt alone. The victors imposed the treaty of 1841 on Muhammad 'Ali, whereby Egypt retained control only over Sudan. In return, however, he was granted hereditary rule of Egypt, and the succession of rule for his family was thus ensured.

The most devastating blow to the industrialization of Egypt was the acceptance by Muhammad 'Ali of the 1838 Anglo-Ottoman Convention, which, by imposing free trade on Egypt, allowed the import of cheap British manufactures into Egypt and effectively destroyed the industrial monopolies.

Egypt's first experiment as a developmental state enjoying total autonomy from internal social forces failed. The failure was due to the imposition of free-market rules on Egypt by foreign powers, while at the same time these same powers were protecting their own industries from foreign competition.

The Withdrawal of the State and Reliance on the Free Market

Forced to relinquish its policies of independent development and industrialization, the Egyptian economy was reintegrated into the international economic system and forced to rely on its exports of primary agricultural products, essentially raw cotton. From 1838 to 1916, the role of the state was restricted to the promotion of agricultural exports and the building of the infrastructure necessary to maximize the production of cotton, its main export crop. The state invested heavily in irrigation projects and the building of railways, ports, and a large commercial navy.

Khedive Isma'il (1863–79) invested not only in agricultural infrastructure to maximize the production of cotton, but also in urban renewal, with dreams of transforming Cairo into another Paris. These large investments were made possible by the boom in cotton prices resulting from the outbreak of the American Civil War. With the resumption of the United States' cotton production, prices came tumbling down, and

Isma'il was forced to complete his projects by taking out foreign loans. To repay the loans, he resorted to selling Egypt's shares in the Suez Canal to the British. But the most important step undertaken by Isma'il to generate revenues was the sale of land to Egyptians, which led to the growth and entrenchment of an Egyptian landowning elite.

Unable to pay the foreign debt, Egypt was declared bankrupt. The European powers intervened in the country's financial affairs on the pretext of administering its debt. Isma'il's resistance to this intervention led to his removal from power in 1879 and his replacement by his son Tawfiq. The government's bankruptcy and its inability to pay even the armed forces' salaries led to the 'Urabi revolt of 1882. That same year, the British invaded Egypt, claiming that they wished to protect the khedive. They would control Egypt's fate for the next seventy-two years.

The 'Urabi revolt was encouraged by the Egyptian landowning elite, which aimed to wrest power from the Palace, which was dominated by Turkish-Circassian and Albanian elites. With the failure of the revolt and the intervention of the British, the landowning elite was dealt a severe blow in its attempts to secure independence from both the Ottomans and the khedive or at least to share power with the khedive.[19]

British rule of Egypt consecrated the rules of the free-market and strengthened the primary product export strategy, based on a single crop: cotton. Britain also encouraged private property and forced the state to privatize landownership. As a result, the landowning elite expanded in numbers, turning Egyptian landowners into a force to be reckoned with.[20] The interests of the land-owning elite coincided, however, with the primary product export-oriented strategy enforced by the British.

Attempts at Industrialization

The primary product export-oriented growth strategy followed by Egypt underwent a deep crisis in the aftermath of the economic recession that hit Europe in 1906–1907. Reduced European demand for Egyptian cotton mired Egypt in a prolonged crisis that extended to the first two years of the First World War during which the British imposed restrictions on cotton exports from Egypt.

The long depression at the beginning of the twentieth century made clear even to the landowning elite the dangers of relying on a single crop for exports and for the generation of the bulk of the country's revenues. Calls were made for the diversification of economic activities and, especially, for industrialization. At the beginning of the First World War, the Egyptian government established a commission for the examination of the state of industry and commerce. The commission's main policy recommendation was to promote industrialization, and the state was subsequently called upon by the commission to promote and help the industrialization process.

In accordance with these recommendations, the state helped to establish the first Egyptian bank, Bank Misr, in 1920. Eight big landowners founded Banque Misr, which in turn established the Federation of Egyptian Industries in 1922 to promote the interests of the new industrial elite. The state granted Banque Misr an LE200,000-loan to lend money to nascent Egyptian industries. By 1938, the state loans had reached LE1.137 million. But the policy was soon to be ended, on the grounds of inadequate loan security.[21]

Following Egypt's achievement of nominal independence from Britain in 1922, big landowners and industrialists came to dominate parliament. The new power elites passed laws to impose minimum land taxes and established a government-sponsored agricultural bank (Credit Agricole) to support landowners in times of crisis. They also passed laws to restrict foreign ownership of land and put pressures on the government to sell them state lands at minimal prices.[22] Poor peasants benefited very little from these measures. By the beginning of the 1950s, 0.1 percent of landowners owned 20 percent of agricultural land while 95 percent of owners controlled only 35 percent.[23]

At the same time, the members of the landowning elite increased their investments in the emerging industries with state support by obtaining tariff protection in 1930. The outbreak of the Second World War promoted Egyptian industrialization to substitute for imports. However, the end of the Second World War led to the resumption of cheap foreign imports, which dealt a harsh blow to Egyptian industry.

To strengthen its position, the landowning-cum-industrial elite passed a law (the Egyptianization Law) in 1947, which required that native Egyptians own at least 51 percent of all shares in new joint stock companies. The share of Egyptian ownership in new joint stock companies rose from less than 5 percent in 1920 to 84 percent in 1948.[24]

Between 1922 and 1952, industrialization resulted in the establishment of consumer goods industries (the easy phase of import-substitution policy), mainly for textiles and food. However, the industrial labor force was small, was paid low wages, and deprived of many rights, such as minimum

30   The Role of the State in Development

wages and health insurance.[25] The domination of the political and economic system by the landowning-cum-industrial elite resulted in high income inequalities. The Second World War added to the economic hardship. Recession and high inflation led to economic stagnation and a further increase in income inequalities. In 1950, wages accounted for 38 percent of Gross Domestic Product (GDP) while profits absorbed 62 percent of GDP.[26]

With the resumption of unfettered foreign trade at the end of the Second World War, increased competition from cheap foreign imports hastened demands for state intervention to protect Egyptian industry and to impose a ceiling on land ownership to ensure the transfer of capital from agriculture to industry. Calls for land reform were made even by members of the elites.[27]

While many intellectuals, politicians, and even some landowners advocated land reform and a state-led industrialization drive from 1916 to 1952, it was impossible to implement these policies for several reasons.

First, the political system was dominated by powerful members of the landed elite. Any call for land reform would have amounted to a threat to their interests. Second, the presence of British troops in Egypt, even after Egypt had gained nominal independence in 1922, would have thwarted any efforts at controlling free trade, so beneficial to British trade with Egypt. Third, the state had no autonomy, relative or otherwise. The King (the largest landowner in the country), the members of the landed elite who dominated the majority parliamentary party at the time (the Wafd), and the British were hostile to any interventionist role in the economy by the state.

To promote industrialization, protect Egyptian industries, and impose land reform, dominant power relations had to be restructured, in other words, there was a need to abolish the power of the King and that of the landowning elite and for Egypt to gain independence from Britain.

The Nasserist Experiment in State-Led Development (1952–70)

The dominant power relations that existed from 1916 to 1952, while leading to some industrialization, especially during the two world wars, prevented further industrialization and development for several reasons. For one thing, the state was subsumed under the power of the landowning and industrial elites. Regardless of calls for land reform to increase the pool of savings and therefore investments in industry, the state was unable to impose land reform laws that would run counter to the interests of these elites.

Second, the members of the industrial elite came from the ranks of the landowning elite. "The same 12,000 families of big landowners who held some 50 percent of all cultivable land also included the 11,000 major shareholders who held some 40 percent of joint-stock companies."[28] A conflict between the landowning and industrial elites in this case was unthinkable, and weakened the ability of the members of the industrial elite to pursue their own interests independently from those of the large landowners. Third, the presence of British troops in the country prevented the Egyptian elites, and the state for that matter, from effectively pursuing a policy of protecting infant industries from cheap manufactured imports. Under the free trade rules, the only comparative advantage obtained by Egypt was in the export of raw cotton to European markets.

After the end of the Second World War, Egypt witnessed the acceleration of a deep societal crisis. Soaring unemployment and inflation rates, growing income inequalities, the inability of the government formed by the Wafd Party (the dominant party in power from 1923 to 1952) to obtain complete independence from the British, and the inability of economic elites to deepen the industrialization process beyond the easy phase of primary consumer goods production, resulted in the fragmentation of social and political forces. Political movements of all stripes proliferated, ranging from clandestine communist movements to fascist parties such as Young Egypt. Governments were formed and dissolved in rapid succession. Finally, unknown dissident groups resorted to the burning of some of Cairo's major landmarks in February 1952.

This spiraling and uncontrolled political turmoil ended with the military coup of July 1952. The Free Officers, under the leadership of Gamal Abd al-Nasser, claimed that the unstable situation in Egypt required their intervention to rid the country of the corrupt monarchial rule of the house of Muhammad 'Ali. The Free Officers did not have a clear economic agenda, just vague calls for independence, development, and social justice. Nevertheless, the Free Officers came to power and resolved to effect policies that had been on the nationalist Egyptian agenda for almost forty years. In their Six Points Program, the Free Officers declared that their regime would rid the country of feudalism and imperialism, build a strong military power, and pursue economic development.

32   The Role of the State in Development

The new regime succeeded in negotiating the complete withdrawal of the British troops that were stationed in the Suez Canal region, and the last troops left in June 1954. Their departure not only accomplished a long-standing nationalist objective, but also led to the liberation of the country from the rules (both political and economic) imposed by the British High Commissioner, who had been the real power behind the throne. A clear example of that power was the return of the Wafd Party to power, after the dissolution of its cabinet in 1942 by order of the King. The Wafd had supported the allies in the Second World War, contrary to the secret support of the King and other political groups for the Axis powers. To enforce the decision to return the Wafd to the Cabinet, British troops surrounded the Palace until the King acceded to British demands. In 1954, following an internal crisis within the ranks of the Free Officers over discussions of a suitable political system, the regime gained autonomy from all political forces by abolishing political parties and instituting a one-party system under its control. This measure would cost the regime the mistrust of the elites and their resistance to the regime's plans for economic development.

In order to abolish feudalism (as the regime characterized large land ownerships), the first land reform law was issued in September 1952. The law put a 200-feddan (approximately 200 acres) ceiling on land ownership, a far less stringent ceiling than that proposed earlier. This was not implemented for the sake of land redistribution per se (which was limited at best), but mostly in the belief that such a law would liberate capital from agriculture and direct it toward industrial investment. The law reduced the share of the large landowners from around 20 percent of total land ownership to only 6 percent, while the share of the poorest owners (95 percent of all owners) rose from 35 percent to 46.6 percent. Two other land reform laws were implemented in 1961 and 1969. The 1961 law reduced the ceiling of land ownership to 100 feddans per person, and in 1969, land ownership was further restricted to 50 feddans per person and 200 feddans per family. By these measures, the Nasserist regime eliminated the economic base of the power of the landed elites and reduced the unequal distribution of agricultural land.[29]

To promote economic development, the regime sought to support the private sector and encourage foreign investment. The Permanent Council for the Development of National Production was established in 1952 to assess the feasibility of private sector industrial projects and advise would-be entrepreneurs. The Council was to collaborate with the private sector in establishing joint ventures, and the new regime issued very generous laws to encourage foreign investment. A decree (Law 120 of 1952) abolished the requirement of 51 percent Egyptian ownership of industrial enterprises. This law had been established in 1947 as part of the Egyptianization drive at the time, but the Federation of Egyptian Industries pressured the government to revoke it, arguing that local entrepreneurs were incapable of achieving the desired industrialization on their own. Law 156 of 1953 allowed foreign enterprises during the first six years of an investment to repatriate profits annually up to 10 percent of capital invested, and after that up to 20 percent annually.[30] Not only that, but it also became legal for foreign capital to own 100 percent of the shares of new industries (Article 2 of Law 26 of 1954). In case of project failure, other laws granted full fiscal exemptions to new industries and allowed foreign companies to re-export all of their capital after only one year of operation.[31]

Notwithstanding the generous investment incentives offered by the new government, both Egyptian entrepreneurs and foreign investors reduced their industrial investments and resorted to disinvesting their firms by distributing very high dividends, reaching 80 percent of the profits, which ate into outstanding capital—or capital plowed back into industry.[32] Private Gross Investments declined from LE112 million in 1950 to just LE39 million in 1956.[33] The private entrepreneurs' (Egyptian or otherwise) reluctance to participate in the state's development policies is understandable. The exclusion of the entrepreneurs from the political system, through which they could protect their interests, did not encourage them to invest in the new system, no matter what incentives were offered by the regime. The land reform laws contributed to the reluctance of private entrepreneurs to invest further in the industrial sector. The regime did not realize that the industrial entrepreneurs came from the ranks of the landowners. The land reform laws of 1952, while mild at best, caused the industrial elites to be wary of the regime's intentions toward their industrial concerns. They feared a government takeover of their industries, especially since the new regime was seen as an intruder on a political scene that had long been dominated by their interests.

The reluctance of the private sector to invest in industry led to a nationalization drive that started in 1956 and grew to form a huge public sector in the 1960s. The emergence of the public sector began with the regime's planning of a huge project, namely, the High Dam in Aswan.

34   The Role of the State in Development

The dam was to provide Egypt with a constant supply of water to increase cultivable land area; but more notably it was to provide much-needed hydroelectric power for the establishment of heavy and intermediate industries. Two main industries were established shortly after the military coup: a fertilizer plant in Aswan and an iron and steel complex in the Cairo suburb of Helwan.

All the economic projects were discussed with the Misr Group of industries and the Federation of Egyptian Industries. Notwithstanding the attempts of the new government to support and include the private sector in its decision-making processes, private entrepreneurs were still reluctant to participate with the government in its ambitious industrialization plans, nor were they moved to increase industrial investments for the reasons mentioned above. Some authors claim that, in a way, the private sector was the instrument of its own demise.[34]

The political battle to build the High Dam resulted in the formation of the nucleus of the public sector. At first, Egypt resorted to the World Bank for a loan to finance the construction of the dam. In the meantime, in its quest to create a strong military, especially after the debacle of the 1948 war and the creation of the State of Israel, Egypt asked to purchase arms from the United States. The U.S., wary that such arms would strengthen Egypt's military hand against Israel, declined. Egypt responded by buying arms from the Soviet Union via Czechoslovakia in 1954. The U.S. and Britain forced the World Bank to withdraw its support for the financing of the High Dam. In a dramatic counter-response to what he perceived as a slight, Nasser nationalized the Suez Canal: a move that triggered the Suez war waged by Britain, France, and Israel against the new regime. The invading forces withdrew in December 1956 under pressure from the United States and the intervention of the Soviet Union, which threatened to use nuclear power. In retaliation for the invasion, Nasser nationalized all British and French assets. To manage the nationalized assets, the Egyptian government created the Economic Organization in 1957. The government formulated a first three-year industrialization plan in 1957. The first plan, with its emphasis on manufacturing, increased investments from only LE2 million in 1957 to LE49.3 million in 1960. The labor force grew at 8.5 percent annually during the same period.[35] Capital stock in manufacturing grew by 82 percent in the period between 1950 and 1960.[36]

The success of the first Three Year Plan encouraged the government to proceed with a Five Year Plan. The weak performance of the private sector since 1952 had been in part responsible for the sweeping nationalizations of Egyptian assets that took place in the 1960s, but there were political factors at play as well. Chief among them was the dissolution of the Egyptian–Syrian Union in 1961, which had been formed in 1958. The declaration of the socialist laws of 1960 met with strong resistance from Syrian industrial and commercial elites and from the military, which led a coup d'état, and the union was dissolved. Fearing that Egyptian elites would resort to the same tactics, Nasser nationalized and sequestrated the majority of non-agricultural assets to undercut any attempt at regime change. According to Waterbury, by 1965, the public sector accounted for 90 percent of total non-agricultural domestic output, 45 percent of domestic savings, and 90 percent of gross domestic capital formation.[37]

Dominating the majority of economic resources, the regime achieved a high degree of autonomy from all social forces, especially from the recalcitrant industrial elite, and engaged in the implementation of the first Five Year Plan, 1960/61–1964/65. The plan emphasized the development of heavy industries and consumer goods and consumer durables, and attempted to promote export-oriented industries. A total of LE500 was invested in the industrial sector in the period between 1960 and 1965. During the period of the plan, industry grew annually at 9 percent, and total GDP growth reached 5.5 percent.[38] In 1964–65 the manufacturing share of GDP reached 19 percent.[39] The labor force grew tremendously through the plan period, from 6 million workers to 7.3 million workers, a total increase of 22 percent.[40] Nevertheless, the industrialization drive of the first half of the 1960s resulted in a high import bill for intermediate products (38 percent of total imports in 1965–66) and capital goods (24 percent of total imports for the same year).[41]

The Nasserist regime, aiming at building a new social coalition to support its policies, implemented several measures to decrease the high income-inequalities obtaining before 1952. In addition to land reform, the regime fixed the rent of agricultural land and real estate at low levels. Rent contracts became inheritable, which reduced the role of property owners to that of recipients of very low rents that would not change for years to come. Tenants effectively became part owners of agricultural land and real estate. If owners wished to sell their properties, they had to obtain the approval of the tenants, who received a 50 percent share of the sale proceeds in exchange for vacating the rented land or real estate.[42] The free public education program was expanded to include all stages of education, including higher education. Public health programs

36   The Role of the State in Development

were initiated, and the government took upon itself the provision of free healthcare for all those unable to afford private treatment. The regime also subsidized major food items, especially bread, and fixed low prices for most manufactured products. It committed itself to full employment by guaranteeing the employment of all graduates of high schools and universities. Minimum wages and generous labor laws ensured workers' economic rights. All these measures resulted in the narrowing of income inequalities. The percentage of poor families decreased from 35 percent in 1958–59 to 27 percent in 1964–65 for rural families, and from 30 percent to 27.8 percent for urban families. The share of wages in total income increased from 38 percent in 1950 to 50 percent in 1967–68.[43]

By these measures, the regime created a strong social base to support its policies. The social base was formed of the middle class (that benefited mostly from free education and the guaranteed employment policies), the workers, and the peasants. A faction of the business elite, engaged mainly in construction and internal trade, joined the social alliance supporting the regime.

The second half of the 1960s witnessed a deceleration of growth, however, and average economic growth did not exceed 3.3 percent per annum. The economic slowdown was the result of multiple factors. The Import Substitution policy of the first half of the 1960s, coupled with the socialist laws of income redistribution and social welfare policies, increased the state financial burden tremendously, while domestic savings, and therefore investment, remained relatively low. In the absence of substantial foreign direct investment, the regime could not maintain the high rates of investment required to sustain a high growth economy. Most production was geared to the satisfaction of internal demand. The lack of a viable strategy for the export of manufactures limited the scope of the market and thereby limited the scope of import substitution industrialization itself.

Other, non-economic factors deepened the economic crisis of the second half of the 1960s. The emergence of a large public sector led to the creation of a new class to manage it: a bureaucratic elite,[44] that is, the top echelons of the bureaucracy in charge of managing the public sector began to act as collective owners of public enterprises, subjecting production to the satisfaction of their personal interests at the expense of public requirements. The bureaucratic elite, by manipulating public sector assets, succeeded in amassing large fortunes through bribery and corruption. A sizeable private sector still existed in Egypt, especially in agriculture, construction, and internal trade. Relations between the

Economic Liberalization and the Emergence of a Rentier Economy   37

public and private sectors created the conduits for corruption and bribery and the private accumulation of profits by bureaucratic elites. Egyptian entrepreneurs were able to generate wealth through the establishment of monopolies in wholesale trade, dealing in black market goods, and by acting as subcontractors for the public sector.[45]

The economic crisis was accentuated by Egypt's involvement in two major wars: the Yemen War (1963–67) and the 1967 Arab–Israeli War. Both wars were very costly and were financed by reducing investments rather than consumption. The regime did not want to alienate its social base by increasing consumer prices, especially after a brief experiment in price-raising in 1965, which had led to mass protests. The crisis led Nasser himself to attempt to revamp the system. In 1965 he tried to run the public sector according to free-market rules, separating production from welfare criteria. He also attempted to set up a free zone in Port Said in an effort to attract Arab funds and encourage an export-oriented industrialization strategy.[46]

In an address to the heads of all public sector companies on March 18, 1967, Nasser reiterated the need to link wages to productivity, claiming that socialism did not mean equal wages but equal employment opportunities. He also sought to depoliticize production by weakening the power of the Arab Socialist Union, the regime's sole political party, by eliminating its interference in production decisions and limiting its role to the implementation of plans and the overseeing of relations between management and workers.[47]

Nasser did not succeed in reshaping the system in the second half of the 1960s. The existing power relations and the social alliance that supported the regime prevented the emergence of an industrialization policy run on market criteria. These power relations had to be restructured to allow the emergence of a new elite capable of steering the society toward economic liberalization.

Economic Liberalization and the Emergence of a Rentier Economy (1974–91)

The death of Gamal Abd al-Nasser in 1970 initiated a power struggle between factions of the dominant political–bureaucratic elites. A faction of the ruling bureaucracy (a faction supporting pro-Nasser policies) sought a solution to the economic crisis in a deepening of the so-called socialist economy, by extending the power of the state over the economic sectors that remained private, especially agriculture, construction, and

38 The Role of the State in Development

internal trade. Another elite faction within the bureaucracy favored a return to the market mechanism, the dismantling of the public sector, and the encouragement of foreign direct investment as the only solutions to the deepening economic crisis. The struggle between the two factions came to a head in May 1971, when President Sadat succeeded in eliminating the pro-Nasser faction through sweeping arrests of his main opponents.

To attract foreign investment, Sadat promulgated Law 65 of 1971, by which many incentives were built in to attract such investment, such as the establishment of 'free zones' in which new companies would be offered special incentives, such as a five-year exemption from taxation for new companies and the assurance of a safeguard against government actions such as nationalization. Joint ventures between foreign companies and public sector units were granted autonomy.[48] Notwithstanding the generous incentives of this law, few foreign investments were generated. The country was still suffering from the ramifications of the 1967 Six Day War, creating a political climate too unstable for this law to be taken seriously by would-be investors.

The Soviet–American détente of 1972 made it clear to Sadat that Egypt could not continue to depend on the support of the USSR. For Egypt to broker an understanding with the west, and especially with the United States, Sadat opted for a limited war in 1973 to bring the issue of the Arab–Israeli conflict to the international agenda and to raise options for settlement of the conflict. One year later, President Sadat declared an Open Door (liberalization) economic policy, and another investment law was promulgated, Law 43 of 1974, to encourage foreign investment and to signal Egypt's intention to reintegrate its economy into the liberal international economic system. In addition to the incentives contained in the 1972 law, Law 43 stipulated that any approved project would automatically be considered part of the private sector even if public sector companies participated as partners in these ventures. The results of this last stipulation were far-reaching. Under this law, private sector projects were exempted from labor laws mandating labor representation in management, profit sharing by workers, and workers' labor tenure.[49] The law lifted the previous requirement of Egyptian majority ownership, and contained explicit protections against nationalization and expropriation.[50]

Sadat was convinced that, to attract foreign investments, Egypt had to ally itself with the west, particularly the United States. An important step toward forging this new alliance was his decision to conclude a peace treaty with Israel, a treaty that led to the isolation of Egypt from the Arab world and the cessation of Arab aid after his visit to Jerusalem in 1977. To compensate Egypt for the loss of Arab aid, and as a reward for the conclusion of a peace treaty with Israel, the U.S. granted Egypt aid estimated at US$2.1 billion per annum.[51]

The Open Door policy failed to attract a credible amount of foreign direct investment. From 1974 to 1982, total investments committed under Law 43 of 1974 did not exceed LE5 billion. Egyptian investment accounted for 61 percent of total investment (24 percent by the public sector, 37 percent by the private sector). Arab investment accounted for 23 percent, and investment by western countries amounted to only 16 percent. However, of all investment committed, only 32 percent was actually implemented. Egyptian capital (both public and private) contributed 80 percent of all agricultural capital, 72 percent of industrial investment, 52 percent of financial investment, 75 percent of investment in construction, and 57 percent of investment in the service sector. The bulk of Arab investments were concentrated in the free zone areas (72 percent of total investment committed to that sector, followed by financial investment (40 percent), construction (16 percent), and services (10 percent). Western capital represented 16 percent of inland investments and 12 percent of free zone investments, while the majority of western investment was directed at the service sector, making up 33 percent of total investment in the sector.[52] Most projects approved under Law 43 were concentrated in banks, tourism, and investment companies.[53] Some of the Open Door ventures were described by John Waterbury as ventures that led to the "rape of Egypt,"[54] for they sought fast and large profits without regard to the law.

Nevertheless, the 1975–85 period witnessed high rates of economic growth. GDP growth rates were uneven during the period, reaching high levels in 1976 (21.5 percent), 1982 (12.4 percent), 1979 (16.3 percent), 1977 (11.5 percent), 1980 (9.7 percent), 1983 (8.8 percent), and 1988 (8.1 percent). The rate of growth was negative in 1981 (-5.2 percent) and 1974 (-2.5 percent).[55]

The large increase in GDP during the 1975–85 period was mostly the result of a shift from directly productive sources of income to various forms of unproductive income or rent. The increase in oil prices after the 1973 war had a large impact on Egypt through remittances earned by workers who had migrated to the Gulf, increased revenues from the Suez

40   The Role of the State in Development

Canal and tourism, and the sale of Egyptian oil. Petroleum exports increased from US$187 million in 1974 to US$3,329 million in 1981–82. Workers remittances increased from US$189 million in 1974 to US$2,855 million in 1980–81, only to decline to US$1,935 million in 1981–82. Remittances increased sharply from US$2,973 million in 1985–86 to US$8,884 million in 1987–88, to drop again to US$3,743 million in 1989–90. Suez Canal revenues increased from US$85 million in 1975 to US$909 million in 1981–82 and from US$1,028 million in 1985–86 to US$1,471 million in 1989–90. Tourism revenues increased from US$265 million in 1975 to US$611 million in 1981–82 and to US$1,472 million in 1989–90.[56]

Arab countries' assistance in the form of grants, cash loans, deposits, and project program loans increased from US$905 million in 1973 to US$1,751 million in 1977, to decline to just US$885 million in 1979, a drop that was caused by Sadat's visit to Israel.[57] While receiving these unprecedented external flows, Egypt also increased its foreign debt from US$3 billion in 1974, to US$19 billion in 1981, to US$37 billion in 1986.[58] This spiraling foreign debt was the result of soaring imports and the decline of traditional exports. The trade deficit increased from US$4,978 million in 1985–86 to US$8,296 million in 1998–90.[59]

Under the Open Door policy, the private sector was given a greater role in investments. Relatively cheap credit was extended to private entrepreneurs. However, most of the private sector investments were concentrated in non-productive activities such as luxury buildings, speculation on real estate, and the import of luxury goods. Some businessmen even succeeded in transferring part of the credit to their personal accounts outside Egypt.[60] The share of manufacturing in total investments by both the private and the public sector dropped from 40 percent in 1967–73 to just 19 percent in 1981–91.[61]

Egypt in the 1980s was transformed into a rentier economy, relying on external sources of income while neglecting its productive sectors: agriculture and manufacturing. The economic liberalization measures were not geared to a strategy of export-oriented industrialization on the East Asian model, but to a relatively open economy that was quickly de-industrializing.

The Open Door policy failed to generate employment for an expanding labor force. In the entire period from 1974 to 1990, Law 43 projects, both inland and in the free zones, accounted for less than 1.5 percent of total employment.[62] The Egyptian economy at large, while achieving high growth rates in the period 1974–85 (averaging an annual rate of 8 percent), experienced a jobless growth, that is, the rate of job destruction was higher than that of job creation.[63] Open unemployment increased from 2.2 percent in 1960 to 4.3 percent in 1976 and jumped to 11 percent in 1986.

The reduction of employment opportunities in the formal sector resulted in the proliferation of informal employment. Informal employment in 1976 was estimated at 2.4 million workers, while total employment in the formal private non-agricultural sector did not exceed 170,000 workers. In 1985, informal employment reached 2.9 million and rose to 4.8 million in the 1990s.[64]

Wage levels in Law 43 projects were uneven. They were relatively high in finance and services enterprises and much lower in industrial projects. The average wage rate in industrial projects was close to that of an unskilled worker in the construction sector.[65] An important corollary of these developments was the decline of real wages. The real wage per worker (US$ per week) declined from US$70 in 1980 to US$11 in 1991. Accordingly, the real unit labor cost declined from US$0.827 in 1980 to US$0.333 in 1991.[66] This trend worsened in the 1990s with the implementation of the structural adjustment program.

At the same time, economic growth in Egypt as a whole, and in Law 43 projects, depended heavily on high capital intensity. In the period 1977–89 the annual average growth rate of output was 6.12 percent. This growth depended on an annual capital growth rate of 7.25 percent and an annual growth in output per worker of 3.65 percent. Capital growth rate per worker for the same period reached 7.18 percent.[67] This heavy reliance on capital in a labor-intensive economy like Egypt's is partly responsible for the increasing unemployment and falling wages of the last three decades.

One of the major consequences of the Open Door policy was a spiraling inflation rate, averaging 25–30 percent per annum during the 1974–85 period.[68] The result was a very low real GDP growth rate. Similarly, real per capita growth of GDP averaged only 0.2 percent per annum during the period 1986–93.[69]

Economic Reform and Structural Adjustment Policies (1991–2005)

By the early 1990s, the Egyptian economy was clearly in crisis. Total external debt stood at $US49 billion, and the total external debt to GDP ratio had reached 150 percent. The budget deficit was equal to 20 percent of GDP and the annual inflation rate stood at more than 20 percent.[70] The Gulf War of 1991 further aggravated the crisis. Over a million workers returned to Egypt in the aftermath of the war, which affected workers remittances negatively, and tourism, a major source of foreign exchange, declined significantly.

To remedy the situation, Egypt turned to the International Monetary Fund and the World Bank for help, concluding an agreement with the International Monetary Fund in May 1991 and the World Bank in November 1991. The International Monetary Fund focused on monetary and fiscal reforms and the reform of exchange rates. The World Bank focused on the reform of the Egyptian economy through investments, liberalization, and privatization. A comprehensive stabilization and economic reform program, the Economic Reform and Structural Adjustment Program (ERSAP), was formulated, and the Egyptian government began implementation in April 1991.

The main targets of ERSAP were to improve the balance of payments so that Egypt could repay its foreign debt, reduce inflation rates, and reduce public debt. This required the lifting of price controls, a reduction in government expenditures (including the reduction of state subsidies), a reduction in public investments, the imposition of new taxes such as the sales tax, and a freezing of wage rates. At the same time, the government had to sell public enterprises and liberalize foreign trade.

An important result of these measures was the undoing of the populist power relations that had reigned supreme in Egypt after the 1952 revolution and which survived the Open Door policies of the 1970s and 1980s. The 1977 riots that ensued after the government decided to lift all subsidies, and which threatened to topple the regime, made the government much more cautious in its attempts to remove the economic privileges granted by the Nasserist regime, which had mainly benefited the middle class, the workers, and the peasants. ERSAP was to have a profound effect on workers; the peasants and the program squeezed the middle class, forcing many to join the ranks of the poor.

The first two years of ERSAP's implementation witnessed very low growth rates. The GDP growth rate did not exceed 1.9 percent in 1991–92 and 2.5 percent in 1992–93. The GDP growth rate reached a peak in 1999–2000 at 5.9 percent, but plunged to 3.4 percent in 2000–2001, 3.2 percent in 2001–2002 and 3 percent in 2002–2003. Starting in 2003–2004, the GDP growth rate improved, to reach 3 percent in 2003–2004 and 5 percent in 2004–2005.[71] Notwithstanding GDP growth rates, GDP decreased from US$90.4 billion in 2001, to US$84.2

billion in 2002, and to US$71.5 billion in 2003. It increased slightly, to US$78.3 billion, in 2004.[72] The sluggish economic performance was due in part to the Asian and Latin American financial crises of 1997 and 1998, the 2001 September 11 attacks, and the depreciation of the Egyptian pound by 25 percent in January 2003, which led to a considerable rise in prices and the cost of living. The final outcome of the recession in the period 2000–2005 was the decline of per capita GDP from US$1,313 in 2002 to US$1,197 in 2003, and to US$1,111 in 2004. It rebounded slightly, to US$1,296 in 2005 but is still below the 2002 level.[73]

The implementation of ERSAP also resulted in a sharp decline in public investment, and at the same time private investment slowed. The contraction of both public and private investment in the period 1990–98 brought the annual capital growth rate down from 7.25 percent in 1977–89 to just 0.19 percent in the period 1990–98, and capital per worker decreased from 7.18 percent in 1997–89 to 0.17 percent in 1990–98. Concomitantly, the annual output growth rate declined from 6.12 percent in 1977–89 to 4.57 percent in 1990–98.[74]

Investment in manufacturing as a percentage of total investment dropped from 21.6 percent in 1990–91 to 9.6 percent in 1999–2000 and to only 7.2 percent in 2003–2004.[75] The share of manufacturing dropped from a high of 40 percent in 1967–73 to 18.7 percent in 1981–91, 16.2 percent in 1992–97, and only 12.2 percent in 1997–2002.[76]

Foreign direct investment (or the lack thereof) contributed to the recession. Foreign direct investment flows did decline by 50 percent during the period 1991/92–1996/97. Despite successive investment laws and incentives offered to would-be investors, Egypt was and still is incapable of attracting large foreign direct investment. Modest to begin with, foreign direct investment further declined from US$1.656 billion in 2000 to US$509 million in 2001 and US$428 million in 2003.[77] It seemed to recover in 2004–2005, reaching US$3.9 billion.

Egypt has received large amounts of foreign aid, especially at the beginning of the 1990s; aid reached US$5.4 billion in 1990 and US$5 billion in 1991. This aid was tied to the participation of Egypt in the first Gulf War. Afterward, foreign aid declined and even U.S. aid has been declining annually, to reach only US$1.9 billion in 2004–2005. U.S. economic aid declined from US$655 million in 2001–2002 to just US$535 million in 2004–2005, while military aid is constant at US$1.3 billion annually. U.S. economic aid is expected to decline further in the coming years.[78]

The impact of ERSAP on employment growth in the 1990s was disappointing at best. The program's implementation led to a sharp decline in public sector investments and thereby employment. The private sector, which was given priority in private investments, increased its share of employment marginally.[79] Thus the private sector was unable to compensate for the decrease in public employment, while the government abandoned the policy of employing new entrants to the labor market. In addition, a substantial amount of credit was squandered by the private sector on unproductive high and rapid-return projects such as speculation on land and real estate, while some of the credit was transferred abroad in shady deals.[80]

Most private sector investments were also concentrated in economic sectors characterized by low labor absorption and high capital–output ratios, such as industry (essentially oil) and social services, while little investment was assigned to the sectors generating high employment, such as construction and trade.[81] In fact, the share of wages in income distribution declined. In 1997, the share of wages in Gross Domestic Output reached 11.4 percent in public firms and only 7.6 percent in private firms.[82]

The situation of labor in manufacturing, the sector that might lead an export-oriented strategy of development, can at best be described as dismal. The Family Budget Survey of 1996 revealed that 42 percent of workers in manufacturing were below the poverty line. The Enterprise Sample Survey of 1998 and the Labor Sample Survey of 1998 indicated that more than 70 percent of workers in private manufacturing were poor.[83] The labor situation in industry worsened in the periods 2000–2001 and 2004–2005, while GDP growth rates improved.

According to the statistics of the ministry of industry and trade, GDP growth rates improved from 3.2 percent in 2000–2001 to 4.9 percent in 2004–2005. The following two years, 2005–2006 and 2006–2007, witnessed an increase in GDP of 6.8 percent and 7.1 percent, respectively. It is too early to predict whether high GDP growth rates will be sustained in the near future. Average labor productivity reached 2.5 percent in 2002 and 7.1 percent in 2004, to drop to 2.4 percent in 2005. At the same time, average annual wage growth rates were negative for the whole period, recording -0.1 percent in 2001–2002 and 2002–2003, 0 percent in 2003–2004 and -0.6 percent in 2004–2005.[84]

Adding to the problems generated by ERSAP was the government's relinquishment of guaranteed full employment, enshrined as a constitutional right. Unable to change the constitution, the government resorted to other measures to nullify the right. The measures included: reduction of the number of the newly employed in the public sector and the civil service; allowing workers in state owned enterprises and the civil service to take long leaves of absence without pay; and opening the gates for labor migration, whether temporary or permanent. At the same time, as indicated above, the private sector failed to generate significant employment opportunities. Open unemployment has become one of the consistent patterns of the labor market since the 1980s. Official statistics estimated the unemployment rate at 12 percent in 1986, 9 percent in 1990–91, and 7.4 percent in 1999–2000. In the period 2000–2004, the average unemployment rate stood at 10 percent.[85] However, these estimates may grossly underestimate the problem. The *Strategic Economic Trends Report* of the al-Ahram Center for Political and Strategic Studies indicates that the definition of the unemployed adopted by the government is deficient. According to official sources, a person is unemployed if he or she has no source of income, contrary to the international and economic definition, which identifies someone as unemployed if he or she is actively looking for a job but has not found one. Accordingly, the *Strategic Report* estimates the real unemployment rate to be in the range of 25 percent to 30 percent.[86]

The privatization of state owned enterprises added to the problems surrounding worker insecurity and increasing unemployment. In the period 1993 to 2003, 197 state owned enterprises were privatized. The government used different privatization techniques: sale of public enterprises to anchor investors (29 companies); sale of the majority of shares on the stock market (38); sale of 50 percent of shares (6); sale of 40 percent of shares on the stock market (10); and sale of all shares to employee shareholder associations (33). They also sold 6 companies in liquidation and 27 companies as production assets; 21 companies and production units were leased on a long-term basis. The value of the companies sold between 1997 and 2003 reached LE12 billion.[87]

In order to sell state owned enterprises, the government resorted to multiple tactics to downsize the labor force. The transfer of workers to remote areas forced many to resign from their jobs. Dismissal from work and the provision for early retirement were two other measures to force workers to resign. Another tactic was to reduce incentives and allowances, which formed a substantial proportion of the very low official wages.[88]

The privatization tactics, the lowering of real wages, and the shrinking labor market caused labor unrest to mount during the Open Door and structural adjustment periods. A few examples may illustrate the escalating conflict between the government and public sector workers. In September 1994, seven thousand workers at the Kafr al-Dawwar Spinning and Weaving Company (one of the strongholds of the textile industry) were barred from entering the factory by the State Security Forces. The workers stormed the factory and staged a sit-in while maintaining production. On October 2, State Security Forces stormed the premises and fired tear gas and live ammunition against the strikers. Four people were killed, 120 people were wounded, and another 90 were arrested. Workers threatened by layoffs and the privatization of their factories waged a series of strikes in the mid-1990s. Major strikes took place at the Misr Helwan Spinning and Weaving factory in 1998. The entire workforce of 8,700 was given three weeks' leave, but only 2,800 workers were allowed to return.[89] During 2006 and 2007, a continuous series of demonstrations and sit-ins forced the government to bargain with industrial workers and state employees about wages, which had not increased since the mid-1990s. The government acceded to some of the demands of the demonstrators. Nonetheless, with increasing food prices (rising by around 40 percent in the last quarter of 2007), protests and demonstrations are on the increase.[90] In agriculture, the government in 1992 passed Law 96 "for regulating the relationship between owners and tenants" to amend the land reform law of 1952. The law was intended to liberalize the agricultural sector fully and to consolidate landholdings, in the expectation that the majority of smallholders would abandon their plots after the large increase in land rents. According to the new law, land rent was raised threefold, a level twenty-two times that of the land tax, for a transition period of five years. After 1997, rent was determined by market mechanisms. The law abolished inheritance of rent contracts, a major element of the prior land reform. After 1997, owners had the right to evict tenants, a right that had been removed by the old Land Reform laws. Rented lands constitute 34 percent of total agricultural land in Egypt. The 1992 law affected 905,000 tenants, supporting at least five million family members.[91] In response to growing popular opposition to the determination of rents by the market alone, the government announced in October 1996 that the transition rent period would be extended for an additional five years, until 2002. However, the extension had not

Economic Reform and Structural Adjustment Policies   47

become effective by the end of 1996; the government had left rents to be determined by market forces. Since then, the goverment has left rents to be determined by market forces. Before 1992, the average rent for agricultural land was LE200 per feddan per year and increased to an average of LE600 in the transition period between 1992 and 1997 and again to an average of LE3,000–4,000 after 1997.[92] Peasants' protests and violence emerged in reaction to the government measures. In 1997 and 1998, 49 people were killed, 956 were injured, and 2,785 arrested in disputes related to the new law.[93] An important outcome of the 1992 law was an increase in the number of landless peasants. Almost half of the affected tenants became landless. Only 12,000 of the newly landless peasants (1.5 percent of those affected) were given land by the government.[94]

Price deregulation and the adoption of flexible exchange rates added to inflationary pressures in the domestic economy. The average LE/US$ exchange rate rose from 3.5 in the late 1980s to 4.33 in 2001–2002, 5.13 in 2002–2003, and 6.16 to 7.15 in 2003–2004, and dropped to 5.75 in 2004–2005. Egypt's high import bill and the greed of wholesale and retail commercial agents exacerbated inflation rates, especially during 2003 and beyond. According to the data provided by the ministry of the economy and foreign trade, the consumer price index (CPI) reached 21 percent in 1991–92, only to drop to an average of 10 percent in the period 1991–95 and to drop further to an average of 4 percent in the period 1997/98–1999/2000. After the floating of the exchange rate in 2003, the CPI jumped to 21.7 percent in January 2004.[95] However, the way in which the Egyptian government estimates the CPI—according to a basket of goods weighted heavily in favor of subsidized fixed-price goods— underestimates the real inflation rate. A better measure is the wholesale price index. The wholesale price index reached a high of 18 percent in 2002–2003 and dropped slightly to 16 percent in 2003–2004.[96]

The inflationary pressures and the economic reform and structural adjustment policies lowered real income by 14 percent in urban areas and 20 percent in rural areas in the period 1991–96.[97]

The final outcome of the Washington Consensus policies pursued by the government deepened poverty in Egypt. There are different measurements of poverty. The ultra poverty line is a measure of food poverty; the lower poverty line is an estimate of the cost of essential food and non-food items; and the upper poverty line reflects the actual consumption expenditure of the poor.

48   The Role of the State in Development

According to the Households Expenditures Survey of 1999–2000, 20 percent of all Egyptians lived at or below the lower poverty line and 50 percent lived at or below the upper poverty line. The urban lower poverty line was slightly lower (18.5 percent) than the rural line (21.5 percent). Forty-six percent of the urban population was at or below the urban upper poverty line, and fifty-two percent of the rural population was at or below the rural upper poverty line. Poverty lines for Upper Egypt and Lower Egypt were the highest, with lower poverty line estimates of 36 percent for urban Upper Egypt and around 35 percent for rural Upper Egypt. The estimates for the upper poverty line skyrocketed to 69 percent for both urban and rural Upper Egypt. The estimates of the upper poverty line are highest in urban areas of the governorate of Asyut (91 percent), Sohag (85 percent), Qena and Beni-Suef (76 percent), and Sharqiya (72 percent). The lowest levels were in South Sinai (7 percent), Port Said (11 percent), and Suez (18 percent). The rural upper poverty line was highest in Asyut (83 percent), Sohag (77 percent), Qena and North Sinai (62 percent), and lowest in Damietta (3 percent) and South Sinai (8 percent).[98]

The World Bank survey of 1995 estimated that the lowest-income 10 percent of the population did not earn more than 4.4 percent of total income, and the share of the lowest-income 20 percent of the population in total income was estimated at 9.8 percent. At the same time, the share of total income of the highest 20 percent of the population was 39 percent, and the share of the highest 10 percent amounted to 25 percent of total income. This demonstrates that the Economic Reform and Structural Adjustment Program resulted in high income inequalities. The World Bank estimates for the international poverty lines for 1995 concur with the results of the Households Expenditures Survey of 1999–2000. The percentage of the population living below US$1 a day did not exceed 3.1 percent. However, the percentage living below US$2 a day spiraled to 52.7 percent of the total population.[99]

The Neoliberals and Their Reform Agenda

The Egyptian government's ruling party, the National Democratic Party (NDP), held an important conference in 2003. The Policy Unit, headed by Gamal Mubarak, advanced a set of policy papers that came to form the basis of the regime's new policies. A new cabinet was formed in July 2004, headed by Dr. Ahmed Nazif. The main assignment for the new Nazif cabinet was to accelerate the Economic Reform and Structural Adjustment Program and to create a business-friendly environment. The

Nazif cabinet included a business tycoon, Rashid Mohamed Rashid, as minister for foreign trade and industry. The appointment of a business-man to head such an important ministry was a novel move rarely seen since 1952, when successive cabinets relied on the appointment of tech-nocrats drawn mainly from academia.

After a year of turbulent political changes and the reelection of Pres-ident Mubarak, Dr. Nazif was charged in December 2005 with forming a second cabinet. The second Nazif cabinet saw the appointment of six members of the business community to six major ministries: trade and industry, housing, transportation, health, agriculture, and social welfare. It seems that the state is not embedded in social networks, as Evans claims, but that business leaders are now in charge of policy making under the rule of Egypt's neoliberals.

The Nazif cabinets embarked on a comprehensive program of eco-nomic reforms that was drafted by the NDP Policy Unit in 2003. A neoliberal economic team, essentially made up of the minister of trade and industry, the minister of finance, and the minister of investment (called the troika by many experts) engaged in far reaching reforms.[100]

The ministry of finance slashed customs and taxes. The weighted aver-age tariff rate was reduced from 14.6 percent to 9 percent and all surcharge and service fees were abolished. A new law (Law 91 of 2005) cut personal and corporate income taxes by 50 percent and imposed a new flat tax rate of 20 percent; thus corporate taxes were brought in line with personal income taxes. The higher rate of 40 percent was maintained for state-owned enterprises, however. Drastically reducing corporate taxes for the private sector, while maintaining the rate for public sector enter-prises was a measure sure to force privatization because state owned enterprises would go bankrupt in no time due to unfair competition (higher prices born of higher tax rates) from the private sector companies.

The 20 percent tax rate is applied to a personal income at or above LE40,000, or US$7,000 per year. Lower rates apply to annual incomes less than US$7,000. A flat income tax is a regressive tax. The tax burden on lower incomes is much higher than that on higher incomes. More astound-ing was the unification of the tax rate on personal and corporate income.

A new ministry of investments was created in July 2004. It oversees all investment authorities (the General Authority for Investment, the Cap-ital Market Authority, the Cairo and Alexandria Stock Exchanges, the General Authority for Real Estate Finance, and the Public Enterprise Office) under one umbrella. The ministry was created to provide more coordinated and coherent investment policies and simpler procedures for establishing businesses in Egypt. Its main task, however, has been to accelerate the privatization process.

In the period July 2004–March 2006, the ministry of investments sold 80 companies, or 27 percent of all companies sold from 1991 to March 2006, for a total sum of LE19,948 billion, or 53 percent of total proceeds for the period.[101] Assets sold to Egyptian investors in the period July 2004–June 2005 reached a value of LE2,071 million, or 37 percent of total assets sold during the period.

Assets were sold at nominal prices. For example, the Qalyub Spinning Factory was sold for just LE4.5 million and the Ammoun Hotel for LE20 million, when in fact the land of the hotel alone could have brought that amount of money. Most sales of assets were not publicly announced. In 2007, the ministry of investment offered one of the country's largest commercial retail chains, with branches in all Egyptian governorates, for LE0.6 billion to one anchor investor (a Saudi investor).

The government is applying a new approach to the privatization program in order to accelerate the privatization process. It has offered a number of Law 203 companies for sale to private investors before completing their restructuring. The government's prices reflect the buyers' commitment to future investment, to assumption of the companies' liabilities, and to the making of investments required to upgrade and restructure the companies before their sale. An example of this new approach is the recently completed sale of the Alexandria Tire Company (Trenco) to the French firm Michelin for US$10 million: Michelin has pledged to invest US$40 million in the plant.[102]

The program under the Nazif government, while accelerating the process of privatization, is in essence subsidizing the private sector at the expense of the nation as a whole. The executive board of the IMF was more than pleased with the so-called reforms undertaken by the Nazif cabinet. According to the IMF:

> The direction of economic policies in Egypt changed sharply in 2004 with the appointment of a pro-reform cabinet led by Prime Minister Nazif. The new economic team moved aggressively on key structural reforms in the areas of trade, taxes, and subsidies, and launched plans to restructure the financial system, privatize most state companies, modernize the fiscal accounts, and strengthen monetary policy.[103]

Despite all of the above, the IMF is pushing the government to radically reduce consumer subsidies. Subsidies on food and fuel as a percentage of GDP rose from 3.1 percent in 1998–99 to 7.4 percent in 2004–2005. Food subsidies rose from less than 1 percent (0.9 percent) of GDP in 1998–99 to 2.1 percent in 2004–2005. Fuel subsidies increased from 1.1 percent in 1998–99 to 4.3 percent in 2004–2005.[104] The increase in fuel subsidy was due mainly to the increase in international oil prices. In July 2006, the government increased the price of octane-90 gas, which is used widely in Egypt, by 30 percent, and of other petroleum products by 20–25 percent. These price increases are expected to lead to a higher overall inflation rate due to a concomitant increase in transportation costs.

To eliminate subsidies, the second Nazif cabinet introduced a new ministry, that of social welfare, the main aim of which is gradual elimination of consumer subsidies. The government is proceeding carefully with the elimination of subsidies because of the political impact this is likely to have. The 1977 food riots are an experience that the government is not eager to repeat.

In July 2006, the government increased transportation, electricity, and communication prices, in an effort to align domestic prices with international prices. By doing so, however, it conveniently ignored the facts of very low wage levels and falling real per capita incomes.

Strong believers in neoliberalism, the new cabinet members are running their ministries according to market criteria. For example, a 25 percent increase in telephone rates was implemented when the publicly owned (80 percent of shares are owned by the government) Egyptian Communication System had just realized a profit of around LE2 billion in the fiscal year 2005–2006. The transportation ministry is considering involving the private sector in the ownership and management of the public communication system, and the health ministry is considering a general health insurance system to increase the ministry's revenues. The higher education ministry is considering the privatization of certain educational institutes and the establishment of a number of universities that would charge much higher fees than the free-state universities. The education system as a whole is allowing for the establishment of a large number of private schools and universities in Egypt. These institutions charge exorbitant tuition, while the public education system is increasingly deprived of good education standards.

The neoliberals of the Nazif cabinet are accelerating the process of liquidation of the populist alliance of the 1960s–1980s. Very few of the original economic rights forged in the 1960s survive, and the public sector is being liquidated ever more aggressively. The overall effect of the reformist Nazif cabinet has largely been the subsidization of the business elite and the impoverishment of the majority of the population. Finally, the state has relinquished its development role and has been taken over by private interests.

Egypt: A Developmental State?

Contrary to the developmental experience of the newly industrialized countries, Egypt's experiment in economic liberalization has resulted in what can be called a predatory state, that is, a state dominated by narrow special interests. The emergence of what some Egyptian economists call a lumpen bourgeoisie, one interested in the accrual of quick profits and benefiting from shady deals at the expense of society as a whole, characterized the period of the 1970s. In the 1980s, so-called Islamic financial companies amassed billions from the savings of Egyptians, promising very high rates of return, reaching 25 percent of original deposits. The companies were subsequently found to be fraudulent, and millions lost their life savings. Widespread fraud in building codes resulted in the collapse of high buildings and the death of hundreds. Some so-called businessmen borrowed heavily from public sector banks and fled the country, with the loans deposited in foreign banks. Economic liberalization thus became a conduit for widespread corruption, which penetrated all levels of the state.

The state's withdrawal from an actively participatory role in the economy was not compensated for by the building of an efficient capacity to enhance economic development. The Egyptian state did not attempt to guide investments but left implementation to an immature and nascent private sector. Can Egypt develop into a developmental state? This remains to be seen. Some members of the new cabinet, however, are trying to build the administrative capacity of the state, training cadres from both the government and the private sectors and improving the state's capacity to plan investment priorities. It is still too early to suggest that Egypt is turning into a developmental state, since it must take an active role in the economy in order to achieve an orderly path of growth and development.

2

The State, Democracy, and Development

Modernization and the traditional Marxist theories have both asserted that economic development leads to democracy. The neoliberal school challenges this assumption, claiming that it is democracy that leads to economic growth and not the other way around.

A plethora of empirical studies has tried to prove the hypothesis of democracy as a pre-condition for economic growth, but the main empirical results indicate that democracy can only survive in a country with a certain level of per capita income. Low levels of per capita income do not guarantee the sustainability of democracy, and democracies are said to be more likely to survive when income inequalities are lower. Other empirical studies show that democracy has either a negative effect on GDP growth or no overall effect. Many authoritarian regimes' economies grow as rapidly as, if not faster than, those of democratic regimes. The *net* effect of democracy on growth performance cross-nationally over the last five decades has been negative or null. Most case studies arrive at the same conclusions.[1]

While most research focuses on a simple causal relationship linking democracy to economic growth, other research explains regime type changes through a more complex analysis of stages of economic development, maturation of social forces, and the interplay of power relations in the context of development. Transitions to democracy in less developed countries are the consequence of important divisions within political regimes, interaction among elites, and the opposition of interests and strategies.

53

54   The State, Democracy, and Development

The historical development of economy, society, and polity in Egypt, like that in many third world countries, has demonstrated that inter-elite power conflict has been and still is the prime factor in the quest for political change (see pages 8–10). Inter-elite power relations have determined to a large extent the struggle for democratization in Egypt, and inter-elite conflict has not stopped at the level of domestic elites. In many instances, the power struggle between Egyptian elites and foreign elites has forced Egyptian elites to form alliances with other classes in society, especially the middle class, in order to protect their own interests and to dislodge the power of foreign elites.

The Relationship between Democracy and Development
The modernization theory assumes that economic growth and development lead to democracy, while the more recent neoliberal school maintains that democracy is the main determinant of development and growth.

Modernization and neomodernization theorists believe that economic development, especially industrial development, results in the emergence of more stratified social structures. Industrialization is responsible for the emergence of a working class and a more educated entrepreneurial and middle class. It dilutes primordial social ties and gives rise to increased urbanization and secularization. Modernization is also closely tied to individualism, that is, the pursuit of one's individual interests, which form the core of a free-market economy. Therefore, the social structure emerging from industrialization supports and encourages the emergence of liberal democracy. Dahl, Moore, and Schumpeter assert that economic freedom is the base for political freedom.[2] Capitalism is then an essential condition for the emergence of democracy. Lipset argues that democracy is related to the state of economic development. The higher the level of development of a country (that is, the level of per capita income), the greater is the chance that it will sustain democracy.[3]

Traditional Marxist theory also adopted an economistic explanation for political democracy. The economic structure is the determining structure, responsible for the determination of other structures, especially the political structure. Capitalism in its industrial phase leads to a class structure, divided mainly between the bourgeoisie and the proletariat. A class struggle between bourgeoisie and proletariat is an outcome of the exploitation of workers by the bourgeoisie, and the democratic political system is an essential means through which to mediate the expected class conflict.

The Relationship between Democracy and Development   55

Both modernization and Marxist theories contend that democracy is an outcome of economic growth and not vice versa. From the 1980s, with the emergence of neoliberalism, that relationship between democracy and economic development has been questioned. Does economic development lead to democracy or is the adoption of political liberalization and democratic values a necessary pre-condition to the promotion of economic development?

A politicist trend in political science argues that since the political system controls the economic system, economic growth is simply a measure of how well the political system is performing.[4] Accordingly, democracy is no longer an effect of economic growth. Therefore, all countries that pursue economic development need first to adopt a democratic political system, as a precondition for growth and development.

Democracy requires that the citizens of a state or country determine the policies that influence their lives. It involves debate over policy and competition for office, participation of citizens in decision-making, accountability of rulers, rule of law, and civilian control over the military. The arguments for the primacy of democracy and the necessity of a democratic political system for the promotion of economic growth and development involve the question of the protection of property rights and a better allocation of resources.

Democracy is supposed to promote development by safeguarding property rights. In a capitalist economy private individuals own economic resources and the role of the state is to protect this property by enforcing the rule of law. The protection of property rights is said to be conducive to capital accumulation and growth. This will only work if the regulations to protect private property rights extend to large social groups and do not simply cover small privileged groups or elites.[5]

Democracies also are believed to have better mechanisms for the allocation of resources to productive uses, because democratic governments are accountable to their citizens. This assumes that authoritarian rulers, because they are not accountable to electorates, have no incentive to increase investment and total growth.

A number of studies show a positive relationship between democracy and development.[6] Sen contends that a 'friendly process of development' should embrace the twin goals of economic growth and the extension of political and civic rights. In this case development is understood as a human process, where people are the target of efforts at development and not economic growth as such.[7]

Londregan and Poole show, however, that democratic regimes might revert to authoritarianism if poverty is widespread. Przeworski et al. claim that democracy is sustainable if it occurs in countries enjoying a certain level of economic development.[8] If democracy occurs in countries with a low level of per capita income, the liberal political system might be overcome by authoritarianism.

Strong support for the democratization of totalitarian regimes emerged with the collapse of the Soviet Union in the early 1990s. Western scholars and western countries now promote what they call "a good governance agenda." The underlying assumption is that the extension of political and civil rights will reinforce democracy and development in a cycle of "mutually beneficial exchanges."[9]

Developing countries are encouraged to adopt democracy and support human rights. The World Bank links liberal democracy to economic growth and urges donor nations to extend aid only to countries pursuing democratic reforms.[10] Major donors such as the United States, France, and Britain, and a number of international donor organizations are now attaching strict conditions to their assistance, requiring recipient countries to respect their citizens' political and human rights.[11]

The proponents of democratic good governance and the Washington Consensus contend that economic and political liberalization work in tandem.[12]

But the key question is: Can developing states engineer economic and political liberalization simultaneously, as suggested by the World Bank and other donor institutions? Kwon compares the development of democracy and capitalism across regions. He concludes that the twin processes of democratization and economic liberalization did work in Eastern and Central Europe but failed in Latin America and Southern Europe. These findings suggest that the historical context might be responsible for the relationship between democracy and capitalism and that the initiation of both processes at one and the same time has to take into account the specificity of regions and independent states.[13] On the other hand, Elster and Przeworski claim that economic liberalization might abort the democratization process due to the economic hardships imposed on large segments of the population.[14]

Notwithstanding the claims of the World Bank and other donor institutions, Houngnikpo argues that the commitment to democracy and the upholding of human rights has always taken a back seat to

The Relationship between Democracy and Development   57

considerations of regional and global security and the economic interests of advanced nations.[15]

Many scholars refute the thesis that democracy is conducive to economic development. Bardhan asserts that the idea that democracy protects private property is recent and far-fetched,[16] for he contends that if the majority of a country's population is poor, private property will be under threat even if the democratic process is properly functioning.

Democracy in a developing country might also lead to populist pressures in the form of heightened demands for immediate consumption, increased subsidies for both private consumption and business inputs (utilities, legal assistance, and so on), protective trade policies, and so forth, which have a negative effect on investments and growth.[17] The reasoning is as follows: When a majority of the people is poor their marginal propensity to consume is very high; therefore savings and investment are low. In a democracy, workers can unionize, increasing wages and thereby lowering profit and investment. In all cases lower investment will lead to lower economic growth rates. Gasiorowski asserts that democracy might have a negative effect on development and economic growth.[18] According to him, democracy results in high inflation and slower economic growth because of unrestrained competition for resources and the development of deficit financing to satisfy increased demand from all sectors of the economy.

On another level, external forces might affect democracy, especially in developing countries subject to the new conditions of economic globalization. A number of studies conclude that globalization, in the shape of exogenous economic forces, can create openings for democracy by increasing competition, and thereby conflict, among elites.[19] Inter-elite conflict is a precursor to deep political fissures and promotes change in semi-democratic or authoritarian countries. Economic crises or the adoption of structural economic changes might affect the balance of power between different elite factions, which will necessarily lead to elite conflict over access to resources and benefits. These same conditions can alienate important social groups, weakened by the crises, and therefore may undermine their political support for the political elites responsible for the adoption of economic policies that lead to the crisis. Rudra claims that the unraveling of the cohesiveness of elites and mass disenchantment will force governmental authorities to adopt a policy either of greater liberalization or of political repression.[20]

58   The State, Democracy, and Development

Another thesis that links economic globalization to political liberalization is that of the development of capital markets. Maxfield argues that the development of capital markets is detrimental to authoritarian elites, who lose a major source of their resources as rent-seeking activities diminish and the power of business increases.[21] Others, however, have advanced the thesis that foreign capital flows will bolster recipient governments regardless of regime type.[22]

Economic globalization is also credited with the creation of new interests and new political coalitions.[23] Social groups harmed by economic globalization, be they workers, bureaucrats, or asset holders, will pressure the government to enact policies in their favor. This might lead governments to liberalize in order to maintain stability,[24] and yet, contrary to these predictions and under the same set of factors, governments might opt for more political repression. There is therefore no necessary correlation between economic globalization and political liberalization.

There has been a plethora of empirical studies aimed at testing the relationship between democracy and development, and the results have been controversial. Some studies find a negative relationship between democracy and development; others show a positive relationship; and a third group concludes that the relationship between democracy and development is unclear.

Przeworski investigated the hypothesis that economic development leads to the emergence and survival of democratic regimes and the hypothesis that political regimes affect economic growth.[25] He concludes that:

1. Democracy can only survive in a country with a certain level of per capita income. Low levels of per capita income do not guarantee the sustainability of democracy. "No democracy ever fell in a country with a per capita income higher than that of Argentina in 1975 (US$6,055),"[26] that is, democracy has a greater likelihood of surviving in wealthier countries.

2. The impact of economic growth on the survival of democracy is hard to determine.

3. An educated labor force increases the probability of a democracy's survival.

4. Democracies are more likely to survive when income inequalities are lower, and they are four times more likely to survive in countries where the labor share of value added in manufacturing is greater than 25 percent.

5. Democracies are more likely to fail when one large party controls a large share of seats (more than two thirds) in the lower house of the legislature. They are more stable when there are constitutional mechanisms in place for the periodic replacement of heads of governments.
6. Parliamentary democracies are more likely to survive than presidential ones.
7. The probability of the breakdown of democracies falls as democracies grow older; this result is nullified, however, once controlled for per capita income.
8. While education, income distribution, political institutions, and the relations of political forces all have some impact on the survival of democracy regardless of per capita income, the role of income in determining the success or failure of democracy is overwhelming.

Persson and Tabellini used a sample of 150 countries for the period 1960–2000 to study the interrelationships between democracy and development and the effects of regime types.[27] Their main findings were that:
1. Enacting economic liberalization ahead of political reforms is more associated with better economic performance than is the opposite sequence of events, that is, the introduction of political liberalization first.
2. The economic growth effect of political reform from autocracy to parliamentary democracy is negative.

Persson and Tabellini classify democracies by their style of government (presidential versus parliamentary) and their form of electoral rule (majoritarian versus parliamentary). They find that parliamentary and proportional democracies are associated with greater government spending, thereby affecting economic growth negatively.[28] Persson argues that parliamentary systems usually have greater spending demands to respond to than do presidential and majoritarian systems, due to the interests of broader coalitions of voters.[29]

Other empirical studies show that the correlation between democracy and economic development is rather weak. In a study of a sample of 130 countries, Svante Ersson and Jan-Erik Lane conclude that the positive impact of democracy on economic development is a rather tenuous one.[30]

60   The State, Democracy, and Development

The established positive correlation between democracy and wealth is cast into doubt by the number of very wealthy countries that can hardly qualify as democratic. A number of cross-national empirical and case studies demonstrate that rentier economies, especially in the Middle East and Africa, while providing wealth to society as a whole, do not encourage democratization; that is, the notion that high per capita income has to be correlated with democratic regimes is not always valid, especially in resource-rich countries. As a matter of fact, researchers agree that resource rents promote authoritarianism.[31]

In any event, the results of the empirical studies point to correlations, not direct causal relationships, so they must be taken with a dose of skepticism, since it has to be assumed that they will not add significantly to an explanation of the relationship between democracy and development.

A number of scholars notice that the third wave of democratization (1990s) resulted in the emergence of a number of hybrid political systems. These regimes proliferated in many parts of Africa, Latin America, and Asia, and combine features of both democratic and authoritarian regimes. Since the beginning of the twenty-first century these hybrid systems have outnumbered democracies in these regions.[32]

These regime sub-types are categorized as hybrid regimes,[33] electoral democracies,[34] illiberal democracies,[35] semi-authoritarian,[36] semi-dictatorial regimes,[37] and so on. The regimes are characterized by having a formal party system, a degree of freedom of speech, and civil society organizations, but elections are mostly controlled, allowing no real competition with the dominant party holding power. While these regimes might be politically ambiguous in terms of the political liberalization they allow, all of them have engaged in economic liberalization. Half-hearted attempts at political liberalization are not endogenous but are forced on these systems either by international financial organizations or as a pre-condition to western countries' extension of aid. These subtypes might further muddy the relationships between democracy and development, although such artificial political liberalization signals that these regimes are unwilling to endanger the economic liberalization process through a democracy that might end in failure of the state itself.

O'Donnell and Schmitter explain transitions to democracy as the consequence of important divisions within the authoritarian regimes themselves and the interaction of elites and opposition of interests and strategies.

The Seeds of Liberalism: From Muhammad 'Ali to the British   61

A number of comparative historical studies extend the O'Donnell and Schmitter thesis by analyzing regime types through changes in economic structures and the concomitant changes in class differentiation and power relations. A study adopting the comparative historical approach is that of Rueschemeyer et al. (see pages 8–10). Rueschemeyer et al. also contend that democracy is a product of the contradictions of capitalism exacerbating social inequalities. However, whereas the process of democratization itself is a product of the subordinate classes' actions, forms of social inequality are not exhausted by class inequalities. Racial and ethnic divisions may either reinforce class divisions, or weaken the cohesiveness of classes if they cut across class lines.

The historical development of economy, society, and polity in Egypt rather demonstrates that inter-elite power struggle, not pressure from subordinate classes, was the prime factor in the quest for political liberalization. Inter-elite conflict did not stop at the level of domestic elites. In fact, the conflict between Egyptian elites and foreign elites forced the Egyptian elites to form alliances with other classes in society, especially the middle class, to protect their own interests and to dislodge the power of the foreign elites.

The Seeds of Liberalism:
From Muhammad 'Ali to the British Invasion of Egypt

Egypt was a province of the Ottoman Empire from the mid-sixteenth century until the British declared Egypt a protectorate at the outbreak of the First World War. However, since the rule of Muhammad 'Ali, Egypt had been highly independent from Constantinople, even if it had continued to pay the Ottomans an annual tax.

Prior to Muhammad 'Ali, Napoleon had instituted various consultative councils. A "Special Council," whose members were appointed by the French, represented the interests of several social groups, such as religious leaders, merchants, the Copts, the army, and the French themselves.[38] This experiment was short-lived, however, and the defeat of the French by the British and the Ottomans and the return of Egypt to its previous status as an Ottoman province abolished these councils.

Muhammad 'Ali established a state that was highly autonomous, whether from internal forces or from foreign powers, including the Ottoman Empire itself. Any attempt at including the Egyptian people or their elites in the dominant power relations was abandoned. Agricultural land was nationalized and put under state control. Muhammad 'Ali's new

62   The State, Democracy, and Development

industries, ranging from textiles to armaments, were owned and run by the state. In the process of industrialization, small industries and guilds were crushed and their owners were forced to work as laborers in state industries.[39] Muhammad 'Ali himself became the ruler, the landlord, the industrialist, the trader, and the monopolist of power, whether political or economic. Despite his monopolistic hold on power, Muhammad 'Ali established an advisory council, made up of 156 members, including thirty-three high-ranking officials, twenty-four district officials, and ninety-nine notables.[40] The council was, nevertheless, purely consultative, and Muhammad 'Ali was under no obligation to abide by its edicts.

This situation can be explained by the extermination of the previous ruling elite (the Mamluks) by Muhammad 'Ali himself and the lack of an Egyptian elite capable of imposing its power and interests on the state. But while Muhammad 'Ali exterminated the previous ruling elite, his habit of granting lands to members of his family and high officials of state, and to army officials, provincial governors, and notables in exchange for their assumption of tax liabilities, led to the reemergence of private property in agriculture. This process was strengthened under Khedive Said and reached its apex under Khedive Isma'il.

Muhammad 'Ali's experiment in state-led industrialization collapsed after the defeat of his army by the European powers allied with the Ottoman Empire. The European powers imposed free trade rules on Egypt and destroyed the state's monopolies. Thereafter, Egypt relied on a single crop for exports (cotton) and a primary-product export-oriented growth strategy. This strategy required heavy investment in such agricultural and transportation infrastructure as irrigation canals, dams, railways (the oldest railway line in the world after that of Great Britain), ports, and a commercial navy. The infrastructure was mostly built by the state under Khedive Isma'il (1863–79). High revenues from cotton, especially in the first half of the 1860s, financed the infrastructure, but the end of the U.S. Civil War and the resumption of American cotton exports led to a steep decline in the price of Egyptian cotton. To continue his infrastructure and urbanization projects, in addition to financing a growing army, Isma'il resorted to foreign loans.

Isma'il tried to raise revenues to cover the debt. The Muqabla law issued on August 30, 1871, reduced taxes on land by half for anyone who paid six years' of land taxes in advance. Owners of lands who did not enjoy full ownership rights (such as the right to pass their land by inheritance), would acquire such rights, along with the tax concession. While

The Seeds of Liberalism: From Muhammad 'Ali to the British   63

the Muqabla law was discretionary at first, it became obligatory in May 1874.[41] The law resulted in the extension of private property rights to nearly all agricultural land in Egypt. Until the promulgation of the Muqabla law, most privately owned land was held by the members of the ruling house of Muhammad 'Ali, Turkish–Circassian elites, and a few Egyptians granted the land by the wali or khedive for services rendered to the ruler himself. However, Isma'il's Muqabla law expanded owner-ship of land, which was the main economic asset of the time, and gave rise to an Egyptian landed elite.

Despite Isma'il's efforts to repay the debt, including the sale of Egypt's shares in the Suez Canal to the British, he failed in his quest. The foreign debt amounted to £91 million in 1875. Isma'il stopped payments that year, and foreign creditors, led by the British and French, established a Public Debt Fund *(La Caisse de la Dette Publique)* to ensure repayment. Egypt was declared bankrupt in 1876. In 1878, a commission of inquiry was formed to examine Egypt's finances. It found that the khedive had mismanaged the finances, and demanded curtailment of his power. A new government was formed, headed by Nubar Pasha and including two foreign ministers (French and British).

In his efforts to resist foreign intervention, Isma'il tried to resort to the Assembly of Delegates instituted by a decree in November 1866. As part of his modernization and Europeanization efforts, Isma'il had tried to emulate European parliamentarism by establishing the assembly, but it had no legislative role. The assembly's deliberations covered internal affairs only. Its main role was advisory, and the khedive could endorse or reject the assembly's advice.[42] The Assembly of Delegates opposed the draconian measures imposed on Egypt and the foreign intervention in Egypt's internal affairs, meeting from January to July 1879 and demand-ing control of the country's finances.

In addition to the Assembly of Delegates' protests and demands for a greater role in the country's financial affairs, Egyptian army officers protested the appointment of foreigners as cabinet ministers and a 50 percent reduction in pay for a group of officers. The protesting officers occupied the ministry of finance building, threatening a long siege if their demands were not met.

The foreign powers were dismayed by the protests, particularly those voiced by the assembly, and pressured Isma'il to dissolve it in April 1879. The members refused to dissolve the assembly, an indication of a real change in role, from mere advisors to true parliamentarians. They

64   The State, Democracy, and Development

claimed that they represented the nation and that the khedive therefore could not dissolve the Assembly of Delegates.

Taking advantage of the army officers' protest and the refusal of the assembly members to dissolve the parliament, Isma'il rejected the declaration of Egypt's bankruptcy, dismissed the foreign ministers and, indeed, the entire cabinet, and took measures to form a new cabinet.

The British and French, in turn, pressured the Ottoman Sultan to depose Isma'il in favor of his son Tawfiq. Khedive Isma'il was deposed in 1879, was subsequently exiled, and died in 1895. Under Tawfiq, the foreign cabinet ministers were reinstated and the assembly was dissolved.

In his conflict with the European powers, Isma'il formed an alliance with the notables (the landed elite of the time). While the alliance gave him the pretext he needed to reject foreign intervention in Egypt's affairs, it did not succeed, for the weak Ottoman caliphate gave in to European interests rather than join Isma'il in his resistance. Nevertheless, this conflict was to mark Egyptian politics for a long time to come. It brought about Egypt's colonization by the British to thwart attempts by the army or the new elites to end foreign intervention, whether Ottoman or European. The appointment of Tawfiq as khedive, the restoration of foreign intervention, and the dissolution of the assembly were moves that took little heed of the impact of such measures on the Egyptian population, particularly on the army officers and the new landed elites.

All of this amounted to the beginnings of a national revolt, starting as an army protest against the financial hardships imposed on the country and military by foreign powers and escalating with the collaboration of members of Egypt's landed elite and leading merchants and heads of guilds. In a now famous confrontation with the khedive on September 9, 1881, Ahmad 'Urabi, who headed the army rebellion, demanded the reinstitution of the Assembly of Delegates, the drawing up of a constitution, the restoration of the army to its original force, and status for Egyptian officers equal to that of the Turkish Circassian officers then dominating the army.[43]

The 'Urabi revolt, regardless of its outcome, is significant because it signaled the birth of Egyptian nationalism. The new Egyptian landed elite was subordinate to the ruling Turkish-Circassian elite and sought an ideology that would deprive the foreign elite of political legitimacy. Egyptian nationalism was the new legitimizing ideology against foreign intervention, the Palace, and the Turkish-Circassian elite. It was flavored with Islamic rhetoric in an attempt to displace the pure Islamic ideology that was the basis of the Ottoman and Turkish-Circassian elite's domination of Egypt.[44]

The Egyptian nationalist movement was associated at the time with strong demands for democracy and constitutionalism. Democracy would serve to check and control the powers of the khedive and the Turkish-Circassian aristocracy, and the foreign powers' monopoly over the country's finances. The nationalist movement, by demanding a democratic system, was attempting, if not to control the political system completely, to at least share power with the khedive and the ruling Turkish-Circassian aristocracy.[45]

The 'Urabi revolt almost stripped Khedive Tawfiq of his powers. The revolt ended with the British invasion of Egypt in 1882, the pretext for which was protection of foreign minorities. The British occupation lasted for seventy-two years (1882–1954).

Restricted Liberalism and the Emergence of an Industrial Elite (1923–52)

British rule deepened the Egyptian economy's dependence on cotton cultivation. Cotton production increased from around 3 million qantars (120 million kg) in 1879 to approximately 8 million qantars (320 million kg) in 1913. Nevertheless, the price of cotton fell steadily until the first decade of the twentieth century, declining from US$22 per qantar in 1870 to just US$7 in 1897.[46] The expansion in cotton production was made possible by large investments in agricultural infrastructure, while industry and manufacturing were neglected. Lord Cromer, the British Commissioner and the real ruler of Egypt at the time, saw industrialization, particularly in textiles, as undesirable, claiming that it would educe the large revenues from custom duties on Egypt's imports of cotton goods.[47] But Cromer's real motive was to prevent any competition to British textile manufacturing: while Egypt exported all of its cotton production, it was one of the main importers of British textiles.

Egyptian landowners were content to concentrate all their efforts on the production and export of cotton. However, the 1906–1907 European economic crisis dealt cotton exports a serious blow. Reduced European demand for cotton led to a sustained economic crisis in Egypt that lasted until the outbreak of the First World War in 1914. The dangers of a monocrop economy were made clear even to the members of the landed elite. An independent economic policy was necessary to

66   The State, Democracy, and Development

avoid such drastic crises, but economic independence first required political independence from Great Britain.

Political agitation for independence reached dramatic heights during the period (1907–14), and Egypt's first political parties emerged during this period. The Nationalist Party, led by Mustafa Kamel, advocated an Islamist orientation and the formation of an alliance with the Ottomans to oust the British from Egypt; it was formed by merchants, a faction of the middle class, and students. The People's Party, formed by secular-oriented liberals, agitated for emancipation from the nominal domination of the Ottoman caliphate and for negotiations with the British to gain independence. The Constitutionalist Party was a creation of the Palace that sought to defend the khedive and his court officials. The People's Party recruited its members from the landed aristocracy, the intelligentsia, and the middle class.[48]

Because of its Islamist orientation and strident Egyptian nationalism, the Nationalist Party found an ally in Khedive 'Abbas (1892–1914). The landed aristocracy of the People's Party, on the other hand, viewed both the khedive and the Ottoman caliphate as the main impediments to their interests and therefore preferred to pursue moderate policies toward the British, hoping to enlist their support in the struggle against Turkish-Circassian hegemony. Independence from the British could be secured later through negotiations.[49] This political stance stemmed in part from a shared interest with the British in securing revenues from the cultivation and export of cotton for some members of the landed elite, but it also grew out of a realistic assessment of the military capabilities of the British and the Ottomans. Particularly after the dire results of the 'Urabi revolt, Egypt was not ready for or capable of withstanding a prolonged conflict with the powerful British Empire, while British forces were certainly capable of wresting Egyptian independence from the Ottomans and ending, once and for all, the reign of the House of Muhammad 'Ali.

The Nationalist Party, while capable of engineering large and tumultuous demonstrations (mainly of students), found itself at odds with the khedive when he changed policies and opted for rapprochement with the British. The Palace resorted to the Constitutional Reform Party to defend the position and privileges of the khedive and the Turkish-Circassian aristocracy. The Constitutional Reform Party relied on an ideology of conservative pan-Islamism and Islamic orthodoxy in its appeal to the masses for their support for the ruling khedive.

Restricted Liberalism and the Emergence of an Industrial Elite 67

The outbreak of the First World War aggravated the political and the economic crises that had begun in 1907. The British deposed the khedive and declared Egypt a British Protectorate in 1914. The Assembly (a caricature of a parliament created by the British) was suspended, and the press was placed under military censorship, which alienated the educated segments of the middle class and the intelligentsia.

The British also imposed restrictions on cotton exports. Inflation soared, and speculation on land and commodities created a new class of nouveaux riches composed of Egyptians and foreigners alike.[50] Workers (especially unskilled workers) suffered from a sharp fall in real income. Peasants suffered the most. The British army commandeered grain and beasts of burden at very low prices, and peasants were recruited by force into the British Camel and Labor Corps.[51]

The economic crisis eased during the last two years of the war, however: the British relaxed the restrictions on cotton exports, and a four-fold increase in the price of cotton exports encouraged landowners to expand cotton acreage at the expense of food crops, which led to spiraling inflation in the wholesale price index, from 100 in 1914, to 211 in 1918, and to 312 in 1920.[52] The rural and the urban poor were the most victimized, followed by the urban middle class. Charles Issawi claims that this situation increased mortality rates from 300,000 per year before the war to 375,000 after 1916 and to 510,000 in 1918, causing mortality rates to exceed birth rates.[53]

While the landlords benefited from the war, they were alienated from the British by the latter's attempts to increase Sudanese cotton production to depress international prices. The war did lead, however, to some local industrialization and the creation of a nucleus of a working class.[54]

By the end of the war, the British had succeeded in alienating all segments of Egyptian society and all relevant political trends. A nationalist movement that agitated for Egypt's independence in accordance with the fourteen points of President Woodrow Wilson's speech of January 1918, and which was headed by Sa'd Zaghlul Pasha, was triggered by the refusal of the British authorities to allow an Egyptian delegation (or *wafd*, later the name of the political party led by Zaghlul) to attend the Versailles Peace Conference to present its case for independence. When Zaghlul protested the British refusal, he and some members of his group were exiled.

Demonstrations spread throughout the country in a continuous wave of protests; the railway system was sabotaged; lawyers, students, railway

68   The State, Democracy, and Development

workers, and government employees initiated strikes; women joined the demonstrations; and the nationalist movement resorted to a general political boycott of all British attempts to end the revolt, including a boycott of the Milner Commission.[55] A one-sided British declaration of Egypt's independence on February 28, 1922, ended the 1919 revolution. The revolution, in any case, was nominal at best. The British attached four reservations to the declaration that limited the country's independence severely. These included clauses for the protection of the British Empire's communications (the Suez Canal), the defense of Egypt against any aggression, direct or indirect, the protection of foreign interests and those of minorities, and the maintenance of a joint government of Sudan and Egypt.[56] There were protests against the reservations, especially by the Copts, who did not regard themselves as a minority and who allied themselves to the Wafd Party. Nevertheless, the declaration of Egypt's independence ended the revolution. Sultan Ahmad Fu'ad changed his title to King Fu'ad, and a constitution modeled on that of Belgium (but with many of its articles derived from the Islamic shari'a) was formulated. In January 1923, elections were held, and the Wafd Party was elected with an overwhelming majority. A semi-parliamentary democratic system gave powers to the landed elite, as against the King and the Turkish-Circassian elite. Nonetheless, the King retained tremendous executive and legislative powers, which aborted the newfound powers of the elites.

The 1923 constitution was liberal in intent, guaranteeing equality before the law, individual liberties (including liberty of opinion and assembly), and a free press. It also guaranteed private property. For the first time, the Egyptian constitution guaranteed compulsory education for both sexes. It established Islam as the state religion and Arabic as the official language. The constitution suffered, however, from the excessive powers vested in the executive, that is, the King. The King also had legislative power (along with the senate and the chamber of deputies), which allowed him to initiate legislation. The wide powers of the King allowed him to veto any legislation passed by parliament. He also had the power to prorogue the parliament or adjourn its sessions for a certain period of time. More significantly, the King could dismiss the cabinet (even if it had been formed by the party that had won the elections) and replace it with another of his choosing. Despite the overwhelming powers granted to him by the constitution, the King (Fu'ad and later Faruk) frequently violated the constitution's provisions and in many instances suspended it.[57]

The parliament was composed of a senate and a chamber of deputies. The King had the right to appoint two-fifth of the senators. Eligibility for the senate depended on income, and the King nominated the senate's president. The chamber of deputies was elected by indirect ballot. Clearly, the constitution conferred great power on the King. The result was a semi-parliamentary system, and the main function of the parliament was consultative in nature and effect.[58]

Nevertheless, the Wafd Party maintained its popularity up to the military takeover in 1952; its resilience and in some way its main weakness lay in the character of its main constituents: its nationalist coalition. Landowners and peasants, workers and emerging industrialists, the educated and the illiterate, and most of the middle class supported the Wafd, although two main groups, the landowners and the emerging industrialist-capitalist class, competed for control of the Wafd. Jean and Simonne Lacouture argue that a national bourgeoisie sought to dislodge the power centers of the cosmopolitan and foreign elites.[59] Members of the landed elite needed to wrest agricultural decisions from British control, and to increase their ownership of land. The new industrial elite that emerged in 1922–23 with the creation of Banque Misr and the Misr group of industries needed state protection to compete against foreign elites and foreign imports. Only a nationalist government could grant these privileges.

While the Wafd was closely tied to a faction of the landed and industrial elites, it catered to the other social groups. The middle class benefited from expanded free education and employment in government, and a welfare program was extended to the poor. Nevertheless, successive Wafd governments were restricted in their welfare programs by the landed and industrial elites that dominated it, and social inequalities increased.

At the same time, factions of other elites formed their own parties. Not as popular as the Wafd, these came to be known as the minority parties, the most important of which was the Liberal Constitutionalists Party by the big landowners (a direct offshoot of the People's Party and the Nationalist Party).

The economic crisis of the 1930s, while accelerating industrialization, due to heavy state protection, also resulted in widening income inequalities, spiraling inflation, and massive unemployment. The Wafd was caught in a dilemma. The nationalist question still lingered, due to the inability of the Wafd to obtain complete withdrawal of the British

70   The State, Democracy, and Development

troops. The economic hardships caused discontent, especially among large segments of the middle class and the poor. New political movements, namely, the Society of the Muslim Brothers and Young Egypt, were able to recruit adherents from the discontented. The Muslim Brothers agitated for a supra-Islamic federation, and Young Egypt adopted a supra-nationalist but Islamic ideology. Both groups resorted to terrorism as a tactic of intimidation and political manipulation.[60]

The Second World War deepened the economic crisis, and the Wafd failed to address the problems of spiraling inflation, high unemployment, and widening income inequalities. The dominant elites of the Wafd succeeded in blocking any legislation or measure that would limit their benefits or contradict their interests. Industries enjoyed strong state protection and were mostly monopolistic, due to the narrow internal market and the inability to export their products, even to neighboring countries. More damaging to the Wafd was the intractability of the nationalist question and the continued presence of British troops in Egypt. The national question became more difficult with the defeat of Egyptian troops in the first Arab–Israeli war, in 1948.

The Palace, the British, and the political parties themselves contravened the so-called liberal and parliamentary system of Egypt between 1922 and 1952. Elections always resulted in an overwhelming show of support for the Wafd, but the party rarely in fact ruled during that period. Out of thirty years of so-called liberal politics, the Wafd ruled for a total of seven and a half years. The minority parties allied with the King and supported by the British dominated the government. Parliamentary elections were rigged, and parliamentary office was confined to a narrow elite. The Palace and the British managed to interfere whenever the electorate brought undesirable representatives to power. For example, the British forced the King to dismiss the Wafd government in 1924, and to bring the Wafd to power in 1942.

The articulation of the political and economic crises, after the end of the Second World War, resulted in massive unrest and the outbreak of violence in the period 1945–52. The elites were fragmented and a severe inter-elite conflict emerged between a faction of the landowning elite on the one hand, which refused any agricultural reform, and a faction of the landed–industrial elite (represented by the Liberal Constitutionalists and the Sa'dists, a splinter group from the Wafd) on the other, which relied heavily on foreign capital and allied itself to the Palace and the British.

Serious restructuring of the economy to alleviate the economic crisis was prevented by the political fragmentation of the elites and the discontent of the poor and the middle class. The intervention of the army in July 1952, while it claimed to be engineering a revolution, was, in fact, an attempt to end the cycle of unrest and violence that ended with the Cairo fire of January 1952.

Authoritarianism, Nationalism, and State Autonomy (1952–76)

The 1952 Revolution prevented a revolution from taking place, but, on the other hand, it did engineer a structural transformation of Egypt, both socially and politically. The leaders of the 1952 Revolution, the so-called Free Officers, were an assortment of officers from diverse political backgrounds. Some of them were members of the Society of the Muslim Brothers and the Young Egypt party; others belonged to the left, while many did not have any clear political identification.

The Free Officers came to power without a definitive program, but once in power they determined their goals as:

1. The eradication of imperialism;
2. The abolition of feudalism;
3. The eradication of monopoly capital;
4. The establishment of social justice;
5. The building of a strong national army;
6. The establishment of democratic rule.

While the goals were vague, they reflected nationalist (eradication of imperialism; the building of a strong army) and populist (abolition of feudalism, eradication of monopoly, and establishment of social justice) yearnings and an indeterminate call for democracy. With the exception of political democracy, these goals would later be pursued through economic and social measures that would change the face of Egypt.

The six goals also indicate that, from the beginning, Gamal Abd al-Nasser, the leader of the Free Officers, while paying lip service to the idea that the army would return to its barracks after stabilization of the political situation, did not intend to return the country to civilian rule. Nasser understood that returning the country to civilian rule would bring back the same old elites, which might welcome the eradication of imperialism but would block implementation of other goals relating to the economic and social restructuring of Egypt. Nasser took the position that an early return

72   The State, Democracy, and Development

to democracy would only bring back the old political parties that were (according to him) centers of political corruption. He claimed that for a democratic system to function it was necessary to guarantee social democracy, whereby class distinctions of wealth and privilege would be abolished.[61] To promulgate their vision of a cohesive national political constituency, in 1953 the ruling coalition (the Revolutionary Command Council (RCC) created a political structure called the Liberation Rally, in lieu of parties. The Rally was designed to provide a political institution and attract followers, but it was stillborn and did not take roots in Egypt's political system. It was an artificial and hollow political structure that never succeeded in mobilizing the different political factions in existence at the time.

The Free Officers designated General Muhammad Naguib as head of the government, to gain the population's confidence. Nasser himself was only thirty-four years old at the time of the revolution, and the rest of the Free Officers were too young and obscure to gain the people's confidence. However, the appointment of Naguib and the varied backgrounds of the Free Officers would soon result in an internal power struggle that would eliminate many of their members from the ruling coalition, the Revolutionary Command Council (RCC), and lead to the emergence of Nasser in 1954 as the leader of the revolution.

For Nasser to apply his vision for Egypt, he had to monopolize power within the RCC and to destroy the old political elites. A power struggle ensued within the RCC itself. The conflict soon emerged between General Naguib, the titular head of the new regime, and Nasser. The main bone of contention between Nasser and Naguib was the return to civilian rule and the establishment of a parliamentary system. Naguib, a reformist at heart, advocated a return to civilian rule. He was supported by a few RCC officers, among them Khalid Muhi al-Din, a member of the Egyptian left and later the head of the Progressive Unionist Party (Tagammu') that would emerge after 1977. Nasser, on the other hand, argued that a return to civilian rule would bring back the old political factions and the system controlled by the old elites. The power struggle came to a head in February 1954. Naguib, the President of Egypt at the time, was forced out. A popular upheaval supported by the old elites, the leftists, and the Muslim Brothers, protested his removal and brought him back as president, but Naguib then nominated Nasser prime minister. By March 25 of the same year, the RCC, after solidifying its position in the army and winning the support of the Muslim Brothers, announced the return of the country to civilian rule and the disbanding of the RCC. Supporters of Nasser, especially trade unions members, staged massive demonstrations against the dissolution of the RCC. The army stood firmly behind the new leadership of Gamal Abd al-Nasser, and Nasser declared the return of the RCC to power on March 29. In mid-November 1954, Naguib was dismissed as president and placed under house arrest.

These very well-orchestrated tactics to get rid of Naguib and those members of the RCC who advocated a return to democracy consolidated the power of Nasser as the head of the RCC. However, Nasser was aware that the leftist movements and the Muslim Brothers were still active and inciting resistance to his rule. Another power struggle ensued between the regime, on one side, and the Left and the Muslim Brothers, on the other. The leftists were easy to dispose off. Their fragmentation weakened their organizations. Leftist elements in the army were purged. The regime harassed the different communist groups, and many communists were arrested and tried on the pretext of conspiracies to overthrow the regime. The Muslim Brothers were more difficult to deal with. Allies of the regime in bringing down the monarchy, they nevertheless opposed the agreement initialed by Nasser and the British on July 27, 1954, for the evacuation of British troops. The agreement provided for a gradual withdrawal of British troops from Egypt, but allowed them to return if Turkey or any Arab state came under attack. The Muslim Brothers opposed the agreement, claiming that it was harmful to Egypt's interests.

The Muslim Brothers' opposition to the agreement was a sign of their dissatisfaction with its inability to dominate the new regime. Nasser was not interested in submitting to the power of the Muslim Brothers or, for that matter, to any other group. The attempt on Nasser's life by a member of the Muslim Brothers on October 26, 1954, while Nasser was delivering a speech in Alexandria gave him the chance to retaliate in force and to get rid of the Muslim Brothers once and for all. Massive arrests of the Muslim Brothers, and especially of members of the Secret Order (an underground branch that used violence to liquidate Muslim Brothers' enemies) and of the Executive Committee members, began that same night. Special "People's Tribunals," headed by Gamal Salem (RCC cadre) and including Husayn al-Shafi'i and Anwar Sadat as members, were established to try them.[62] Those arrested were handed hefty indictments and received harsh penalties.

74   The State, Democracy, and Development

The elimination of the old elites and competing political forces such as the Muslim Brothers and the leftists were steps that would allow complete state autonomy. The state autonomy envisaged by Nasser would propel a development process that would deepen industrialization, widen the social base of the regime, and eliminate any threats to the new ruling elites. At the time, any democratic system would have blocked revolutionary economic policies such as land reform, the deepening of industrialization, and the control of financial institutions (see Chapter 1).

In effect, the land reform programs implemented by the regime not only improved land distribution but also brought a substantial section of the peasantry into the social coalition supporting the regime. However, more economic restructuring was needed to gain the support of other social forces for the new rulers. After eliminating competing political forces, the Nasser regime embarked on policies to strengthen its rule and to promote development and social justice, although one of the main problems that needed to be addressed was the failure to establish a meaningful political structure.

Convinced that a return to the old political liberal system would defeat the purposes of the revolution, Nasser said that Egypt would not have a parliament until the regime liquidated the influence of the landowning elite and the so-called exploiting capitalists.[63] In order for the regime to block the return of the old elites' domination of the political system, a coalition of social forces would form the basis of the new political structure.

A new constitution was promulgated on January 16, 1956. Instead of a parliamentary system, it formed a new political organization, the National Union. The National Union was to gather the different political forces into a political coalition. The constitution established a national assembly. The members of the assembly had to be screened and nominated by the National Union. Only those nominated by the National Union could run in elections, supervised by the ministry of interior. The regime had in fact created a corporatist political system effectively run by the state.

The 1956 constitution gave major powers to the president. The parliament was under his control. The first national assembly was short-lived, for it was in effect terminated by the announcement of the union between Egypt and Syria in 1958.

The Syrian secession from the union in 1961 ushered in a new stage in political institution building. The major tasks of this period, heralded by Egypt's move toward massive nationalization of economic institutions, required a new constitution. A preparatory committee of 250 members was formed to plan for a new constitution and to prepare for the establishment of a National Congress of Popular Forces. The committee was charged with the task of determining the qualifications of individuals running for the congress. Certain categories of people were banned from running for elections: convicted criminals, landlords who had lost land to agrarian reform laws, those whose property fell under sequestration, and so on. Clearly, the regime wanted to isolate its enemies from participating in the new political system. Since the congress was to represent the coalition of working forces in society, quotas were assigned to each group. Peasants were assigned 25 percent of seats, workers 20 percent, the so-called nationalist capitalists 10 percent, trade unionists 15 percent, unorganized wage earners 9 percent, university teachers 7 percent, students 7 percent, and women's organizations 7 percent.[64]

Thus formed, in May 1962 the National Congress of Popular Forces approved a national charter, which presented an outline for a new constitution, and proposed a new political institution that Nasser decided to call the Arab Socialist Union. The Arab Socialist Union was to become the only political party in Egypt and would vote for a national assembly.[65]

The 1964 constitution allocated 50 percent of the seats of the national assembly to peasants and workers. This stipulation is said to have increased the power of the executive. Workers were drawn mostly from the public sector, where the government had ultimate control, and the peasants were beholden to an intricate system of cooperatives managed by the state.[66]

The new political institutions reflected the new economic policies of Nasser's regime. The socialist laws were designed to increase state autonomy, the state becoming the country's main capitalist and entrepreneur. The elimination of the industrial elite in the 1960s and its replacement with a public sector was a major step toward the establishment of a populist system that would perform the basic function of solidifying the regime's social, and therefore political, base.

The populist system of the 1960s rested on economic inclusion of important social groups in the supporting social coalition, while excluding those same forces from political participation. The nationalization measures of the 1960s and the economic hegemony of the state increased the scope of economic inclusionary measures. More radical land reform laws and rent controls on urban real estate and rural agricultural land shifted power from owners to tenants. The public education program was extended, and wider public health programs were initiated. In addition, the regime implemented a large-scale program of subsidies and ensured full employment through a system of guaranteed employment for all graduates of secondary schools and universities. All these measures not only reduced income inequalities, but also strengthened the regime's political base.[67]

A new bureaucratic elite emerged to manage the sprawling state sector. The lack of accountability and the absence of a politically viable democratic system led in time to widespread corruption and gross administrative inefficiencies. The power of members of the bureaucratic elite reached unimagined heights, and they managed to create strong power centers within the state. The lack of open political forums, together with repressive policies, eliminated any effective challenge to the power and greed of such bureaucrats.

The slowdown in economic growth and the growing economic problems that emerged after the Arab defeat in the 1967 Arab–Israeli confrontation, in addition to the heavy costs of the war, contributed to a new power struggle between the two factions of the bureaucratic elite. One faction agitated for a return to the mechanisms of the private market, claiming that the system was hampered by the inefficiencies of the public sector, and that the role of the state should accordingly be restricted. Moreover, foreign capital would help to deepen industrialization. Therefore, and in order to solve the economic crisis, Egypt should seek a rapprochement with the west, particularly the United States, make peace with Israel, and concentrate its efforts on economic growth and development. Another faction claimed that the economic crisis would not be solved by a return to freewheeling, unfettered capitalism. Egypt had to extend the centralization of the economy, to maintain the support and aid of the Soviet Union and to put and end to the Israeli occupation of the Sinai, either through military action or a comprehensive settlement of the Arab–Israeli conflict.[68]

The power struggle between these two factions within the bureaucratic elite would come to a head after Nasser's death in September 1970 and the appointment of Sadat as president. By May 1971, the faction in favor of a return to capitalism and rapprochement with the west had managed to dislodge the other faction from power and thus a new stage in Egypt's history was begun.

The Arab Socialist Union was to remain the regime's only political institution up to 1976, when President Sadat began a new experiment in limited democracy by creating three pulpits within the Arab Socialist Union to represent the right, the left, and what he called the center. The center was ultimately his own party, first called the Egypt Socialist Party, then replaced summarily by the National Democratic Party, which remains the majority party of the ruling regime to this day.

Restricted Political Liberalization, the State, and the Emergence of a New Capitalist Class (1976–91)

After his so-called Corrective Revolution of May 1971, Sadat called for a new constitution. The new constitution of 1971, adopted by national referendum in 1971, and still in force, continued the tradition of concentrating power in the hands of the ruler. The president has the right to rule by decree, to dismiss the legislature, and to appoint and dismiss ministers.

The 1971 constitution also included an article that contained clause, "*al-shari'a al-islamiya masdarun ra'isiyun li-l tashri'*" ('Islamic shari'a is a principal source of legislation'). This departed from the previous constitution, which had only declared Islam to be the official state religion. Sadat also granted amnesty to political prisoners, many of whom were Muslim Brothers members who had been jailed by the Nasserist regime after an alleged coup d'état attempt in 1965. Also in September 1971, Sadat issued the first law to encourage Arab and foreign investments, signaling the regime's intentions to adopt a different economic philosophy.

One of the main outcomes of these measures was the alliance forged between Sadat and the Muslim Brothers, who had been staunch enemies of the Nasserist regime. This signaled Sadat's intention to embark on a deep restructuring of political and economic power relations to point Egypt in a new direction. Obtaining the support of the Muslim Brothers was a necessary step toward dismantling the Nasserist social base, formed of large sections of the middle class, the peasantry, and the workers. Political power relations had to be changed in order to build a new alliance among top members of the bureaucratic elite favoring a liberal and market-oriented economic system, the traditional wing of the old elite, and private sector magnates.

These new policies could not be implemented, however, while Sinai remained under Israeli occupation. The limited success of the 1973 war

78   The State, Democracy, and Development

gave Sadat the necessary legitimacy to embark on his new policies. In October 1974, the regime issued the October Paper, which stressed the need for Arab and foreign capital and western technology to boost economic development. He claimed that economic liberalization was a necessary condition to attract foreign capital. For economic liberalization to occur, the state had to relinquish its monopoly over the economy and reverse the previous regime's inclusionary economic policies. A market-oriented regime could not operate in the shadow of the Nasserist populist alliance. One major step toward economic liberalization would be the elimination of the political structure that had supported Nasserist policies: the Arab Socialist Union.

In August 1974, Sadat circulated a paper to members of the Arab Socialist Union considering the future of the polity, and especially the future of the Arab Socialist Union, in which he suggested the need for multi-parliamentarism. The third National Congress of the Arab Socialist Union, which convened in July 1975, strongly resisted the creation of a multi-party system. Members advocated, instead, the democratization of the party's own structure and suggested the establishment of opinion forums that would reflect different political trends, as suggested by President Sadat. Accordingly, in March 1976 Sadat called for the establishment of three forums, representing the right, the left, and the center. The newly established forums participated in the 1976 elections. Once the elections were over, Sadat moved quickly to declare, in his inaugural address to the People's Assembly on November 1976, that the forums were political parties. Consequently, political parties were formed in June 1977, and the Arab Socialist Union was eliminated.[69] The elimination of the Arab Socialist Union, previously dominated by Ali Sabri, Sadat's arch rival and enemy, marked an end to the Nasserist political institution that might have resisted the desired fundamental changes to the economy.

The formation of political parties notwithstanding, the political liberalization experiment proved to be restricted. The multi-party system was not designed to establish a truly democratic system in Egypt but to facilitate the implementation of much-needed economic reforms in order to attract foreign capital and mobilize internal savings. The multi-party system performed another function for the regime, that of creating structured and recognizable opposition parties, thereby providing the appearance of opposition to the regime. This enhanced the regime's ability to divide the opposition and to gather information on the nature and scope of its activities. President Sadat called democracy a safety valve that enabled him to gauge his opponents' strategies.[70]

During the 1970s, economic liberalization proceeded slowly. The reshaping of economic power relations was strongly resisted by the Nasserist social base, especially by peasants, workers, and university students. New year's day in 1975 was marked by widespread workers' riots protesting inflation and repression. In March the workers of Mahalla al-Kubra textile factories staged a massive strike demanding higher wages and better working conditions. The state resorted to widespread arrests of the workers, but they staged another strike in August of the same year. In September, public transportation workers waged a three-day strike that paralyzed Cairo.[71]

The social unrest, prompted by the regime's economic policies, reached a peak in January 1977. After the government announcement of the cancellation of subsidies, especially food subsidies, riots engulfed the whole of Egypt, from Alexandria to Aswan, for two days (January 18 and 19). The government had canceled the food subsidies due to pressures exerted by the IMF and the U.S. to stabilize the economy, reduce the budget deficit, and restore the market mechanism. Violence reigned for two days and abated only when the government backed away from the proposed measures. Massive arrests followed, and Sadat blamed the Left for the riots.[72] Nevertheless, the food riots were to make successive governments wary of attempting to eliminate subsidies suddenly, particularly food subsidies.

Despite the changes in economic policies and the introduction of a restricted political liberalism, the state remained an authoritarian-bureaucratic state, retaining its strong grip on the public sector, a means for enrichment of the bureaucratic elite and for pursuit of highly interventionist policies. Similarly, the state dominated the country's political structure through the overwhelming power wielded by the NDP, the majority party, which was headed by the president himself and which had inherited all the privileges of the defunct Arab Socialist Union. The regime was also highly repressive, preferring coercion to political compromise.

President Sadat's high-profile trip to Jerusalem in November of 1977 and the Camp David Accords alienated the allies of the regime, especially the Muslim Brothers and radical Islamist groups. In September 1981, Sadat cracked down on all his opponents. Security forces were ordered to arrest over three thousand people, whose political leanings ranged from far right to far left. On October 6, 1981, Sadat was assassinated by Islamist extremists (al-Gihad group).

While the assassination of President Sadat precipitated and was precipitated by a crisis, the transfer of power to vice-president Hosni Mubarak was achieved swiftly and peacefully according to the rules of the Egyptian constitution. Mubarak continued Sadat's policies but in a more conciliatory manner. One of his first actions after he was sworn into office was to free everyone arrested in September 1981, in a gesture of national reconciliation. Nonetheless the regime declared a state of emergency after Sadat's assassination that is still in effect today.

The 1980s saw little in terms of systemic political changes, and more liberalization was unthinkable during that decade due to the deep economic crisis that plagued Egypt from the mid-1980s on. The steep decline in oil prices of the 1980s, when the price of oil decreased from US$41 per barrel in 1980 to US$8 in 1986, had a deep recessionary impact. The lower oil prices had a direct impact on the revenues derived from the sale of Egyptian oil and an indirect impact through workers' remittances, especially from workers in the Gulf, and through proceeds of the Suez Canal. Egypt's external debt increased from around US$21 billion in 1980 to US$41 billion in 1991. In this context, Egypt resisted pressures for the full implementation of a structural adjustment program that would increase inflationary pressures, unemployment, and income inequalities, particularly with the 1977 food riots still fresh in the regime's mind.[73]

Steps Toward Democracy: The Consolidation of the Capitalist Class and the Gradual Retreat of the State from Its Developmental Role (1991–2005)

The participation of Egypt in the 1991 Gulf War on the side of the coalition forces gave Egypt some respite. Half of the country's foreign debt was either forgiven or rescheduled, but in exchange Egypt was forced to implement fully structural adjustment and economic liberalization programs sponsored by the IMF and the World Bank. The 1990s were thus characterized by profound structural economic changes (see Chapter 1 for a full description of the implementation of structural adjustment policies).

Economic liberalization, with its inflationary and recessionary effects, affected the majority of the people negatively. Only the wealthy took advantage of the process, through the increased entrepreneurial opportunities offered by the privatization process and the growing private market. The privatization process created an industrial and rural elite dependent on the state for access to public economic resources.

The top echelons of the bureaucratic elite joined forces with the new elite, their efforts centered on access to political power for the appropriation of state assets through privatization. As a result, the state effectively built the capitalist class of the 1990s. The divestiture programs of the state transferred the privatized state assets, usually monopolies, to special members of the elites. In an uncompetitive economic environment, the privatized assets continued as monopolies, yielding high profits because of the absence of competition. While the privatization of state assets meant that they changed hands, it did not alter the regime's protective policies with respect to them.

Privatization also led to collusion between state bureaucrats and businessmen for the sale of public sector enterprises at prices much lower than the market.[74] Some companies were sold at prices lower than the value of the real estate on which they were built.[75] El Najjar identifies some of these industries: the Egyptian Pepsi Cola Company, al-Nasr Boilers, al-Ahram Beverages, Asyut Cement, and the Meridien Hotel.[76] Most companies were sold to investors through loans provided by state banks. In some instances, investors bought state-companies with loans backed by false guarantees and retained ownership of the companies even after they defaulted on the loans. In the last few years of the 1990s, many cases of fraud which had taken place with the banks' collusion were referred to the courts, only for many of the defendants to be released after just a few years in prison.

The Egyptian government's practice of selling assets to anchor investors (single individuals) or to a small group of investors is increasing the monopolization of the economy. Monopolies or near monopolies exist in iron and steel, cement, telecommunications, and food and beverages. The process of privatization was accelerated during the last two years of the Nazif cabinet, with the majority of sales assigned to anchor investors. The changes in land tenancy regulations occurred in the 1990s (see Chapter 1) and these changes in turn altered land distribution dramatically, creating a new landed elite, with 7 percent of the population owning 60 percent of the land. The land reforms of the 1950s and 1960s have almost disappeared, so that there are now no longer controls on rents or tenure for peasants.[77]

With such a privatization process, few, if any, of the members of the new elite would be interested in democratization. Most members of the industrial and landed elites have opted to join the dominant party, the NDP. The last parliamentary elections (2005) saw the elite flock to the NDP, and seventy-seven members of the new parliament are from the private business sector. Not only are members of the private sector elite members of the NDP and the parliament, but the last cabinet included six private sector magnates (see Chapter 1). These ministers were handed portfolios corresponding to their sphere of expertise, so, for example, the minister of transportation owns a car company in the private sector and the minister of health comes from one of the most prestigious private hospitals in Egypt. It would seem that the government is not averse to recruiting ministers from the private sector, ministers whose policies might raise questions about conflicts of interest.

Nevertheless, those segments of the population that have suffered from the processes of privatization and economic reform (workers, peasants, and white collar workers) still prefer to be included in the dominant party. As far as public sector workers are concerned, the government follows a policy of divide and rule. In order to make public sector companies more profitable, managers were advised to lay off temporary workers, while wage supplements were withdrawn from other workers to force them to resign. The government also established a policy of early retirement to bribe workers to voluntarily submit their resignations. At the same time, the workers' upper echelons were kept employed and awarded wage increases. Another tactic used to subvert workers' discontent was the formation of shareholders' collectives among public sector workers. Usually, the shares sold or given to workers were few and were sold directly by the workers through the stock market. While some of these policies inflamed the rank and file, the workers' leaders became more cohesively tied to the state in order to protect their own interests. The government has attempted to formulate a new labor law that would do away with many of the benefits awarded to workers in the 1960s, and has so far shied away from promulgating such a law.[78]

Although the peasants have suffered with the cancellation of the rent controls and inheritance rights in tenancy of the agricultural land reforms of the 1960s, the lifting of price controls on most agricultural products has appeased them. Moreover, most peasants vote for the NDP due to the persistence of voting according to family loyalties or political clientelism. By integrating the rural elite into its ranks the NDP has guaranteed the rural vote.

This state of affairs has affected the ability of opposition parties to recruit adherents. The liberal Wafd Party has been deserted by members of the business elite, who prefer the nexus of rent-seeking activities that they gain from their closeness to the party in power. The Progressive Unionist Party (Tagammu'), the natural party for the defense of the workers and the peasants' interests, cannot rival the NDP in access to state patronage.[79] Most of the members of the party represent the left-leaning intelligentsia, who have little appeal to the electorate, a state of affairs that has left the party unable to compete in parliamentary elections.

On another level, while the opposition political parties are restricted in their efforts to fill the political vacuum, a trend of a strengthened civil society emerged in the 1990s. Unable to maintain welfare policies, the state in the 1990s encouraged non-governmental organizations (NGOs) to shoulder some of the burden by establishing programs in health, education, micro-enterprises, and so on. Professional syndicates became substitutes for political parties. Syndicates of businessmen, lawyers, journalists, doctors, engineers, and academics evolved into centers of political dissent and opposition. Some analysts argue that the growing activities of NGOs and professional syndicates served the purposes of the regime, which benefited from the fragmented nature of civil society.[80]

The 1990s also witnessed the highest level of conflict between the regime and radical Islamist groups, which reached its peak with the massacre of tourists in Luxor in 1997. The government responded with a policy of massive arrests of Islamic radicals. The Islamist groups reversed policy after 1997 and declared a truce with the regime. However, the most threatening group to the regime is the Muslim Brotherhood. The Brotherhood opted to compete with the regime in parliamentary elections. In the 2005 parliamentary elections, the Muslim Brothers, despite being members of an outlawed organization, were nevertheless left to campaign under their logans and to use the name of their society. They won an unprecedented eighty-eight out of 454 seats (see Chapter 3). No other opposition party garnered more than 4 percent of the seats.

These results were the outcome of external pressures on the Egyptian government to democratize the political system (mainly pressures by the Bush administration, which adopted the stance that democracy in the Arab region is the best antidote to terrorism). In February 2005, the president announced the first multi-party elections for president. Since the 1952 Revolution, the majority party had nominated one person for the post. Yes/no referendums always returned the head of the majority party to the presidency. The announcement of a constitutional change to allow for multi-party presidential elections led to a storm of discussions and demonstrations, the formation of new political groups, and an

84   The State, Democracy, and Development

unprecedented national dialogue, led this time by a new independent press. The existing press was, until very recently, formed of state owned newspapers and a few party newspapers. The emergence of an independent press, mostly funded by businessmen, or supported by unknown political groups, has given a new tone to the Egyptian media. Even state owned television now airs a great number of political programs running the gamut of the political spectrum from right to left.

The presidential elections ended with the reelection of President Mubarak, an expected outcome due to the relative obscurity of his competitors. His victory was also the result of a strong presidential campaign waged by the new, younger NDP leadership headed by Gamal Mubarak, the president's son, heir apparent, and the secretary of a new committee established in the NDP, the Policies Committee. On the other side, the opposition parties ran a mostly negative campaign against the incumbent and failed to articulate strong platforms that addressed the problems of everyday life that plague Egyptians. A few opposition parties boycotted the elections, while others tried to form a national alliance to oppose the incumbent. This alliance never materialized, which weakened significantly the position of the opposition parties.[81]

But more important were the parliamentary elections that followed in November 2005. The legislative elections witnessed a high degree of violence from all parties, vote buying, and the use of force by the security forces, especially in the last two rounds of the vote.[82] Dr. Husam Badrawi, an influential member of the NDP's Policies Committee, who ran as an independent, lost his seat to a rival (another NDP member), and after the elections rejoined the NDP, declared that "people are not looking to policies or reform or to what really can be done institutionally . . . . They are very locally directed to personal favors and gifts, which usually ends by an opening up to votes for money, which is very, very bad."[83]

More telling is the fact that only 20 to 23 percent of registered voters voted. Urban areas witnessed the lowest turnout, at 10 percent, while rural areas, which usually have higher rates as a result of the clientelism and family ties referred to above, had a turnout of 40–50 percent.

The legislative session of 2006–2007 witnessed a high number of constitutional changes proposed by the president. The changes included an amendment to allow voting on proportional lists. This amendment will allow smaller opposition parties to be better represented and will limit the number of independents (especially from the ranks of the Muslim Brothers, who usually run as independents). The amendment will also strengthen the party system, which seems to be withering even while the number of political parties exceeds twenty-three; most of these are in fact very small parties with no following or presence in Egyptian politics.

The amendment was proposed not only to limit the number of seats held by the Muslim Brothers, who are not allowed to form a party (the party law does not allow the formation of parties on a religious basis), but to discipline NDP members themselves. Many NDP members defied the candidates' list proposed by the NDP secretariat, resigned, and ran as independents, then rejoined the party after winning the elections. The official NDP candidates won only 30 percent of the parliamentary seats. After independent candidates rejoined the party, this percentage rose to almost 70 percent.

Is there a future for a more democratic system in Egypt? The answer to this question depends on the maturity of social forces, progress in economic and social restructuring, and the future of the semi-secular state.

Egypt: A Hybrid Regime?

The constitutional changes and attempts at democratization in Egypt during the last two years have engendered a system that researchers have variously labeled as a hybrid regime, an electoral democracy, an illiberal democracy, a semi-authoritarian democracy, and a semi-dictatorial democracy. The Egyptian system exhibits all the characteristics of hybrid regimes. Egypt has a formal party system, a large measure of freedom of speech, and civil society organizations. Nonetheless, elections are mostly controlled, allowing no real competition with the dominant majority party.

Pressure from the United States and major European powers for political liberalization forced Egypt to enact some changes in the political system. Such changes do not go deep enough to threaten the power of the dominant regime, however, and increased political liberalization can even threaten economic liberalization by threatening the state system itself. Most businessmen are members of the majority party and derive economic power from the political power of the regime itself.

3

Politicized Religion, Conflict, and Development: The Islamists and the State

R ecent studies of the relationship between religion and development have neglected the use of religion as a political tool (see Introduction). This is of particular interest for Egypt, where politicized Islam has always played a major role in the constitution of national ideologies. The modernization of Egypt that began under Muhammad 'Ali created a conflict between a conservative ideology based usually on religion and an ideology of secularization and modernization. Successive ruling regimes have manipulated Islam to support their policies and to fight competing elites.

The transition crisis of the 1970s led anti-Nasserist elites to use Islam as a tool of political mobilization, directed at large sectors of the population against Nasserist economic policies, to end the economic policies of import substitution and reintegrate Egypt into the international economic system through the policies of economic liberalization. In response, the regime allied itself to its old foes: the Muslim Brothers. The Sadat regime went as far as creating Islamist groups on university campuses, which later developed into radical groups that threatened the regime that had created them.

This mutating use of Islam—from a tool to fight particular economic policies to an ideology seeking creation of an Islamic state—resulted in periods of intense conflict between the state and Islamist groups. From the 1970s onward, the relationships between the regime, the Muslim Brothers, and other Islamist groups vacillated between periods of accommodation, whenever the Islamist groups kept peacefully to their

87

designated role of ideological and cultural mobilization, and periods of conflict, whenever they attempted to dominate the regime and even replace it.

Religion and Development: Theoretical Approaches

A growing literature on the interrelationships between religion and development attempts to study the impact of religion on economic development and, conversely, the effects of economic development on religion. The literature indicates that religion might affect development either positively or negatively. It can have a positive impact on development if it promotes favorable attitudes toward work and capital accumulation. It can have a negative impact if religious groups and institutions incite conflict and violence that impede development. Conversely, development may lead to lower levels of religiosity. With increased per capita income, people may become less religious, and religion may come to play a smaller role, not only in the economy but in social and political processes as well.

Modernization and Marxist theories both postulate a decline of religion with the advent of economic growth and development. However, recent years have witnessed a resurgence of religion around the world, both in the number of adherents and in their overall visibility. Resurgent religion is characterized by a conservative bent all over the world, from the evangelism of the United States to fundamentalist Islam in the Middle East and the rest of the Islamic world.

The Impact of Religion on Development

The notion of interrelationships between religion and development is not new: Weber was one of the first theorists to address the topic. In his seminal work *The Protestant Ethic and the Spirit of Capitalism,*[1] Weber explores the relationships between capitalist economic rationality and religious ethics. He argues that the economic development of northern Europe is associated with Protestant ethics: the encouragement of frugality, the concern with savings and entrepreneurship, the emphasis on hard work, and the demand for education to read the Bible, all contributed to economic development. The emphasis of Lutheran and Calvinist doctrines on fulfilling one's calling in life through diligence and discipline created a path to the capital accumulation necessary for development. Religion can also have a positive impact on development if it promotes positive attitudes toward honesty, thereby increasing levels of trust and reducing

Religion and Development: Theoretical Approaches   89

levels of corruption and crime.[2] Religion can contribute to a country's openness to outsiders, thereby promoting interaction with others in domestic and international economic interactions.

Religion may also affect capitalist development negatively if it discourages capital accumulation, encourages negative attitudes toward work, interferes with the free-market mechanism, or diverts resources from economic activities toward the promotion of religious attendance and the building of religious halls of worship. The endorsement of mendicity and ascetic ways of life also encourages non-work attitudes and diverts resources from development, thereby lowering capital accumulation and economic productivity.[3] Religious groups and institutions might also promote violence and conflict, which will divert resources to the purchase of arms, increase poverty levels, and dampen economic growth.[4]

The modernization and Marxist theories assume that economic development reduces the level of religiosity as measured by attendance of religious services or by religious belief. With development, religion is assumed to play a lesser role in political decision-making and in social and legal affairs. Economic development reduces the level of religiosity due to increases in per capita income, education levels, life expectancy, and urbanization. It also leads to a reduction in fertility levels and changes in the age structure of the population.

Education weakens religiosity by promoting scientific reasoning and rejecting beliefs based on ignorance, superstition, and reliance on supernatural forces. Yet education might promote religiosity. Religious beliefs, because they are non-verifiable, need a level of abstraction that can only be attained through education.[5] Education is also said to increase returns from social networks and other forms of social capital, thereby increasing the level of participation in religious networks and activities.[6]

Economic development might also reduce attendance of religious services and time spent on religious activities. The opportunity cost of these activities increases as development raises the value of time measured by wages or per capita income. Time spent on religious activities would decrease as their opportunity cost increases. Urbanization is said to affect religiosity negatively, as urban areas might offer social opportunities that compete with religious activities, such as museums, theaters, and political organizations.

Glaeser and Glandon argue that people become more religious with age, and they predict that religiosity increases with higher fertility and lower life expectancy.[7] If development decreases fertility and increases

90 Politicized Religion, Conflict, and Development

life expectancy, then developed countries will tend to have lower levels of religiosity than developing countries.

Religious Pluralism: Supply Side or the Market Approach

Adam Smith argued that established state religious institutions turn into monopolies or oligopolies providing religious services, a fact that reinforces religiosity and increases the potential for these institutions to impose their ideas on the public. By contrast, the presence of many religious denominations (the existence of an open market in religion) that do not depend on the state but on the contributions of their members, pressures all denominations to cater to their constituents' needs and demands. Therefore, religious plurality, that is, an open market in religion, will foster moderation and reason.[8]

Building on Smith's argument, a number of researchers (Iannaccone, Stark, Bainbridge, and Finke) developed what they call a market or supply-side model of religious participation.[9] Contrary to Smith's notion, they argue that state-established religious monopolies discourage religious participation, while a multiplicity of religious denominations in a competitive market of religions will increase attendance and encourage religious belief. This is based on the assumption that in a competitive market, religious institutions will provide better services, thereby encouraging attendance. The natural corollary of these arguments is that if religion is more in demand the less the state intervenes, then states should not support a religious monopoly. However, an argument can be made that a state monopoly of religious institutions might raise attendance, especially if the state is subsidizing its activities.

Empirical Evidence

Barro and McCleary tested many of the assumptions about the interrelationships between religion and development.[10] They based their study on a large sample of fifty-nine countries, the predominantly Muslim ones including Bangladesh, Malaysia, Pakistan, and Turkey. Countries professing eastern religions were also included (China, Hong Kong, Japan, South Korea, Singapore, Taiwan, and Thailand), in addition to developed Christian majority countries. However, the authors acknowledge that coverage is better for rich countries rather than poor ones.

Their most important empirical results are as follows:

- The overall effects of economic development on religion are negative, that is, an increase in economic development leads to less religiosity, as measured by attendance of religious services and professed beliefs.

The results demonstrate different patterns for individual measures or dimensions of economic development:

1. Education is positively related to attendance at religious services and religious beliefs, but measures of superstition, fortunetellers, and good luck charms are negatively related to education.

2. Urbanization is negatively associated with religiosity.

3. There is a highly significant negative relationship between attendance at religious services and life expectancy, and there is a negative relationship between life expectancy and beliefs (beliefs in heaven, hell, and the after-life). This means that while older people may physically attend fewer religious services (due to illness or lack of communication), they tend to have higher levels of belief, which is natural because of a higher expectancy of death.

4. There is a negative relationship between religious beliefs and development (as measured by the level of per capita income), all other development indicators remaining constant.

5. There is a significant positive correlation between the imposition of a state religion and attendance of religious services, which reinforces Adam Smith's postulates but runs counter to the supply-siders' predictions. However, government regulation of religious institutions decreases attendance and might also depress the level of religious belief.

6. Religious pluralism is positively associated with attendance.

Nevertheless, overall results of studies of the impact of religion on economic development tell a different story. Differences in the composition of the population among different religious denominations have little impact on economic growth, assuming all other explanatory variables are held constant. Another major result is that more or less religiosity overall (as measured by attendance and beliefs) does not have a great impact on economic development. However, some evidence indicates that increases in religious belief and decreases in church attendance tend to stimulate economic growth.

Religion and the Crisis Explanation

The literature on the relationships between religion and development still lies in the realm of testing for correlations between the two. The empirical results are not clear-cut, and the line of causality between religion and development is a tenuous one. Nor do the explanations proferred cover the emergence of radical religious movements; at best, they attempt to explain the increase or decrease of religiosity in societies at the end of the twentieth century. But what are the reasons for the emergence of movements that use violence and terrorist tactics to attain their goals?

A predominant explanation in the sociology literature for an emergence of radical groups is the Crisis Explanation. People are said to join radical movements because of a complex set of grievances. The most important, as mentioned in the literature, are the failure of modernization projects, the legacy of colonialism and imperialism in third world countries, cultural westernization processes that alienate people from their own cultural legacies, economic crises, blocked social mobility, dissatisfaction with authoritarian political systems, and defeats in major wars.

While some or all of these factors may have contributed to an increase in religiosity and/or the emergence of radical groups, radical groups might exist even without the recent increase in violence that was witnessed in the Middle East and many other parts of the world. And on a more basic level: Is there a relationship between these elements of crisis and development?

The Social Movement Theory posits a number of criticisms of the simple Crisis Explanation. First, while grievances might provide the impetus for joining radical religious groups, there are other factors that have to be taken into account, such as the level of political and/or societal repression and the availability of resources to fund the groups' activities. Second, the simple Crisis Explanation cannot explain why some members of deprived or alienated groups join religious movements, while others suffering from the same conditions do not. Third, the thesis stressing the psychological reasons behind joining fails to explain differential patterns of response to the same stimulants of grievances and levels of distress.[11]

In the Social Movement Theory, the resource mobilization thesis stresses that the person who joins a radical group is a rational actor whose decision is based on utility calculations.[12] Others advance the thesis that

Religion and Development: Theoretical Approaches   93

social networks are the most important factor in mobilization. In this situation, grievances are said to create the conditions for alienating individuals from their social and political backgrounds, but they have to be exposed to networks, which actively and consciously recruit them.[13] On the other hand some dissatisfied individuals might actively seek networks that address their grievances.[14]

Framing, that is, the presentation of an interpretation that provides a framework for understanding the surrounding environment, is also said to be important to enable dissatisfied individuals to make sense of their experiences and the events they are exposed to. Snow et al. stress that frames are important in guiding actions. When the individual's frame and the movement's frame correspond, then recruitment and the mobilization of dissatisfied individuals become possible.[15]

Baylouny adds the qualification that radical religious movements are essentially oppositional political groups.[16] Such movements are said to be governed by political considerations and strategic calculations. The actions of the movements are conditioned by the available political opportunities. Exclusion from the political system is a major cause of radicalization of these movements. If offered the opportunity to participate in the political system, radical movements will opt for nonviolent means of persuasion. For Baylouny, the way to moderate radical religious groups is to adopt a democratic political system. Democracy is the only means to moderate political parties and political movements. Within a democratic system, previously radical groups can turn moderate because they choose to work within the system peacefully. Once such groups have a vested interest in the system, they will pressure more radical groups to moderate their actions and positions.[17]

Misztal and Shupe attribute the increase in active social movements to globalization.[18] Activist social movements in third world nations are an outcome of the western cultural and economic domination that threatens their cultural and national identities. Religious movements are on the increase because they offer cohesive rallying points and a suitable means for collective action, relying upon well-known values and traditions.[19] By reducing economic and cultural barriers and frontiers, globalization compels active groups to seek and reassert their identities through their religious beliefs and traditional values. Misztal and Shupe claim that with globalization, especially during the twenty-first century, religious and semi-religious social action groups will support collective action and protest movements.[20]

While the Social Movement theory offers an explanation of the mechanisms of recruitment and reasons for adherence to religious social movements, it relies on the Crisis Explanation for the reasons that facilitate recruitment into the movements. Balouny's thesis that these movements are oppositional political movements is correct, but it does not explain why they take on a religious character. In addition, the complete trust that she puts in the efficiency of the democratic system as a means of moderating these movements might be justified if such groups believe in a mechanism of checks and balances and are ready for compromise. Most of the time religiously active social movements think in terms of absolutes, and their reliance on religion as political interpellation indicates that they believe they are the only holders of truth, because their truth is God's truth. Moreover, fundamentalist religious groups have emerged in democratic countries as well. Consider the Christian evangelist movement in the United States. It is true that its members resort to the ballot box at election time, but some splinter groups carry out terrorist attacks. So democracy does not necessarily provide security, especially in new democratic systems, where democracy might pave the way for these groups to take control of the state itself.

Most of the theories and theses advanced complement each other. The Crisis Explanation is a valid one, but not every crisis triggers deep changes in a country's socioeconomic structure. As previously discussed (see page 11), a Transition Crisis can fracture economic paradigms, political structures, and ideological beliefs, signaling changes in development paradigms and dominant power relations.

The Transition Crisis

In previous research I advanced a specific crisis explanation for the prevalence of religiosity and the emergence of radical groups, especially in Egypt, namely, the Transition Crisis theory.[21] Some developing countries are more prone than others to transition crises propelled by deep changes in power relations in the course of development. Most developing countries, especially in the Arab world, depend at present on two main economic strategies: one relies on the export of primary products and the use of the financial proceeds of these exports to promote internal development; the other is an export-oriented industrialization strategy. For some countries, the export-oriented industrialization phase has followed a stage of internally oriented, import-substitution industrialization.

During the colonial period, developing countries depended heavily on the primary product export-oriented strategy. The economic crisis of the 1930s and the coming of the Second World War allowed some third world countries partial industrialization along the lines of an import-substitution strategy. Nationalist regimes reinforced that strategy after independence in a quest to replicate the European industrialization process. However, economic globalization and the extension of the role of multinational corporations, together with the collapse of the Soviet Union and Eastern Europe, forced many third world countries to pursue an export-oriented industrialization strategy, especially after the meteoric economic success of East Asian and South Asian nations such as South Korea, Hong Kong, Singapore, Taiwan, and more recently China, India, and Malaysia.

The change in development strategies may lead to the eruption of violent conflict if it destabilizes social and power relations and triggers struggles between different social groups and/or classes. Social groups represent different social and economic interests that are usually incompatible. Different development strategies bring benefits to some groups and losses to others. A new development strategy requires the restructuration of dominant power relations. Different ideologies (religious or non-religious) are used for the mobilization of different social forces to support the competing strategies, which, in turn, reflect competing interests.

An ideology is generally understood as a set of values and beliefs. These values and beliefs can be drawn from religion. The use of religion as the basis for a political ideology is a potent means of transforming individuals into active political actors either supporting or combating competing political groups that seek hegemony over state and society.

Nationalism and Islamism: The Case of Egypt

A very large literature is devoted to Islamist radical groups or what they call in the social movements literature Islamic Social Movements (ISMs). The literature conflates the rise in levels of religiosity in the Muslim world with the salience of some radical groups that use violence and terrorism with the goal of establishing a so-called Islamic state based on a strict interpretation of Islamic law (shariʿa). While there is correspondence between the two phenomena, they are not identical.

Many analysts of the Middle East have explained the resurgence of Islamism (political Islam) as a reaction to the dislocations of the modernization process. The failure of development programs to improve the

96 Politicized Religion, Conflict, and Development

living standards of the majority of the population led to widespread dissatisfaction. Islamists took advantage of this to establish their welfare networks designed to help the disenfranchised. The extension of welfare services to the poor or the impoverished in the process of transition is referred to by Gilles Kepel as "Islamization from the bottom."[22]

To these economic factors, other scholars add political repression by Middle East governments. Authoritarianism and the use of brute force create political opposition that manifests itself in the form of Islamist groups, which resort to violence to counter the state's tactics. Ghassan Salama, one of the Arab world's leading political thinkers, contends that the growth of Islamic-based opposition forces is a reflection of the failure of the ruling elites and the secular opposition forces to bring about democratization in the Middle East.[23]

Michael Hudson finds the significance of Islam lies in its potency as a political ideology; as such it can play a cohesive and integrative role in the Middle East state system. While regimes resort to Islam to enhance their legitimacy, opposition movements use Islam to discredit the incumbent regimes. Thus, Islam performs a unifying social role, transcending the traditional divides of class, region, and ethnicity. Hudson claims that Islam as solidarity strengthens national identities and enhances consensus in the political community at large. However, he warns us that where Islam as ideology results in inequality or intolerance, it will weaken cohesiveness.[24]

Huntington argues that radical Islamist movements indicate the existence of a deep cleavage between Islamic and western cultures. "The underlying problem for the west is not Islamic fundamentalism, it is Islam," writes Huntington in *The Clash of Civilizations*.[25] Bernard Lewis and Daniel Pipes,[26] even more than Huntington, seem to indicate that Islam is so alien to the concepts of modernization, understood in this context to be synonymous with westernization, that Islamic culture is the biggest hurdle in the path, for countries with a Muslim majority, to development and integration into the global world of the early twenty-first century. Lewis examines in particular modern Islamic developments in the context of a long historical wave. He claims that the Islamic world has always been in confrontation with the west and that in the context of this long confrontation, the Islamic world has undergone phases of revival and resistance, confrontation and rejection.[27] Therefore, Islamic revivalism is a recurrent phenomenon to be expected whenever there are conditions that facilitate it.

Gellner explains Islamic resurgence in the context of postmodernism. He claims that there are three positions regarding faith: religious fundamentalism, relativism, and the rationalism of the enlightenment. Islam is still at the phase of religious fundamentalism. Neither secularism nor the relativism of the postmodern phase has had a significant impact on Islam as faith. Therefore fundamentalism is at its strongest in Islam in the current historical period.[28]

These interpretations of the conflict as one between the new radical Islamic movements and the west, or as a form of arrested development through the phases of modernity and postmodernity, disregard two very important considerations: the Islamists are in conflict with their own states, and they are themselves a product of modernity. Bruce Lawrence argues that Islamic fundamentalism is a product of modernization. In his view, the fundamentalists are modern, accepting the benefits of modernity (the use of technology), while at the same time rejecting modernity as a worldview.[29]

Nevertheless, the radical Islamist phenomenon has emerged since the 1970s, initially as a political force supported by the state and as a counterweight to nationalist and socialist trends, in an attempt, first, to reshape internal power relations, and, second, as an opposition force to the regime, when radical groups sought to wrest control from the state itself. In addition, most Islamic forces are not antagonistic to modernization, when understood as economic liberalization.

The conflict between the Islamists and the state or other social groups is a conflict over power and access to economic resources. The resort to an ideology heavily steeped in religion is an outcome of the state's use of religion as an ideology with which to marginalize its opponents, creating a religion-dominated political culture affecting society as a whole. This religiously dominated political culture created the conditions for opposition groups to use religion as a weapon of political confrontation with the state.

Not only did the state use Islam as a legitimizing tool in shaping internal power relations, but also dominant powers in the west have also contributed to the spread of Islamic fundamentalism. The United States government encouraged Saudi Arabia to establish the Islamic Conference Organization to counter the trend of Arab nationalism that reigned supreme in the 1960s. The U.S. also supported the oil-rich Gulf States in establishing the Islamic Development Bank. The Bank advanced generous loans to countries that agreed to implement Islamic law (shari'a).[30]

98   Politicized Religion, Conflict, and Development

More than that, the U.S. prompted Saudi Arabia to fund fundamentalist groups fighting the Soviets in Afghanistan. Some of these groups established an umbrella organization: al-Qa'ida, which was held responsible for the September 11 attacks carried out against the U.S. in 2001.

In the Egyptian context we can distinguish two major political ideologies that have coexisted in Egyptian political culture for the last two centuries: A conservative ideology that resorts to religion as legitimizer, and a nationalist ideology based on a strong sense of nationhood steeped in seven thousand years of uninterrupted recorded history. There is interpenetration between the two trends, that is, nationalist ideology that nevertheless advocates religion as a form of legitimation, and a religious trend that seeks to integrate the concepts of the universality of religion and nationalism.

The Modern State: From Muhammad 'Ali to Isma'il
Egypt was ruled by the Ottoman caliphate through its representative (the *wali*) as a province of the Ottoman Empire from the Ottoman invasion in the middle of the sixteenth century to the imposition of the British mandate in 1914, at the beginning of the Second World War. Ottoman rule rested on the concept of the Islamic *umma* (world) and imposed a version of shari'a steeped in a centuries-long interpretation of Islam. The *ulama* had tremendous power within this system. They advised the ruler in political matters, interpreted the laws, and set the rules for society as a whole. Whatever education existed was religious, confined to the traditional primary level school *(kuttab)*, where the only lesson was that of learning the Qur'an by rote. Higher levels of learning were attainable only through the Egyptian religious institution, al-Azhar. The *ulama* were not only religious leaders, but the nation's political leaders as well. Two incidents illustrate the fact: The *ulama* arranged for resistance against the French invasion led by Napoleon in 1798, and the same *ulama*, in conjunction with the traditional leaders of Egypt at the time (merchants, guild leaders, and so on) rejected the candidate nominated by the Ottoman caliphate to assume power in Egypt after the departure of the French. Instead, in 1805 they succeeded in installing as Egypt's *wali* their own nominee, Muhammad 'Ali, the Albanian soldier who came to Egypt with the Ottoman troops to wrest the country from the French.

Muhammad 'Ali had a vision of building a strong and modern nation in Egypt to serve as a base for expansion in the region. To implement his strategies, he had to have complete power, without competition from either a political or a politico-religious elite. Through a series of intrigues and military clashes, Muhammad 'Ali wrested power from the Mamluks and became sole political leader in 1811. However, he needed to subsume the political power of the *ulama*, who used to advise the rulers and interfere in the decision-making process. By eliminating all forces of opposition, Muhammad 'Ali could venture into the deep structural transformation of the Egyptian economy required to modernize a long-stagnant traditional economy.

Nevertheless, Muhammad 'Ali justified his rule as Islamic rule for an Islamic country under the tutelage of the Ottoman caliphate. He could not repudiate the religious legitimacy that brought him to power, but he succeeded, in the period 1809–13, in breaking the *ulama*'s political power in a series of innovations that gave the state power over religious institutions and the *ulama* themselves. First and foremost, Muhammad 'Ali disposed of the *ulama* who had real power in the religious institutions and who opposed him, simply by deposing them. He also arrogated to the state the right to appoint all the sheikhs (religious clerics) and transformed them into salaried employees of the state. However, the revenues of the *awqaf* (religious endowments) lands were appropriated by the state. By expropriating the sources of independent income and monopolizing the appointment of the *ulama* and the sheikhs, Muhammad 'Ali brought religious institutions and their leaders under state power.

To subvert the power of the *ulama*, he also refused to heed the *ulama*'s advice in matters relating to state councils *(shura)*, a privilege that the *ulama* had had under the caliphate system. Thus, Muhammad 'Ali gained complete control of religious institutions. In return, he upheld shari'a as the basis of government. He retained the tradition of consulting the *ulama* for official approval of his policies, but the loss of independence by religious institutions forced the *ulama* to give appropriate legal opinions *(fatawa)* whenever Muhammad 'Ali requested them. In addition, while he introduced modern educational institutions, he left religious education under the control of religious institutions and upheld the *ulama*'s power to prescribe moral codes of behavior for the whole of society.[31] This system of subjugating religious institutions to the state, while leaving the functions of religious education and the upholding of public morality to the *ulama*, has survived to this day and created the enduring dichotomy between modern (state) and traditional (religious) institutions.

By eliminating the opposition and vested interests, Muhammad 'Ali achieved complete state autonomy and was thus able to build a strong modern army. In fact, his ambitious industrial and agricultural projects were designed to create that army. Extensive industrial projects were implemented, for products ranging from textiles to armaments. All factories were owned and run by the state, and agricultural land was confiscated and became state land. To run the projects, Muhammad 'Ali established a modern education system to provide the state with the educated cadre required to supervise the state monopolies.

As mentioned in Chapter 1, the Muhammad 'Ali experiment came to a halt in 1839, when his army was defeated by the coalition of western countries (Britain, France, Russia, and Prussia) and the Ottoman caliphate ranged against him. The last ten years of Muhammad 'Ali's rule (1839–49) witnessed the collapse of Egypt's first industrialization drive. His factories were dismantled, state monopolies were destroyed, and the Egyptian economy was forcibly reintegrated into the international economic system. The Egyptian economy, in accordance with the so-called comparative advantage theory, had to fall back on agriculture as the main source of income. A primary-product, export strategy, based on the cultivation and export of cotton, was adopted and remained dominant from 1839 to the 1930s.

The structural changes implemented by Muhammad 'Ali in the relation between the state and religious institutions were reinforced under his successors. More important, the modern education system and the growth of a modern intellectual elite (who were sent to France for their education) remained one of the major developments inaugurated by Ali. Even after the modern schools were closed down, emergent intellectual elites with roots in al-Azhar's religious education started to rethink the relationship between traditional religion and the new sciences of the west. Tahtawi, Jamal al-Din al-Afghani, Muhammad 'Abdu, and others fought for a modern interpretation of Islam, without renouncing the basic tenets of the faith.

Concomitantly, Muhammad 'Ali's successors yearned to continue in his footsteps of modernization, by gradually following a cautious policy of secularization. Khedives Said and Isma'il followed Muhammad 'Ali's policy of tolerance toward religious minorities. The major step of basing citizenship on nationalist rather than religious identity came in the form of the abolition of the special tax on non-Muslims (the *jizya*), and the imposition of the military draft on all Egyptians, irrespective of religion.

Khedive Isma'il (1863–79), more than any of his predecessors, strived to Europeanize Egypt. He opened modern schools, enlarged government functions, and rebuilt the army. A growing state bureaucracy formed the nucleus of the middle class. In conjunction with the growth of an Egyptian landed elite, the new social groups desired to play a larger role in society as a whole. At the same time, traditional religious groups witnessed an erosion of their role. Under Isma'il secular legal codes of law displaced the traditional role of the *ulama*. The modern schools (reopened under Isma'il) undermined the *kuttab*s (primary religious schools that taught students to learn the Qur'an by rote and recite it) and religious education at large. Isma'il intensified the dichotomy, which began under Muhammad 'Ali, between the secular and the religious in Egyptian public life.

The new social groups nurtured by the modernization policies of Muhammad 'Ali and his successors found themselves at odds with the foreign ruling elites. The top ranks in the new modern institutions, whether in the government or the military, were still the province of the Turkish-Circassian elites. An Egyptian landed elite grew quickly under the policies of Isma'il, but the biggest landowners, including the khedive himself, were non-Egyptians. The intellectuals were promoting the idea that Egypt should belong to the Egyptians.

The 'Urabi revolt in 1882 was the first movement of national revolt led by the military. The revolt started as a protest movement against the financial and economic burdens placed on Egypt after it was declared bankrupt by the western powers, especially Britain and France. This revolt developed very quickly into a full-fledged revolution against Isma'il's successor, Khedive Tawfiq. The new Egyptian landed elite and the new middle class, including the intelligentsia, supported 'Urabi in a bid to wrest power from the Turkish-Circassian elites and to remove western impositions on the country.

> The importance of the 'Urabi revolt pertains to the fact that for the first time in Egypt, a genuine nationalist movement had emerged. The rising Egyptian landowning aristocracy in its fight to displace the foreign (Turkish and Circassian) ruling class had to appeal to Egyptian nationalism as such. Even though it was flavored with Islamic rhetoric it could not rely on a pure Islamic ideology since that would have legalized the power of the foreign aristocracy as fellow Muslims. The slogan of the movement was Egypt for the Egyptians and a demand for a constitutional government able to check and control the khedive and the Turkish-Circassian aristocracy as a whole.[32]

102   Politicized Religion, Conflict, and Development

Egyptian nationalism was born as a secular movement, one that did not reject religion but which attempted to base the legitimacy of the state on the concept of the national identity of its citizens rather than their religious affiliations. The 'Urabi revolt ended with the British invasion of Egypt in 1882. The fall of Egypt to British colonialism marked a watershed in the confrontation not only between the new social classes and the colonizers, but also between the religious leaders and the British. A reform school that attempted to achieve a synthesis between religion and modernism emerged from the ranks of the religious *ulama*.

The attempts at modernization of Muhammad 'Ali and his successors, the openings to the west, the birth of Egyptian nationalism, and the colonization of Egypt prompted religious thinkers to review the reasons for the political, economic, and military weakness of Islamic countries. A major attempt at rethinking the major intellectual paradigm of Islamic countries resulted in the emergence of a group of religious reformers preoccupied by the relationship between Islam, modernity, and the west. Two of the most important reformers were Jamal al-Din al-Afghani and Muhammad 'Abdu.

The trend of reform started with Jamal al-Din al-Afghani, who endeavored to find a middle way between Islam, as interpreted by the traditional *ulama*, and encroaching western modernism. Like Tahtawi before him, al-Afghani cautioned against a wholesale acceptance of modernization and held that modernity does not imply disregarding the precepts of the faith. Afghani's main activism, however, was directed at the fight against imperialism. His main prescription was to unify the Islamic *umma*, and he preached pan-Islamism as means of liberation. Afghani stressed the concept of the right to self-determination and independence.

Muhammad 'Abdu may be called the father of the Salafiya (fundamentalist) school of Islamic modernism. 'Abdu argued that all the precepts of modernity are included in Islam. Islam stresses the equality of all believers and enjoins rulers to consult with the ruled and therefore to rule according to their wishes. Islam is also tolerant and urges Muslims to protect non-Muslims. Not only that, but Islam stands against forced conversion. Interpreting Islam in this way allowed Muhammad 'Abdu to accept and defend modern innovations in many fields, such as economics (including his ground-breaking *fatwa*, or religious opinion, on interest rates) and social and family relations (he supported Qasim Amin's call for women's liberation and education).[33]

Liberal Nationalism and the Crisis of the
Primary-Product Export-oriented Strategy

The primary-product export-oriented strategy came to a crisis with a generalized economic recession that hit Europe in 1906–1907. Egypt's heavy reliance on cotton as its main export and income earner transformed the European crisis into an internal crisis. The collapse of European demand for Egyptian cotton resulted in a deep economic crisis that plagued Egypt from 1906 to 1914.

The strains of exhaustion of the primary-product export strategy for economic growth and the British occupation resulted in two main developments: First, landed Egyptian elites realized the dangers of relying on only one crop for export and national income and began to agitate for the diversification of products and, more interestingly, for industrialization as a counter to the vagaries of extreme changes in foreign demand. Second, British colonization coupled with weak internal rule resulted in the emergence of political parties that demanded political independence and/or reformation of the political system.

The Nationalist Party under the leadership of Mustafa Kamel blended nationalism with Islamism. Following in the footsteps of al-Afghani, it advocated a pan-Islamic alliance under the tutelage of the Ottoman caliphate to oust the British from Egypt. The party was supported by Khedive 'Abbas Helmi II, who yearned for independence and the return of Egypt to his full authority. On the opposite side, the People's Party, which emerged at almost the same time, was led by a group of liberals who were secular in orientation. The liberals stressed Egyptian nationalism and Islamic reform along the lines of Muhammad 'Abdu's ideas. Their main goal was to eliminate the hold on power of the Turkish-Circassian elite that still ruled through the Palace. They agitated for emancipation from the nominal rule of the Ottoman caliphate in order to weaken the Palace and, contrary to the Kamalists, who wanted to engineer a revolution to get rid of the British, they advocated negotiations rather than direct confrontation. A third party, the Constitutional Reform Party, was created by the Palace to defend the khedive and his court officials.[34]

The political parties, while calling for Egyptian independence, followed different strategies and resorted to different ideologies to achieve their ends. The Nationalist Party recruited its members mainly from students. Merchants and a faction of the middle class were also attracted to the Nationalist Party. Since the first priority of the party was independence from the British, it resorted to Islam as an integrating ideology with which to mobilize the Muslim world against the foreign west. The impact of al-Afghani's ideas on the Kamalists is very clear. On the other hand, the People's Party recruited essentially from the landed elite, the intelligentsia, and the growing middle class. Its members were modernist and secular in approach, although their secularism did not lead them to renounce religion; instead, they advocated religious reformism according to the Muhammad 'Abdu school. The main goal of the People's Party was to secure Egypt's independence from the Ottoman caliphate, thereby depriving the khedive from any legitimacy that rested on the concept of Islamism. The members of the party wanted to establish a modern, secular state that preserved their interests so that they could rule as Egyptian nationalists. Their attitude toward the British was pragmatic. Britain possessed a superior army and exercised power over all its colonies. To gain independence from the British, the People's Party thought that negotiations were preferable to an armed revolt. It was still smarting from the consequences of the 'Urabi revolt, a bitter experiment that had revealed the clear imbalance of power between Egypt and Britain.

The parties also disagreed in their visions of an independent Egyptian state. The Constitutional Reform Party (the defender of the Palace) wanted to establish an Islamic state. It relied on an ideology of pan-Islamism and used Islam to defend the khedive's right to rule and to preserve the privileges of the Turkish-Circassian aristocracy.

The Nationalist Party wanted an independent Egypt allied with the Ottoman caliphate. It adopted an ideology of fierce nationalism blended with Islamism. The People's Party, on the other hand, sought independence from the caliphate as a first priority and was willing to ally itself to the British in order to achieve this goal. The party's vision was to establish a constitutional government to limit the power and privileges of the khedive, and to build a modern state resting on secularism and a reformist Islamic ideology.

The long economic crisis that started in 1906 was aggravated by the first two years of the First World War. The British declared Egypt a protectorate and Egypt was finally freed from the tutelage of the Ottoman caliphate. To finance their military campaign, the British resorted to harsh economic measures. They restricted cotton exports and forced Egyptian peasants into their Labor Corps Battalions. High inflation, together with stagnation and high unemployment, aggravated the crisis and demonstrated to the elites that Egypt had to follow a different economic course.

However, the last two years of the war witnessed a shift in Egypt's economic situation. The British relaxed the restrictions on cotton exports, and landlords resumed cotton cultivation on a large scale. But most of the middle class, the rural classes, and the urban poor were still suffering from unemployment and inflation. Intellectuals and the political parties were repressed. Even landlords were weary of the British, who tried to expand cotton production in Sudan at the expense of Egyptian landowners. The war also gave rise to some industrialization to compensate for the interruption of imports. A nucleus of an industrial work force emerged, formed of foreign and Egyptian labor.

The end of the First World War was a watershed in Egyptian politics. During the war, the British had managed to antagonize all classes and all relevant political forces. The hardships of the war, growing inequalities, mass unemployment, and the exploitation by the British of Egyptian resources, created the conditions for a revolutionary upheaval that swept the country. Egyptian elites were convinced that continuation of the same economic strategy of reliance on the export of primary products would be economic suicide. The need to diversify and industrialize was considered more urgent than at any previous time. The same elites realized that to follow a different economic strategy required independence from the British, who would never accede to such a policy. The elites were heartened by the Wilsonian doctrine, which called for the liberation of countries suffering from colonialism and foreign rule. A group of Egyptian activists, headed by Sa'd Zaghlul Pasha, organized a delegation to attend the Versailles Peace Conference to submit Egypt's demands for independence and the end of the British protectorate. The British refusal to allow the delegation to attend the conference led to the 1919 Revolution, which marked the height of Egyptian political secularism. Muslims and Copts, men and women, urban and rural dwellers, and workers and peasants marched in demonstrations and attacked British communications centers and personnel, and even bureaucrats went on strike. The exile of Sa'd Zaghlul by the British intensified the revolt. The chain of revolt and violence forced the British to unilaterally declare Egypt an independent state in 1922, although the maintenance of British troops in the Suez Canal zone cast a pall on that independence. The British domination of Egypt continued, and determined, to a large degree, the country's subsequent political and economic fortunes.

The delegation that began the process of independence was transformed into a political party: the Wafd (Delegation) Party. The Wafd, which would dominate Egyptian politics up to 1952, was secular in orientation. Its ideology rested on the concept of national unity between Muslims and Copts and an inter-class coalition of all Egyptians, calling not only for independence from the British, but also for restriction of the King's powers. Egyptian nationalism, political independence, and democracy, based on a secular ideology, received their best formulation at the hands of the Wafd's founders. The Wafd represented a major stage in the evolution of Egyptian secularism, one founded on Islamic reformism.

The declaration of Egypt's independence, even if only nominal, led to the establishment of a constitutional monarchy. A constitution was approved in 1923. Egypt was declared an Islamic country, although citizenship was based on nationality and not on religious identity. The constitution did provide for a democratic political system. Nevertheless, the same constitution gave the King ample power over the executive and, more importantly, over the legislature. The first parliamentary elections, held in 1924 and 1929, saw the reemergence of the political Islamic trend. The minority parties used Islam as an ideology to counter the great appeal and popularity of the Wafd. The Liberal Constitutionalists, while they started as secularists, moved to the adoption of a strident Islamist ideology in the hope of attracting followers and as a means of countering the Wafd's appeal to the Egyptian masses. Both the Wafd and the Liberal Constitutionalists were dominated by the landed elite. Competition within the landed elite moved the Constitutionalists to resurrect Islam as a political ideology to split the Muslim majority of the Wafd and to gain adherents. The Constitutionalists went so far as to claim that Copts were conspiring within the Wafd to manipulate it toward narrow sectarian interests.

Capitalizing on the revival of Islamism as political ideology, the Palace, headed by King Fu'ad, adopted an Islamist ideology to counter the Wafd's popularity. After Kamal Ataturk's declaration of a secular state in Turkey and the abolition of the caliphate, King Fu'ad used his supporters from the ranks of the traditional Islamic elite to claim the caliphate for Egypt. As caliph, the King would have been able to dissolve the parliamentary system and restore full autarchy.

One of the most important opponents of the establishment of a caliphate in Egypt was a religious scholar, Sheikh Ali 'Abd al-Raziq. He published a very important and controversial book entitled *al-Islam wa usul al-hukm*, where he claimed that Islam is a religion and not a state. A committee of *ulama* subsequently defrocked him.[35]

The attempt to establish an Islamic caliphate in Egypt under King Fu'ad was defeated, and the Wafd managed to win the ideological battle by warning his followers that by trying to establish a caliphate, King Fu'ad was attempting to deprive Egyptians of their newly gained democratic rights. The Islamist trend that had emerged with the minority parties as an antidote to the Wafd expanded very quickly with the economic pressures of the 1930s. High inflation and unemployment led to increasing inequalities. The Wafd failed to improve the economy and to force Britain to withdraw its troops, and the nationalist question remained unsolved. Two main Islamist organizations emerged in the 1930s in reaction to perceived injustices, whether social or economic: the Society of the Muslim Brothers, which called for an Islamic state, and Young Egypt, which blended an extreme nationalism with Islamism. These organizations, but especially the Muslim Brothers, rallied many Egyptians around the concept of an Islamic state ruled by shari'a, a state that would also be built on the concept of the equality of all Muslims regardless of their level of wealth or knowledge. The *zakat* (alms) is the main mechanism for alleviating poverty and attaining social justice in Islam. The wealth of the nation is God's wealth, and through *zakat* people are carrying out His will for the achievement of a just society. The Society of the Muslim Brothers expanded dramatically from five branch offices in 1930, to fifteen in 1932, and three hundred in 1938. In 1949, it had more than two thousand branches all across Egypt and an active membership estimated between 150,000 and 300,000 members.[36]

In the 1930s, the landed aristocracy managed to divert some of its savings toward industrialization. Under state protection, an import-substitution strategy led to the establishment of a broad base of primary consumer products. This industrialization did not decrease income inequalities, however. The very low wages received by industrial workers and the limited market for industrial products prevented the industrialization of the 1930s from significantly affecting income distribution. The Second World War deepened the economic crisis. Furthermore, the stunning defeat of the Arab armies in the Palestine war of 1948 increased the political crisis that the regime faced because of its inability to resolve the nationalist issue of the continued presence of British troops in the country.

108   Politicized Religion, Conflict, and Development

The coming together of economic and political crises after the end of the Second World War produced a massive wave of unrest and violence in Egypt between 1945 and 1952. The old elites lost their legitimacy because of their inability to conclude an agreement with the British to completely remove their troops from the country and because of the failure of an economic policy that was geared to the advantage of the landed and industrial elites that left the majority of the population suffering from low incomes and high levels of poverty. The Islamic trend represented by the Muslim Brothers gained many adherents, and a war of attrition was waged between the government and the Muslim Brothers. Taking advantage of the 1948 Palestine war, the government announced emergency laws and dissolved the Society of the Muslim Brothers. In response, the Brotherhood ordered the assassination of Mahmud Fahmi al-Nuqrashi, the Prime Minister at the time. The government retaliated by assassinating the *murshid* (leader) of the Brotherhood, Hasan al-Banna, the founder and head of the association, in February 1949.[37]

The Nasserist State, Arab Nationalism, and Independent Development

Antagonized by the government, the Muslim Brothers were moving toward the idea of the use of violence to establish a new Islamic regime in Egypt. The Brotherhood attempted and succeeded in infiltrating the army and the police force. From as early as 1940, there were contacts between Hasan al-Banna himself and Anwar Sadat, a member of the Free Officers clandestine group that would later carry out the 1952 coup d'état. A close friend of Sadat, 'Abd al-Mun'im 'Abd al-Ra'uf, became the liaison between the army and the Brotherhood. The Free Officers helped the Muslim Brothers by training their members in the use of arms and by supplying them clandestinely with arms from the armed forces' caches. In 1951, when the Wafd government decided to wage a guerrilla warfare against the British in the Suez Canal zone, due to their intransigence regarding the withdrawal of their troops, the main guerrilla fighters came from the ranks of the Brotherhood, and the Free Officers supported them with the provision of arms.[38] In 1950, King Faruk is said to have received a report alleging that 33 percent of army officers had links to the Muslim Brotherhood.[39]

The army's coup d'état on July 23, 1952, carried out by the Free Officers, ushered in a new phase in Egypt's economic and political development. The Muslim Brothers were the first to declare their support for the movement, on July 26. The Free Officers had an understanding with the Muslim Brotherhood, whereby the Brotherhood would support the Free Officers' movement in exchange for the inclusion of Brotherhood members in the new government's decision-making processes. Some members of the Free Officers who were also members of the Muslim Brotherhood mediated the relations between the Free Officers and the Brotherhood. Once the Free Officers who formed the Revolutionary Command Council (RCC) were in power, the Brotherhood demanded that shari'a should rule the new state, and they presented nominees for three ministerial posts. Two of the nominees were unacceptable to the RCC. A meeting of the Muslim Brotherhood's Guidance Council discussed the matter and decided not to include any of its members in the government. More important was the Brotherhood's demand for veto power over all legislative matters, a demand that was rejected at once by the RCC.[40] On January 12, 1954, after the refusal of the RCC to accede to the Brotherhood's demands, the Muslim Brothers staged a confrontation between their members and supporters of the new regime. On the following day, the RCC dissolved the Brotherhood, and on January 14 it declared a state of emergency and 450 Brotherhood members were arrested.[41]

As problems overshadowed the RCC—Brotherhood alliance, on January 16, 1954, the RCC announced the abolition of all political parties and groups except for the Society of the Muslim Brothers. The new government was clearly not yet ready for an all-out conflict with the Brotherhood, which had a massive following. A Muslim Brotherhood delegation met Nasser the following day to congratulate him on his decision and demanded a commanding role in the government. Faced by this challenge to the new government's authority, the RCC, on July 23, created the Liberation Rally, a so-called political organization charged with rallying the population to the RCC's goals. The Brotherhood viewed the creation of this organization as a challenge to its position as the regime's popular voice.[42]

The real breaking point between the RCC and the Brotherhood centered on the government's negotiations with the British to obtain the withdrawal of British troops from Egypt. Hasan al-Hudaybi, the then Supreme Guide of the Muslim Brothers, attacked the negotiations with Britain and accused the government of selling the country short. Mitchell alleges, however, that while it attacked the negotiations publicly, the Brotherhood itself had been in contact with the British. He claims that in February or April 1953, the British Embassy Oriental Counselor met with Hudaybi to seek his opinions on the evacuation of British forces.[43] The government went ahead despite the Brotherhood's objections and concluded an agreement with the British on the evacuation of British troops on July 27, 1954. In a sermon delivered during Friday prayers, the Brotherhood accused the government's members of being heretics who did not comply with the teachings of the Qur'an. Angry demonstrators erupted in violent riots following the sermon.[44] The power struggle between the Brotherhood and the members of the RCC, especially the strong prime minister at the time, Gamal Abd al-Nasser, came to a head when a member of the Brotherhood attempted to assassinate Nasser while he was delivering a speech on October 26 in Alexandria, celebrating the signing of the Evacuation Treaty. The government moved swiftly, arresting Hudaybi and dissolving the Society. On December 9, six defendants were hanged and thousands of Muslim Brothers members arrested. The RCC commuted the death sentence received by Hudaybi to life imprisonment.[45] Taking advantage of the mention of the name of Muhammad Naguib, then president, in the trials' proceedings, Nasser moved swiftly to put Naguib under house arrest, thus removing his chief competitor. Shortly afterward, the RCC nominated Nasser for the presidency. He won the referendum (in which he was the only candidate) and became president of Egypt.

Ten years after the mass arrests of Muslim Brothers, Nasser granted all Brotherhood prisoners a general amnesty. A year later, the regime claimed that the security forces had discovered that the Brotherhood was plotting to assassinate Nasser and overthrow the regime. Twenty-seven Brotherhood members were re-arrested, and three of the leaders were sentenced to death. One of the leaders, Sayyid Qutb, is considered the ideological father of the new Islamist groups that emerged in the 1970s. During the trials of Brotherhood members, charges were made that Saudi Arabia, too, had been involved in the plot.

The Muslim Brotherhood was obscured not only through repression but also because the new regime adopted a different and populist ideology, that of Arab nationalism and, later, Arab socialism. The Nasserist period can be characterized as the high point of Egyptian secularism. The majority of Egyptians adopted wholeheartedly the new direction taken by the populist regime, which pursued economically inclusionary policies that benefited many sectors of the population. The essential population base of the regime was a broad coalition of the urban and

Nationalism and Islamism: The Case of Egypt   111

rural poor and, most importantly, the lower middle class (the basic support of the Brotherhood). In addition, especially after the big nationalizations of economic assets during the 1960s, the top echelons of the middle class, especially the technocrats and the professionals, became the new elites under the Nasserist system. Nasser also managed to popularize the new ideology of Arab nationalism by winning the Suez conflict in 1956 and by positing Egypt as the leader, not only of the Arab World but of the third world as well. Egypt was one of the three countries that established the Non-Aligned Movement, and Cairo became the Mecca of third world leaders who emulated the 1952 coup and gained independence for their countries. Nasser also manipulated the media to inculcate the new ideology in the minds of the populace, and educational institutions became tools in that process.

Nevertheless, Nasser did not disregard the importance of Islam as a source of political ideology. His approach to Islam was two-pronged. On the one hand, he brought most Islamic institutions under the power of the state, and, on the other, he used Islam to legitimate some of his policies.

In order to break the power of the Muslim Brotherhood and that of other potential religious political groups, Nasser brought all mosques, mosque preachers, imams, and others under state control. He also brought the *waqf*s, religious foundations, and religious NGOs under state power. Al-Azhar University was modernized, and new, modern curricula were introduced in an attempt to secularize the thousand-year-old institution. The shari'a courts were also brought under the power of the state and transformed into regular courts. In addition, the Charter of 1962 (a political document that would give rise to the 1964 constitution) did not list Islam as state religion. However, to mitigate the wrath of the religious *ulama*, the 1964 constitution did list Islam as the state religion.[46]

Nonetheless, while the shari'a courts were brought under the secular court system, shari'a still ruled in matters of family law. The change was in the form of the institution, not in the law practiced. The same is true about religious schools: they were brought under state control, but what was taught remained the same. Not only that, but the number of mosques and religious schools expanded rapidly under Nasser, and al-Azhar University taught religious and modern curricula simultaneously (the secular curriculum came under the power of the religious *ulama* and not vice versa). These policies have in fact deepened the dual or eclectic character of secularism in Egypt.

112   Politicized Religion, Conflict, and Development

The Transition Crisis, the State, and the Use of Politicized Islam as State Ideology (1970–2005)

The emergence of radical Islamist groups in the Middle East has received a great deal of attention in the political science literature. Two main factors are stressed in most of that literature: the defeat of the Arabs in the 1967 Arab–Israeli war and the failure of modernization and westernization in Arab projects.[47] While these crisis explanations might be partly true, we can nevertheless trace the emergence of radical groups to the 1970s. The defeat of Egypt in the 1967 war was a harsh blow to Egyptians, especially after they were led by the state propoganda machine to believe in the invincibility of their army. Yet, the same people erupted in massive demonstrations on June 9, 1967, when President Nasser, taking responsibility for the defeat, resigned from the the presidency. Nasser was returned to office on June 10. Once in office, he started to rebuild the army, and in 1967–68, a war of attrition was waged against Israel. The population was heartened by this war and yearned for the final battle to be fought to free occupied Sinai.

As for the argument that it was the failure of the projects of westernization and modernization that fueled radical Islamism, nothing could be further from the truth. As mentioned above, the modernization project had begun under Muhammad 'Ali at the turn of the nineteenth century. While the process was not a linear one, it deepened through a century and half, reaching its peak under the Nasser regime, even if in the guise of Arab socialism and nationalism.

Rather, I contend that the emergence of radical Islamist groups in Egypt is the result of a deep transition crisis, that is, a generalized economic, political, and ideological crisis engineered by the state itself.

Sadat and the Transition Crisis of the 1970s

With the death of Nasser in September 1970, Sadat, the vice-president, was elected president through his nomination by the Arab Socialist Union, the only political organization at the time. The members of the bureaucratic elite controlling the regime thought that the nomination of Sadat as president would allow them to continue their domination of the system. They believed that they could control him and continue to exercise their power through him. Little did they know that President Sadat himself was scheming to get rid of the leftist wing of the bureaucratic elite (see Chapter 1 for a detailed explanation of the split in the bureaucratic elite of the 1960s).

The Transition Crisis, the State, and Politicized Islam as State Ideology   113

By the beginning of the 1970s, Egypt was exhausted economically because of the large expenses of the rebuilding of the military and the war of attrition. Economic growth rates slowed. But more importantly, the country's infrastructure was deteriorating rapidly due to the decline of investment in this sector and the direction of most investment funds toward the military.[48]

With declining rates of economic growth, the bureaucratic elite was divided on the strategy required to revive the economy. A right-leaning faction advocated a strategy of reintegration into the international economic system. According to the proponents of the free market, the deepening of the industrialization process could no longer depend on internal capital formation. A reorientation of the economy to the free-market model would attract foreign capital and alleviate the problems of internal savings and investments. They advocated the renunciation of the import-substitution strategy adopted by the Nasserist regime and the reorientation of the economic system toward an export-oriented strategy. On the other side, the left wing members of the bureaucratic elite advocated a deepening of the import-substitution policy and the spread of state control to the sectors still in private hands, such as internal trade and the construction sector. President Sadat was in favor of the policy of economic liberalization and the reorientation of the economy toward a free-market model.

The implementation of this policy meant a frontal attack, not only on the left wing of the bureaucratic elite, but also on the Nasserist populist alliance, in other words, the middle class, the peasants, and the workers, that had dominated the system when President Sadat assumed power on October 15, 1970.

The first sign of a different socioeconomic strategy came in December 1971, through a decree restoring properties sequestered under Nasser to their owners, most of whom had been opponents of the Nasser regime. Sadat had prepared for restoration of the properties six months earlier, in May 1971, by apprehending the most prominent leaders of the left wing, including the powerful secretary of the Arab Socialist Union, Ali Sabri. Prior to that move, the left wing was still in power and would have prevented the implementation of more radical laws canceling the Nasserist policies.

After removing the core Nasserist leadership, a step greatly welcomed by conservatives, Sadat sought an alliance with the Muslim Brothers (the enemies of Nasserism) as a counterweight to the Nasserist populist

114   Politicized Religion, Conflict, and Development

alliances. He released most political prisoners, mainly Muslim Brothers apprehended by the previous regime in 1965. He also allowed the Muslim Brothers who had taken refuge in Saudi Arabia to return to Egypt. Another major step indicating the new alliance between the Sadatist regime and the Muslim Brothers was cemented by the government declaration of Islamic shari'a as a principal source *("masdarun ra'isiyun")* of Egyptian legislation in the 1971 constitution.

By succeeding in forging an alliance with, and therefore placating, the Muslim Brothers, Sadat courted the private sector by issuing in September 1971 a law on foreign and Arab investments. For international and foreign investments to flow into Egypt, certain conditions had to be created. First, foreign investors had to be assured that their investments would not be threatened by nationalization. Second, the scope of the private market had to be increased. Third, the continued occupation of the Sinai and the threat of a new war in the Middle East had to be dealt with.

In February 1971, in a grand gesture signaling the willingness of Egypt to accept a political solution for the liberation of Sinai, Sadat offered to end hostilities and reopen the Suez Canal for international navigation if Israel would accept a partial withdrawal of its troops, east of the canal. To enact these deep changes in Egypt's economic and political policies, Sadat could not depend on the ideology of Arab socialism that had held sway in the 1960s and so turned for a justification of his policies to Islam as political ideology. This was also intended to counter the growing student movement that dominated the universities from 1970 to 1973 and clamored for a resumption of military operations to liberate Sinai. Most of the students at the time were Nasserists, and they accused Sadat of being soft on the occupation. To counter the student movement, especially after the workers and other political groups joined them in criticizing the regime, Sadat decided to plant Islamist groups in the student body. The plan for the Islamization of the universities was conceived by Muhammad Othman Isma'il, then a presidential adviser, and Othman Ahmad Othman, a construction mogul and friend of Sadat with strong ties to the Muslim Brothers.[49]

The Islamist groups in the universities were allowed to set up religious camps during summer vacations for the purposes of indoctrination.[50] Prominent sheikhs were invited to educate the youth, and the government went as far as to arm these groups with light weapons that were used against Nasserist students during the demonstrations that swept the universities between 1970 and 1973. In addition, the Youth Organization was

The Transition Crisis, the State, and Politicized Islam as State Ideology   115

given a new orientation stressing religious education.[51] These Islamist organizations, established and funded by the government, gave birth to the fundamentalist Islamist groups that were to use violence against the state itself and society, such as al-Gama'a al-Islamiya and al-Gihad.

With the partial victory of the 1973 Arab–Israeli war, Sadat embarked on his most challenging offensive against the strategy of import substitution that had dominated the Egyptian economy since the 1930s. In October 1974, Sadat announced the 'Open Door' or economic liberalization policy. "According to this policy, generous incentives were offered to attract foreign and Arab capital. Free areas, completely exempt from labor regulations, were created. In addition the new investment laws lifted the previous requirements of local majority ownership. Explicit protection clauses against nationalization and expropriation measures were guaranteed."[52] However, the results of this first wave of economic liberalization were disappointing to the regime. Most investments came from local entrepreneurs. The majority of Arab investments were located in the free zones and were directed mostly to financial investments, construction, and services. Western capital in the period of the 1970s did not exceed 16 percent of total investments and was confined to the service sector, especially banking.[53]

Mark Cooper argues that economic liberalization during the 1970s was an utter disaster since it led to the expansion of commercial activities and the de-industrialization of Egypt. Huge import bills led to increasing budget deficits, and the trade deficit was estimated at 20 percent of GDP, creating increasing pressures to rely on a policy of foreign indebtedness. Economic liberalization was in essence a commercial liberalization that fueled an explosive inflationary trend. This altered the structure of Egyptian society by creating a small wealthy class and a large destitute class while the middle class fought to stay afloat.[54]

Such conditions allowed the Muslim Brothers and other Islamist groups to extend a network of welfare services to the poor. Drawing on Arab funds, especially from the Gulf, the Muslim Brothers established hospitals and schools that offered their services at much cheaper rates than in the private sector and a better quality of service than in the government sector.[55] These welfare networks expanded the Islamists' popular base.

The alliance between the regime and the Islamists began to falter in the second half of the 1970s. In the food riots on January 18 and 19, 1977, Islamist groups participated on the same side as the students, workers,

116 Politicized Religion, Conflict, and Development

and the poor, signaling the first serious break between the regime and the Islamists. After that, the Islamists moved on to more daring exploits. Some of them kidnapped and murdered Sheikh al-Zahabi, a prominent religious figure and the former Minister of Charitable Endowments (*awqaf*) in March 1977. A series of bombings of theaters, video shops, and other public places ensued. The regime reacted swiftly with a slew of arrests and by increasing the level of official religious propaganda, claiming that the perpetrators of the assassination and other violent acts were not Muslims but killers and saboteurs.

The real break with the regime came with the visit of President Sadat to Jerusalem and the signing of the Camp David peace treaty in 1979. The Islamists resorted to open confrontation with the regime. *Al-Da'wa* and *al-Itissam* magazines issued by the Muslim Brothers attacked not only the signing of the treaty but also the ineffectual economic policies of the regime and increasing income inequalities. In response, the regime tried to placate the Muslim Brothers by passing a constitutional amendment in May 1980, which altered the wording of Article 2 of the 1971 constitution, which had said that "Islamic shari'a" was "a principal source of legislation," (see page 77) to say that "mabadi' al-shari'a al-islamiya" ('the principles of Islamic shari'a') are "*al-masdar al-ra'isi li-l-tashri*" ('the principal source of legislation'). At the same time, the regime made widespread arrests of Islamist activists.[56] The clash between the Islamists and the state resulted in the assassination of President Sadat on October 6, 1981 by a neo-Islamist group (an offshoot of the Muslim Brotherhood), al-Gihad.

The Islamists and the Mubarak Regime
A month prior to the assassination, President Sadat had ordered the arrest of more than 1,500 opposition leaders, including Islamists, priests, the Coptic patriarch, Wafdists, secularists, and Muslim Brothers. The arrests followed violent sectarian strife that had erupted in one of the poorest quarters of Cairo (al-Zawya al-Hamra). For the first time in Egypt's history, members of all political groups and affiliations were arrested in one stroke. Sadat wanted to crack down on the members of his alliance, namely the Islamists. To counter accusations of bias, he decided to arrest notable members of all other groups as well, including prominent independents such as Muhammad Hasanayn Haykal, the renowned journalist who served briefly as a minister in Sadat's cabinet. The opposition against Sadat mounted after the

The Transition Crisis, the State, and Politicized Islam as State Ideology   117

arrests, especially by neo-Islamists, who staged massive demonstrations in the run-up to the assassination.

The assassination was followed quickly by the nomination of the vice-president, Muhammad Hosni Mubarak, for the presidency and by an attempt on the part of the neo-Islamists to take control of the state through a series of violent takeovers of the state administrative offices. Most groups did not follow that plan, but in the province of Asyut the neo-Islamist groups attacked the police headquarters. The attempt ended in violence and bloodshed, and the overwhelming of these groups by state forces. The neo-Islamist groups (al-Gihad and al-Gama'a al-Islamiya) had thought that the population was ready to join them in a revolution to wrest control from the state, but they were not supported in their efforts and were left to battle with the security forces.

In October 1981, Mubarak was elected by a high percentage of votes in the referendum on his presidency, a signal that Egyptians were weary of militant Islamist groups and wanted stability and security. A first sign from Mubarak's regime of a new phase of leniency was the release of all those arrested in September 1981. For the first three years after his election, and after the crackdown on the militant Islamist groups, especially al-Gihad, which had assassinated President Sadat, a period of relative calm, without too many incidents, prevailed. This encouraged the regime to allow the Muslim Brothers to participate in the 1984 parliamentary elections. While the Society of the Muslim Brothers was legally banned, it participated in the elections under the banner of the Wafd Party (Egypt's most secular party, which indicates an opportunistic stand on the part of the Wafd, to gain more seats in parliament through the Brotherhood's support). Nine Brotherhood members were elected, although the honeymoon between the two parties dissipated quickly due to irreconcilable differences in their political outlooks and strategies.

From 1985 to 1992, the state, while allowing its controlled media and the Society of the Muslim Brothers to spread the Islamic message, attempted to curtail the influence of a number of radical Islamist provocateurs, such as sheikhs Hafiz Salama, Muhammad Kishk, and Omar 'Abd al-Rahman, the Mufti (legal religious leader) of al-Gihad. Salama and another forty-four activists were arrested but released in a matter of a few weeks.[57]

In 1986, the troops of the Central Security Forces broke out in massive riots in Giza, the southern end of Greater Cairo. The troops were protesting in response to rumors that their term of service would be extended from four to five years (all the troops are army conscripts), and they were also protesting their meager salaries (around US$2 a month). The Islamists took advantage of the demonstrations to wreak havoc on nightclubs, movie theaters, liquor stores, and any other places that they regarded as places of sin. The riots also led to the smuggling of large quantities of Central Security arms to Upper Egypt where they were sold to individuals, many of whom were members of radical Islamist groups.[58]

Militant Islamist groups began agitating on university campuses, especially in Upper Egypt. In order to finance their activities, the radical groups carried out attacks on so-called stores of sin (selling videos or liquor) that extended to the country as a whole. The government responded swiftly by arresting militants. The parliamentary elections of 1986 witnessed sectarian clashes between Copts and Muslims and provocation from the Islamists claiming that Islam was in danger, to promote the election of Islamists. The 1986 elections resulted in the election of thirty-six Brotherhood members, this time in alliance with the Labor Party, which moved from a secular stand to a strident Islamist nationalist one led by a former Marxist, 'Adil Husayn.

Shortly after the elections, radicals attempted to assassinate a former minister of the interior, Hasan Abu Basha. On June 4, 1986, the editor in chief of *al-Musawwar* magazine, Makram Muhammad Ahmad, barely escaped an assassination attempt. Two months later, another former minister of the interior, Nabawi Isma'il, escaped an assassination attempt. The attempts on officials' lives culminated in 1990 with the assassination of Dr. Rif'at al-Mahgub, the speaker of the parliament at the time.

It seemed that the period of relative calm that had followed Mubarak's accession to power had come to an end, especially from 1985 onward. However, the worst part of the killing rampage carried out by radical Islamist groups extended from 1992 to 1997. The violence started with the assassination of a leading secular thinker, Farag Fuda, his son, and one of his guards in retaliation for his stand against the idea of the establishment of an Islamic state. Fuda voiced the same arguments that Sheikh Ali 'Abd al-Raziq had made in the 1930s: that Islam does not require the establishment of a religious state or caliphate. While religious institutions at the time defrocked 'Abd al-Raziq, the radical Islamists assassinated Fuda and his son (see the discussion on Ali 'Abd al-Raziq above, page 118). The revival of radical Islamist attempts to establish an Islamic state would crescendo into a series of violent acts previously unseen in Egyptian politics.

The Transition Crisis, the State, and Politicized Islam as State Ideology   119

According to Kepel, the radical Islamist groups in the period 1992–97 engaged in the following acts of terror: (1) assassination of prominent persons; (2) murder of tourists, and (3) penetration of the most poverty stricken areas of Cairo, which ended up with the ironic proclamation of the Islamic Republic of Imbaba.[59] Radical Islamists took over Imbaba, the population of which is estimated at one million, with the help of some criminal elements. They enforced their own rules on the inhabitants, which they claimed was an implementation of shari'a law. People paid the radicals protection money, which was claimed as taxes, and were terrified of the radicals. All this happened under the auspices of a government that claimed to be protecting its population. Finally, the government moved massive forces into Imbaba in 1990 and liberated its inhabitants. Imbaba was a prototype of a Taliban regime in the heart of Egypt's capital, Cairo.

During the 1990s, the radical Islamist groups were also responsible for the following acts of terror:

1. On February 4, 1993, a Molotov cocktail was lobbed at a tour bus with South Korean passengers. No injuries were reported.
2. On April 20, 1993, there was an assassination attempt on Safwat al-Sharif, minister of information;
3. On February 19, 1994, unknown assailants fired upon a passenger train and wounded two tourists and two Egyptian citizens in Asyut;
4. On February 23, 1994, a bomb explosion aboard a passenger train in Asyut injured six foreign tourists and five Egyptians.
5. On March 4, 1994, September 27, 1994, and January 12, 1995, unknown gunmen opened fire on Nile cruise ships and wounded a German tourist near the Sohag Governorate. A number of tourists were injured;
6. On June 26, 1995, the Gama'a al-Islamiya and al-Gihad groups attempted to assassinate President Mubarak in Addis Ababa, Ethiopia;
7. On November 8, 1995, radical Islamists opened fire on a train en route to Cairo from Aswan, injuring two tourists and one Egyptian;
8. On November 19, 1995, a suicide bomber drove a vehicle into the Egyptian Embassy in Islamabad, killing at least sixteen people and injuring some sixty others. The bomb destroyed the whole compound;
9. On April 28, 1996, four radical Islamists attacked a group of Greek tourists in front of the Europa Hotel in Cairo, killing eighteen and

injuring twelve. The attackers had mistaken the Greeks for an Israeli group which they thought was visiting Egypt at the time;

10. And finally, on November 17, 1997, radical Islamist gunmen shot and killed fifty-eight tourists and four Egyptians and wounded another twenty-six people at the Hatshepsut Temple in Luxor. This horrific incident was the last such attack by the Gama'a Islamiya.

In the same period, in 1994, Nobel laureate Naguib Mahfouz was stabbed in the neck by an extremist, an attack motivated by the declaration on the part of some sheikhs that Mahfouz was an apostate because of one of his novels *(Children of the Alley)*. They claimed that the novel attacked Islam.

Mahfouz was not the only intellectual to be attacked. Nasr Abu Zeid, an associate professor at Cairo University, was denied promotion to the rank of professor after some of his colleagues declared him an apostate, claiming that his works on the Qur'an were blasphemous. Some Islamists took Abu Zeid to court to force him to divorce his wife on the grounds that a Muslim woman should not be married to an apostate. The first level court annulled his marriage, thereby legally confirming his status as an apostate. Since shari'a law holds that apostates are punishable by death, Abu Zeid and his wife fled to the Netherlands. Although a higher-level court reversed the ruling, the threat remains should any radical Islamist attempt to carry out the death sentence himself.[60]

Egyptians' strong reaction against the Luxor massacre, and the government's massive crackdown on Islamist groups, forced the radical al-Gama'a al-Islamiya to publicly renounce violence. A period of calm therefore reigned after the Luxor massacre, but from 2003 to 2005 a new militant group was active in the Sinai Peninsula. In October 2003, this group bombed a hotel in Taba, killing thirty-four people. In April 2004, it bombed a busy marketplace in Sharm al-Sheikh, killing over fifty people, most of them Egyptians. And in October 2005 it bombed tourist establishments in Dahab. Once again, the government reacted swiftly and with massive force against the Sinai's inhabitants, which alienated many of the tribes living in the region.

In 2007, the leaders of al-Gihad renounced the use of violence against the state. However, their retractions make it clear that the renunciation of violence was a tactical reaction to the reality of a strong state, defeating their attempts at the establishment of an Islamic state in Egypt. Very little changed in terms of their basic ideology. It would seem that

The Transition Crisis, the State, and Politicized Islam as State Ideology   121

Islamist groups (including the Muslim Brothers) are now more disposed to seek change through the party political system than through violence.

During the last few years, the regime has attempted to curb the power of Islamist groups. This is clear from the most recent constitutional amendments, which banned the formation of political parties on the basis of religion. However, the regime still upholds religion as a political ideology in the face of mounting pressures from within and without to liberalize the political system. As long as the state is unable to steer its political ideology to secularism, the crisis between the state and the Islamists will be perpetuated, with dire consequences for the country as a whole.

4

Gender and Development: Women's Rights, State, and Society

Gender Inequalities and Development

The relationship between gender inequalities and development is complex and rarely unidirectional. Gender intersects with social class, ethnicity, and race in the determination of societal power relations, which in turn impact development. Development itself, by restructuring social and therefore power relations, affects gender inequalities.

The Impact of Gender Inequalities on Development

A growing body of literature on gender and development indicates that the persistence of gender inequalities hampers development through its impact on the development of human capital, employment opportunities, the flow of direct foreign investment, and the rate of savings.

A major constituent of human capital is investment in education. Gender inequality in education can affect economic growth through its impact on fertility levels and population growth. The traditional theory posits a causal relationship among a higher illiteracy rate for women, a higher fertility rate, higher population growth, and therefore, a lower economic growth rate.[1] The link between lower fertility and economic growth can be explained by the impact of fertility on dependency burdens, the labor force, and, in turn, investment in human capital.

More educated women can use contraceptive methods effectively and bear the desired number of children. Educated mothers also increase the probability of lower infant death rates due to their better knowledge of healthcare and nutrition. High infant death rates tend to promote high birth rates, as parents have more children in order to reach the desired number of children. Lower fertility tends to decrease the dependency burden, that is, the number of dependents in a family. A lower dependency burden increases the household's and the country's savings, because of a decline in expenditures on consumption by the young and unproductive and on infrastructure such as schools and hospitals. Higher savings leads to higher investment and economic growth.

A lowering of fertility rates will also increase the proportion of people in the higher age brackets of the productive labor force. If increased savings results in a higher demand for investments, a larger share of the working population will be absorbed in gainful employment, and the rate of economic growth will tend to increase. As pointed out above, lower fertility rates also increase investment in children through education and nutrition, which, in turn leads to a more productive labor force in future generations.

Dollar and Gatti, in an extensive international empirical study for the period 1975–90,[2] show that gender inequality in education affects economic growth negatively. They conclude that an exogenous increase in girls' education creates a better environment for economic growth. This result is pronounced for middle-income countries. At very low levels of development, an increase in girls' secondary school education leads to little improvement in female attainment. However, the result is reversed in middle-income countries, where girls' educational attainments accelerate progress.

Klasen claims that gender inequality in education acts as an impediment to economic growth by distorting incentives and through its impact on investment and population growth.[3] His research reveals that Africa, South Asia, and the Middle East have the worst records in terms of initial conditions and records of change in female education during the period 1960–92.

Filmer, in an empirical study using internationally comparable household data sets and investigating the impact of gender and wealth on educational disparities, finds that women in western and central Africa, North Africa, and South Asia have the highest disadvantage in education.[4] Gender gaps are large in many of the countries studied, but wealth gaps are larger in all the countries, and the interplay between gender gaps and wealth gaps results in large gaps in educational outcomes. In some

Gender Inequalities and Development   125

countries, such as Egypt, where there is a high degree of gender inequality in education, the wealth gap interacts with the gender gap to exacerbate the gap in educational enrollment. Filmer also finds that the education of adults, especially of mothers, has a significant impact on the education of children, and that the presence of schools within communities has a great impact on children's school enrollment. Finally, we can expect that the education of women would influence women's economic participation and the types of occupations where women are concentrated.

Some researchers argue that gender inequality in employment might lead to the employment of sub-average male workers, while better-trained female workers are rejected due to gender discrimination. This, they argue, will reduce the average level of skill of the workforce and therefore reduce economic growth.[5]

Barriers to the entry of women into the labor force can also restrict labor supply, thereby increasing the level of wages, leading to higher prices and hampering competitiveness in international markets. Klasen shows that the use of a largely female labor force in labor-intensive manufacturing for exports in Southeast Asian economies is responsible for the success of the export-oriented industrialization strategy adopted by these countries.[6] Other research, however, concludes that the extensive use of women in export processing zones marginalizes women by concentrating them in low-paying jobs with poor working conditions, and that gender inequalities in earnings are the reason for the low prices of these products.[7]

In general, women's earnings are lower than men's (for most countries, estimated at 70 percent of men's earnings). Gender gaps in earnings are usually explained by a large female labor supply, gender gaps in education, and state policies that impose benefits for women, such as maternity leave, that raise the cost of their employment. Discriminatory practices and the devaluation by society of women's labor contribute to the existence and perpetuation of gaps in earnings.

Gender earning gaps may result from women's multiple roles, that is, work both outside and inside the home, which increases the female labor burden. Multiple roles push women toward jobs that allow them time flexibility (such as part-time jobs or home-based employment), which in turn pushes their wages downward.[8] The human capital theory explains earning gaps by the tendency of women to choose occupations that do not require a high investment in human capital (especially education and

126   Gender and Development: Women's Rights, State, and Society

training), and to demand jobs that use skills that do not require constant upgrading, due to women's need for flexible schedules to suit their roles as housewives and mothers. In this case, the lower level of female human capital justifies the earnings gaps. The occupational crowding thesis claims that gender-specific social roles, socialize women and men from an early age to consider some occupations gender specific. Accordingly, gender socialization influences the type of human capital investments seen as appropriate for women. This results in a concentration of female labor seeking certain occupations, thereby increasing demand and lowering wages.[9]

Others have attempted to study the impact of foreign direct investment on gender inequalities in employment and earnings. Foreign direct investments may affect the demand for female labor. In East and Southeast Asia, and in the early stages of export-oriented industrialization, foreign direct investment inflows were large and concentrated in the labor-intensive, export-oriented assembly and manufacturing sector. This generated high economic participation rates for women, narrowing the gender gaps in employment. However, foreign direct investment did not narrow the gender gaps in earnings. In fact, foreign direct investment profited from women's lower wages, which brought down the cost of labor-intensive goods.[10] Increased female employment resulted in increased production, contributing to rapid development. In turn, female earnings, even if lower, increased demand, which in turn promoted economic growth. Still, there are indications that the demand for female labor is declining in export-oriented zones. In Malaysia, South Korea, and the Philippines, the proportion of female labor in the workforce declined in export processing zones between 1980 and 1990.[11] Since 1990, the share of women in manufacturing has been declining for a number of other countries.[12]

While, defeminization is occurring in export-oriented zones, women are still concentrated in certain manufacturing sectors, such as electronics, textiles, and garments. In a highly competitive international market, employing women in these industries depresses labor costs, which are a particularly important cost factor, and therefore reduces prices. Lower wages are not the only explanation for the concentration of women in these manufacturing industries. Employers prefer to hire women for the following openly stated reasons: Women have nimble fingers, are more obedient, exhibit a high tolerance for tedious work, and are more reliable than men.[13]

Gender Inequalities and Development   127

While foreign direct investment may lead to investments in less industrialized countries, it can also be very disruptive, owing to its high mobility. Relying on internal savings ensures the stability of investment and mitigates the risks of capital flight. One of the effects of female employment and earnings is an increase in women's bargaining power within the household. A rich literature on the intra-household allocation of resources demonstrates that gender affects greatly the allocation of resources to types of household expenditures and, therefore, to savings.

The empirical research of Guyer (1988), Handa (1994), and Quisumbing and Maluccio (1999) indicates that women spend their income on the household and children's needs, especially food, at a much higher rate than men.[14] Another empirical study, of twenty semi-industrialized countries for the period 1975–95, demonstrates that women's control of their earnings and an increase in their bargaining power within the household significantly increases the household's aggregate savings.[15] If these savings are directed toward investment, it will necessarily increase development and economic growth.

On another level, some empirical research has found that women's attitudes toward competition differs from men's. Women in business are said to be less likely to pay bribes to government officials, either due to risk aversion or to higher moral standards. Lower corruption is said to result in higher investment and thus growth. The study also finds that corruption falls as the proportion of parliamentary seats held by women increases. Kaufman claims that a one standard deviation increase in the percentage of women in parliament from the sample average of 10.9 percent results in an at least 10-percent decrease in corruption levels.[16]

The Impact of Development on Gender Inequalities

If gender inequalities can hamper development, does development increase or decrease gender inequalities? Successive issues of the UNDP Human Development Report indicate that gender inequalities tend to decrease with the increase of per capita income, a major indicator of development and growth.

Economic development may in effect reduce gender inequalities. Economic growth does expand job opportunities and increase worker productivity. Investment in infrastructure, especially in the provision of services such as water and energy, reduces the time women spend providing their households with these basic services. Higher per capita income increases investment in human capital (especially education and health), thus promoting gender equality between girls and boys. A better provision of public services also increases workers' productivity and decreases gender inequalities.

Economic growth is the outcome of higher demand for products and services, which will necessarily increase demand for labor. Increased demand for labor will, by necessity, especially in full employment markets, increase demand for women's labor in the formal sector of the economy. However, a growing demand for labor, while it may lead to an increased demand for women's labor, does not necessarily affect women and men in the same way. Men and women do not necessarily have the same skills, access to information, and social connections. Consequently, women and men may be allocated to different market positions. According to Dijkstra, if different market positions are not due to different capabilities, then the allocation is sub-optimal and will lead to lower economic outcomes.[17]

While economic growth may lead to increased demand for female employment, it also leads to shifts in employment according to changes in demand and/or productivity. A trend that emerged from the 1990s in export processing zones, especially in the newly industrialized countries, as mentioned above, is the defeminization of labor in the formal sector of the economy and the emergence on a large scale of home-based industrial work, leading to what some researchers call the casualization of labor.[18]

Technological innovation through computer-aided design and manufacture has allowed big corporations to decentralize production by subcontracting. Workers do not have to be held to the traditional manufacturing systems of production or the work shift. Subcontracting allows workers to work at home. This kind of work is more suitable for women and gives them the desired flexibility to accommodate their household chores with the new work environment. However, this type of work often means greater insecurity (there is no obligation on the part of the subcontractor to continue to provide work), no insurance, and no benefits. It may also mean shorter working hours and therefore less pay.[19]

As mentioned above, economic growth, by increasing per capita and household incomes, promotes investment in human capital in general and in women's human capital in particular, especially in the areas of nutrition and education. This leads to higher female labor force capabilities and levels of attainment. Higher capabilities do not necessarily lead to a narrowing of the wage or earnings' gap, however, if the other

Gender Inequalities and Development 129

determinants of the demand for female labor do not change. This is especially true if social norms and traditions perpetuate the typecasting of occupations according to gender. If gender-specific occupations are maintained, even in the process of economic development, this might discourage investment in female human capital due to lower expected returns.[20]

Nonetheless, there are no necessary and mechanistic relationships between development and gender equality. For example, the rapid economic growth in East Asia led to a high demand for women's labor, which narrowed gender gaps in employment. But this higher female's economic participation was achieved at the expense of a growing gender gap in earnings, even with the great gains in women's education and work experience. Women's earnings as a percentage of men's do not exceed 59 percent in Japan and 51 percent in South Korea.[21]

The perpetuation of gender gaps in education, employment earnings, and access to technology and credit, even in the context of economic growth, have increased the proportion of women in the ranks of the poor to the degree that we can claim that there is a trend toward the feminization of poverty. Female poverty has been rising over the last two or three decades. A noticeable increase in female-headed households, the increasing proportion of women's participation in the informal urban sector relative to men, where wages and returns are much lower than in the formal sector, and the gaps in earnings indicate that women suffer from a higher incidence of poverty than men.

The lack of access to resources, coupled with divorce, widowhood, and sometimes simply abandonment, forces women to provide for their families, especially if they have young children, in a hostile and harsh environment. Women heads of households face great challenges to earn enough income to sustain the livelihood of their children, while carrying on their household chores, which puts pressure on their time and meager resources. With lower education levels, work experience, and income, these households can be expected to become more deeply mired in poverty. Buvinic and Gupta contend that there has been a consistent increase in the proportion of female-headed households in most regions of the world since the late 1970s.[22] Thirty-eight out of sixty studies investigating the relationship between female-headed households and poverty, demonstrate a strong interrelationship.[23]

Many researchers found that in periods of reform under structural adjustment policies adopted in many developing countries, female vulnerability to poverty tends to increase. Structural adjustment policies resulted in many cases in the deepening of poverty. Women, with their characteristic lack of control over resources, benefit much less from liberalization of markets. Poor urban working women are especially vulnerable to the effects of economic reforms, such as increased prices and indirect taxation, which, in effect, lower real wages. Women also suffer disproportionately from unemployment due to the decline of state employment, a result of cutting state expenditures as part of economic reform policies.[24] Employment in the state sector has favored females because of state adherence to the principles of equal opportunities and equal pay.

The Role of the State in the Determination of Gender Inequalities

The role of the state in the determination of gender inequalities hinges on an interplay of complex factors. The choice of development and economic strategy influences gender inequalities. State policies can affect gender relations by maintaining, increasing, or decreasing inequalities.

Development Strategies and Gender Inequalities

Since the emergence of the industrial revolution in the west, most developing countries have moved through three stages of economic policy. The first was dominated by colonialist economic policies that depended mostly on a primary-product export-oriented strategy to feed the needs of the industrializing countries. After independence, most post-colonial states adopted an industrialization policy as a development strategy, and used an import-substitution policy to protect infant industries from foreign competition. Finally, with the development of a global economic system and the emergence of the giant trans-national corporations , third world countries had to reintegrate their economies into the global system and adopt an export-oriented industrialization strategy, relying on foreign direct investment to increase their investment and thereby industrialization rates (see Chapter 1). Every one of these stages had an impact on gender relations either by reinforcing traditional pre-capitalist unequal relations or transforming them.

Pre-colonial economic structures in third world countries relied mostly on labor power. Agriculture relied on labor-intensive techniques, where the reproduction of labor was an essential component of the economic process. A sexual division of labor was necessary to perpetuate this economic system. Women, because of their biological reproductive powers, were entrusted with the perpetuation and maintenance of the labor force. Women also performed economic functions that did not come into conflict with their reproductive functions. In order to ensure the labor supply, the pre-colonial economic structures subsumed women's productive and reproductive labor to male domination. Such unequal relations relied on the codification of male authority and superiority and women's obedience and dependence. A patriarchal system based on male superiority and female dependency started as a division of labor but developed later into an ideological and cultural system of gender relations that was perpetuated even in cases where the structure of gender inequalities detracted from development and progress.

Industrializing Europe absorbed the majority of its industrial labor from rural areas. Europe's increasing urbanization required an increase in food and non-food agricultural products that were not available domestically. Colonialism was one of the strategies by which a steady flow of primary products and food staples to industrializing Europe was ensured. Colonialism modified the traditional agricultural structures of colonized countries and oriented them away from subsistence agriculture to a primary-product export-oriented cash economy.

Colonialism also introduced aspects of the capitalist system that dominated Europe, such as monetization, the introduction of private property in land, and the building of roads and communication systems to facilitate the export of raw materials. However, the colonialist powers did little to change the traditional labor-intensive techniques that required higher reproduction rates of the labor force, especially with the intensification of agricultural products designated for exports to the Metropolis. The conversion of most agriculture to cash cropping and the involvement of men in the cash economy, receiving meager wages, forced women to intensify their unpaid labor in the small subsistence sector, in addition to their household duties and obligations. Such policies did nothing to alter the patriarchal gender relations and may have intensified the burden on the majority of women.

The intensification of independence movements resulted in the emergence of sovereign states, especially after the end of the Second World War. The new independent or post-colonial states adopted industrialization, especially import-substitution industrialization, as their main development strategy. The new industrialization strategy required a larger educated and better trained workforce. The new post-colonial regimes encouraged greater education and employment of women. The regimes also introduced a set of reforms to encourage women's participation in the new economy, such as granting women their political rights, the introduction of family planning policies, and the setting of a minimum age for marriage. However, most regimes shied away from meaningful reform in family or personal status laws, where gender inequalities were enshrined either in a rigid interpretation of religious laws or in cast-iron patriarchal civil codes imported mostly from the Metropolis's legislations.

Import-substitution strategies of development led to a fast rise in women's education and employment, especially in the state public sector, but gender inequalities persisted in education, employment, political participation, and so on. The persistence of these inequalities despite formal policies to the contrary may be explained by the state's fear that enforcement of women's rights would cost it the support of religious or traditional leaders, by the inability of women to enforce their new legal rights, and by the resistance of the state bureaucracy, which was predominantly male, to new women's rights. However, the most important reason for the failure of the post-colonial regimes to grant women their full rights, even if in the public sphere only, is the perpetuation of patriarchal relations within the family, cemented by state laws that did little to change these laws in women's favor. While import-substitution industrialization policies did not achieve gender equality, they nevertheless reduced gender inequalities, especially in the fields of education and, to some degree, employment, if not in the area of personal status laws.

The failure of import-substitution strategies, or their exhaustion due to international and national economic and political factors, and the international economic crisis of the 1970s resulted in the emergence of a new global economy relying on free-market and trade rules. In the new global economy, giant transnational corporations succeeded in internationalizing not only trade but also the production process itself. Third world countries had to move from inward-looking policies, relying on the fulfillment of internal market demand, to export-oriented industrialization policies, where comparative advantages and international trade became the engine of growth and development. The effects of these strategies on gender inequalities are contradictory. As described above, where export industries relied on labor-intensive and routine methods of production, the employment of women increased very quickly, to such a degree that analysts began to talk about the feminization of certain industries, such as textiles, ready-made clothes, and electronics. Most women employed in these industries, especially in the export zones, have much lower wages than men and no social or legal protection. The new trends also pushed women away from the formal sector into the informal sector of the economy, where protection is even more tenuous. The increase in women's economic participation should not be considered apart from the growing gaps in earnings and the increased marginalization of female labor. In addition, this type of increase in employment is not accompanied by a social policy directed toward the achievement of gender equality in other dimensions of women's lives, particularly in the context of the family.

State Policies

As discussed in the introduction to this book, Caroline Moser does not view the state as an impartial or neutral agent in the constitution of gender relations within the family, but as an active player. The most obvious policies affecting gender relations are in the realm of family, but other factors impact gender relations, such as state policies concerning legislation, the provision of social services, and the extension of welfare measures.

In many cases, personal status laws reinforce unequal gender relations by granting spouses different rights and obligations. Many countries in the Middle East, while signing the UN Convention on the Elimination of All Forms of Discrimination Against Women, have made reservations with regard to articles that conflict with their own legislation, on the pretext that they contradict shari'a. The excluded articles were not the same for all countries. In addition, some countries, after making these reservations on the basis of shari'a, changed their legislation in accordance with the convention's articles, claiming that the new legislation actually conformed to shari'a. What is more interesting is that most Arab countries in the Middle East had modern constitutions, based on European legislation in all fields except personal status.

The direct intervention of the state in the legislation of relations within the family is not the only means by which it regulates gender relations. Much gender research has been directed at the study of the impact of social policies (or what are known as welfare state policies in liberal regimes) on gender relations. Many liberal regimes attempted to ameliorate the undesirable effects of unregulated market forces not by interfering in the market mechanism itself, but by intervening through the use of cash transfers to support families and by developing social insurance and social benefit systems. Social insurance systems are based on employment in the labor market, but most transfers to help and support families are allocated to the head of the family (the breadwinner). Child allowances and tax reduction schemes are usually granted to the breadwinner in order to help him maintain his dependents. These social provisions are based on the traditional view of the male as breadwinner and the female as housewife and chief carer for home and children. Social insurance systems, especially health insurance, benefit not only the worker but his family members. Such systems may discourage women from participating in the labor market and reinforce their dependency on their husbands. While the state grants all support to the male breadwinner, it does not grant the same benefits to women, even to working women. The work of the wife in many countries is looked upon as supplementary to that of her husband. The system assumes that she is not the main breadwinner (even if she is in reality), and she does not enjoy the same tax breaks or the same social insurance benefits even if she is performing the same job as her male counterpart. In addition, most working women are pushed down to the lower rungs of the job scale, thereby receiving lower incomes and benefits to support their families. Such social welfare systems strengthen unequal gender relations, deepen women's dependence, and maintain the traditional sexual division of labor.[25]

States also claim that certain regulations of women's employment are for their physical and moral protection and the protection of their families. Der Lipp and Van Dijik claim that women's employment is affected by state policies favorable to the accommodation of women's increased participation in the labor force,[26] such as the level of public childcare and arrangements for parental leave. Liberal conservative regimes pursue policies to encourage women to stay home by providing little or no public childcare services and limited parental leave arrangements. Social democratic regimes enact better policies and provide a higher level of state income for mothers, thus depending less on the market system. Socialist regimes expect men and women to be equal, to be fully incorporated in employment, and to work full-time. They provide parents with extensive arrangements for public childcare and parental leave. The state can also restrict women's employment in some sectors or during certain times of the day on the pretext of protecting their physical well-being or morality, by, for example, forbidding women from working in mines or during night shifts.

Such gender-related legislation might in fact undermine women's employment and their full integration into the labor market. It might also justify lower pay for women and even make their employment undesirable from the perspective of certain employers. Rodgers indicates that social policies designed to protect women raise production costs for employers.[27] The restrictions on women's work in certain occupations or at certain times limit the firms' ability to run work shifts and tend to increase the cost of production. Accordingly, employers might opt to curtail women's employment or they may lower their wages to compensate for the increased costs. Thus, these state measures perpetuate gender gaps in employment and earnings and/or force women to stay home.

Gender Relations and Development in Egypt

Egypt's modernization, starting with the rule of Muhammad 'Ali at the beginning of the nineteenth century, changed dramatically the socioeconomic structures of the country except in one domain, namely, gender relations within the family. This had repercussions on gender relations in all other spheres of society. The perpetuation of pre-modern laws in family or personal status legislation and the failure to bring them in line with the rest of the legislative codes are among the main causes of the perpetuation of underdevelopment in Egypt, not only with respect to women's status but to the whole system, whether economically, socially, or culturally. I contend that the perpetuation of women's dependency by family and state patriarchy is a challenge to the concept of a civilian state that the current regime touts as a main component of major constitutional changes implemented in 2007.

Family Laws or Personal Status Laws

Muhammad 'Ali strived to centralize state power to modernize Egypt's socioeconomic structure without challenge from any competing group. In addition to getting rid of the Mamluks (the previous, semi-independent rulers of Egypt under Ottoman rule), he extended state controls over all other power holders and their institutions including the *ulama*, especially in two important domains, those of education and of legislation. Prior to Muhammad 'Ali, the only available education was provided by al-Azhar, the main educational center of Sunni Islam, and the *kuttab*s in the villages. The *ulama* were also the main source of legislation, attempting to apply shari'a laws according to the four legal schools of Islam inherited from the tenth century. According to Lama Abu Odeh, from the tenth to the nineteenth century,[28] Muslim jurists and judges abandoned the previous school of Islamic jurisprudence that depended on *ijtihad*, or coming up with new rules of law directly inspired by the sources of the faith, and relied more on the consolidation of the existing doctrine of the legal school they followed. This resulted in the codification of rigid legal schools for almost ten centuries without any attempt to review the laws according to changing times and circumstance.

As discussed above (pages 98–99), Muhammad 'Ali brought religious institutions and their *ulama* under his direct control, and instituted a modern education system that competed with the traditional religious one, but he left family laws unchanged. This duplication of modern and pre-modern legal systems has been retained in the Egyptian state up to the present period.

Men's rights and duties differ fundamentally from those of their wives. Under the different personal status laws implemented in Egypt, the main duty of a husband is to provide for his wife and children, while in return wives owe their husbands complete obedience. Because the husband is the breadwinner, he can marry more than one woman (up to four) and can divorce a wife simply by pronouncing the words "I divorce you" three times. He can marry non-Muslim women (Christian and Jewish). He has to offer the bride a dowry, part of which is paid at the beginning of the marriage and the rest whenever the wife demands it. He can impose obedience on his wife through the legal system and, until recently, with police enforcement. In cases of divorce, he has automatic custody of the children when they reach a certain age. He inherits twice as much as a woman, and he pays a divorced wife alimony for no less than one year but no more than three years.

In return women have the right to choose their husbands, to receive a dowry as explained above, and to maintain and dispose of their own income or assets unless they volunteer to participate in household expenditures or willingly grant assets to their husbands. Women must be monogamous, and they do not have the right of interfaith marriages. Women cannot unilaterally divorce their husbands: they must petition a court for divorce, and the court can grant it or withhold it. In cases of divorce, women have the right to alimony for themselves and for their children until they are transferred to the father's custody. In certain cases men can prevent their wives from attending educational institutions or from working outside the home. Finally, women have the right to inherit but a share smaller than the male inheritance and according to very specific and detailed rules.

Gender Relations and Development in Egypt   137

The unequal but complementary relationships within the family consolidate men's power over women in an intricate patriarchal system that is based on the concept of men's superiority over women. Andrea Rugh, in her study of the family in contemporary Egypt, explains the persistence of the traditional family structure as an outcome of a corporate society that curbs individuality and stresses the complementarity of roles. The family is hierarchical. Sex roles within the family are rigid: males are the breadwinners; women are responsible for the children and the household. This kind of family is based on male dominance and female accommodation, male authority and female obedience. Women gain status through their traditional roles as wives and mothers. Employment of women is not a measure of higher status: in reality, it might be a measure of economic need and the inability of males to care for their families. While women in their traditional roles can be overworked, physically abused, suffer from restricted rights, and be denied free movement, they still have some advantages derived from their traditional roles within the family. Women control the organization of the domestic domain and financial dispensation for a good part, if not all, of the day. They control those things most valued by men: sex, honor, children, and a well-organized household. Rugh explains the reluctance in Egypt to modify family status laws by the reformers' fear of destabilizing society. The argument against equality within the family is that it will reduce spouses' dependence on each other, consequently reducing the very need for marriage and family life.[29]

Attempts to modify personal status laws met with resistance from the more traditional *ulama*, who saw in the family code the last vestiges of their power over society and the traditional patriarchal culture that did not even allow fair implementation of some, if not much of the traditional system. To this day, while family laws allow women a share of the inheritance,[30] many families deprive their daughters of their share in favor of their sons, especially when the inheritance is in the form of agricultural land or common real estate. Families believe that women, due to their dependency on men, would be too weak to prevent husbands from taking over the land and disposing of it in ways that might endanger family lands as a whole. While the family laws do not deprive women of education, poor families prefer to invest in boys' education because it is assumed that women will move out of the household and the education in question will benefit the husband and his family, not the paternal household. On many occasions, while women have the right to choose their husbands, they are forced to enter into matrimony according to their fathers' or male guardians' wishes, even if they are in complete opposition to their own. Islam grants women the right to set conditions in the marriage contract that uphold some of their rights, such as a condition of monogamy on the part of the husband; protection of rights to education, employment, and travel; and the right to divorce without resort to the courts.[31] However, very few women take advantage of the conditionality rights. Women who do so are stigmatized by the patriarchal culture and are perceived either as unfeminine or as women of loose morals. Society and public opinion in Egypt remain, to this day, very hostile to women who take advantage of conditionality measures in marriage contracts.

At end of the First World War, a nationalist movement led by Sa'd Zaghlul erupted, demanding the liberation of Egypt from British colonialism. After independence, the Wafd Party, the nationalist party at the time, headed several cabinets, and a new constitution was established in 1923. Unfortunately, the new constitution left personal status laws untouched. Upper and middle class women, who participated in the nationalist movement, formed the Egyptian Feminist Union (EFU) on March 16, 1923. Huda Sha'rawi (a prominent upper-class feminist) headed the Union to defend women's rights and advocate improvement in women's status. The EFU did not challenge the existing family code in its stipulations of different roles for males and females within marriage. Rather, it critiqued the abuses of the personal status laws and attempted to improve the status of women within the family. The EFU's first demands for legal reforms centered on the establishment of a minimum age for marriage and the extension of the period of the mother's legal custody over her children. The nationalist government at the time granted these requests, setting a minimum marriage age of sixteen for females and eighteen for males in 1923. Extension of the mother's legal custody was granted in 1929. The law extended the mother's custody of boys to the age of nine and of girls to age eleven; previous custody laws had granted mothers legal custody to age seven for boys and nine for girls. These were the only changes that the EFU accomplished. The EFU's demands to curb husbands' abuses of the personal status laws met with great resistance, and to date the laws remain in force, albeit with certain modifications. The EFU demanded that men's right of unilateral and immediate divorce (without the need to go to court) be regulated, that men's rights to polygamy be restricted, and that the "house of obedience" institution be abolished. This law allows men to force women to return to the marital home against their wishes in cases where they have deserted it or left without the husband's permission. The police could arrest such women and force them back into the marital home or any home judged to be eligible for matrimonial life. It was not until 1967 that Egyptian feminists managed to put an end in practice to the power of the police force to implement the house of obedience rulings, even while the law itself remains on the books. If a woman fails to return to the house of obedience after the husband obtains a court ruling, she is considered *nashiz*, or disobedient, and her rights to maintenance by the husband are revoked.

The personal status laws of 1929 remained in existence despite the efforts of many women to change or modify them, until 1979, when President Sadat passed the most extensive changes ever to the Egyptian Family Code. The new laws (Law 44 of 1979) were publicly (and sometimes pejoratively) called Jehan's Laws due to the perception that the changes were forced through by the First Lady, Jehan Sadat. Law 44 of 1979 stipulated that in cases of divorce, husbands have to register the divorce with the courts or inform their wives of the decision. In many cases, husbands continued to live with their divorced wives, who were not informed of the divorce. In other instances, the divorced wives were kept in the dark about the divorce to prevent them from demanding either the rest of their dowries or from applying for alimony rights for themselves and for their children. Husbands' rights to polygamy were restricted by the legal stipulation that taking a second wife is great injury to the first wife, who therefore has grounds for immediate divorce. Divorced wives, if they had legal custody of their children, were given the right to remain in the conjugal home. The law also extended the duration of alimony for women to three years if the divorce took place without the wife's consent (usually the duration is only one year).

These changes attempted to qualify and restrain men's rights of instantaneous divorce and polygamy granted in the previous code. Unfortunately, after Sadat's assassination, the constitutional court reversed the law, in 1985, by ruling that it was unconstitutional because it was passed when parliament was in recess, even though the Egyptian constitution gives the president ample powers to pass any laws. The reversal of Law 44 of 1979 was prompted by the concerted actions of Islamists, and even by leftist organizations that agitated for the reversal of the law because it was issued by the Sadat regime.

The reversal of the law prompted women's organizations to fight back to reinstate it. The pressure of these groups resulted in the repassing of the law by parliament, albeit in much diluted form. Once women's organizations recognized the new threats posed by the strong resurgence of Islamist organizations, they concentrated their efforts on introducing more changes to the personal status laws, by working closely with governmental organizations such as the National Council for Motherhood and Childhood, non-governmental organizations (NGOs), and UN organizations such as UNICEF, UNFPA, and others.

The convening of the 1994 UN Population Conference in Cairo gave a new impetus to women's organizations, which participated actively in the NGO Forum, and co-ordinated with the then existing ministry of population and with the National Population Council in planning the conference. The convening of the UN Women's Conference the following year in Beijing kept up the dynamics of women's organizations' activism. All these efforts resulted in President Mubarak signing a new personal status law on January 29, 2000. This allowed women to file for divorce without having to claim harm and prove ill-treatment, as previously required. Just by claiming incompatibility, women can obtain immediate divorce, on condition that they renounce any financial claims on the husband and return the dowry he paid on consummation of the marriage. This law was met with considerable hostility and resistance from the more conservative elements of society and from the Islamists, even though it is based on shari'a.

Since 2000, a number of laws have been enacted to enhance women's rights in other areas. Two of the most important legal restrictions on women's rights to be reversed were the nationality laws and the ministerial decree restricting women's travel abroad.

The Nationality Law 26 of 1975 prevented women who were married to non-Egyptians from conferring their nationality on their children. Men, however, automatically conferred their nationality on their children, regardless of the mother's nationality. Non-Egyptian wives can apply for Egyptian nationality only after two years of marriage. The new nationality law grants women the right to confer their nationality on the children, regardless of the father's nationality, a great step forward in the equalization of gender rights.

Women also could not travel outside the country without the permission of their husbands, who could prevent their wives from traveling simply by giving notice to airport passport authorities. The issuance of a passport for married women was contingent on their husbands' approval. A decree of the ministry of interior (article 4 of Decree number 3937 of 1996) required the husband's approval of issuance of a passport to a married woman. This decree was ruled unconstitutional by the Supreme Court in November of 2000, because it was in diametrical opposition to Article 7 of Law 97 of 1959, which stipulated that Egyptian nationals, irrespective of gender, have the right to apply for a passport. Married women now have the right to obtain a passport without the approval of their husband or any other so-called guardian. Nonetheless, this right might be threatened if the government heeds the recommendation of the Constitutional Court. For a while the court decreed the unconstitutionality of the ministry of the interior's decree. It recommended codifying the required approval of the husband or legal guardian's into law, claiming that such restrictions on women's travel preserve the unity of the family. Feminists claimed that many men left their families for years when they migrated to the Gulf, which was of great harm to the families, but men were not legally required to seek their wives' approval for travel.

Such recommendations from an all-male court are not surprising. Until recently, women in Egypt had not managed to become judges, despite President Mubarak's decision to appoint a female judge to the Constitutional Court in 2000. The majority of judges in Egypt block the appointment of female judges, claiming that women's nature (emotionality and soft-heartedness) does not qualify them to be efficient and impartial judges. Worse, women have been denied membership in the Office of the Public Attorney, even though a large number of women have been working as defense lawyers for decades. The barring of women from important judicial posts is based on assumptions about women's nature that are an extension of the traditional concepts of women's roles in the family as exclusively those of mothers and submissive wives. This is telling of the long shadow cast by the family code over the integration of women into the public sphere. Women cannot be submissive and obedient to male members of their families and at the same time become judges in public courts, since this poses a contradiction between the status of women in the private and public spheres.

Women in the Public Sphere

This conception of the role of women in the family has had its impact on women's integration in the public sphere and might explain gender inequalities in employment and political participation. Unequal rights within the family, the assumptions about women's dependency, and their duty of complete obedience to males, whether fathers, brothers, or husbands, have seeped into other areas of the socioeconomic system and led to women's inferior status not only within the family but also in the public sphere.

These assumptions stand in contradistinction to those of the modernization theory, which is premised on the notion that development will move women from roles embedded in traditional societal structures to modern roles, through education and participation in the modern economic sector and the modern political system. Development strategies as a means of modernization, especially through industrialization, are considered the vehicle for women's liberation. Integration into the modern economy and other modern state structures is perceived as a crucial means of changing traditional perceptions of women in society, thereby achieving women's liberation and gender equality. Progress for women, therefore, hinges on ending their seclusion within the home and integrating them into the public sphere. This has led to the adoption in most women's studies of the famous dichotomy between the private/female and the public/male domains as a major analytical tool with which to describe actual positions and measure changes in women's status.

Furthermore, the modernization theory assumes that the integration of women into the public sphere will automatically lead to changes in family relations. Education and work in the modern sector are assumed to give women economic independence, change their traditional cultural perceptions, and enable them to renegotiate their relations within society and the family toward greater equality and democracy.

Indications that integration into the public sphere does not automatically lead to changes in family relations in favor of gender equality or to changes in traditional cultural perceptions about gender roles are explained as anomalies arising from the dominance of a traditional culture or of religion. Culture is therefore the focus of most research on the obstacles to improving women's status in Egypt, especially in reference to the position of women in Islam.

In reality, the perpetuation of the traditional family structure in Egypt might offer a better explanation for the low status of women in the public sphere. Nevertheless, women's integration into the economy also depends upon the particular phase of development in question and the role of the state in encouraging or discouraging women's integration into the modern sector.

One of the uncritical assumptions often made about women's integration into the public sphere concerns the role of modern education in increasing women's chances of entering the modern formal sector of the economy. Prior to the attempts of Muhammad 'Ali to establish a modern educational system and to integrate females into that system through the founding of a midwifery school for women in 1830, women in Egypt did not receive any education, except at home in certain elite circles. Nevertheless, the attempts of Muhammad 'Ali to educate women were resisted to such a degree that the only girls who enrolled in the midwifery school were slaves. Education for women was claimed to increase the risks to women's morality, for by leaving the seclusion of the home to enroll in public schools, they tarnished their reputations and those of their families as well.

At the end of the nineteenth century Qasim Amin, in his famous book, *Tahrir al-mar'a (The Liberation of Women)*, had to defend the right of women to education by resorting to traditional norms, stating that education would improve women's abilities to carry out their traditional roles as wives and mothers, and that the education of women is not only allowed but actively encouraged by Islam.

If women's education in Egypt was minimal during the whole of the nineteenth century, the same was not true of women's participation in the workforce. For the great expansionary projects of Muhammad 'Ali in agriculture and industry, and the building of a modern army, men were recruited in such great numbers for public works and the army that villages became depleted of male labor. Women in Egypt have always worked, especially in agriculture, as unpaid family labor. The high demand on male labor necessarily increased the burden on female labor, particularly since, at the turn of the century, the whole population of Egypt did not exceed 2.5 million. Very little research has addressed women's labor at that time, but during periods of severe labor shortage, women had to compensate by increasing their work in agriculture.

The collapse of Muhammad 'Ali's experiment returned Egypt to reliance on agriculture and to dependency on a single product—cotton—for export. This pattern was reinforced under British rule, when Egyptian cotton became not only the main export but also the main earner of national income. Cotton cultivation is labor-intensive. Women are engaged in the whole production process, but especially during crop harvesting. It is essentially women and children who carry out cotton harvesting, a tedious and backbreaking process, under the supervision of

144   Gender and Development: Women's Rights, State, and Society

men. This process of using mainly women and children in harvesting still exists today, not only for cotton but also for vegetables, wheat, and other products. Harvesting is still done manually in Egypt. Only relatively wealthy women stay at home.

The industrialization drive of the 1930s coincided with an emerging pool of educated middle-class women. The demand for female labor was directed mainly at lower-class urban women, who got involved essentially in the textile factories established by Banque Misr. The post-independence nationalist state attempted to draw middle-class and lower-middle-class women into the areas of education and health then staffed mostly by foreign women.[32] However, conservative opponents fought against the inclusion of women in the workforce, by stressing that the real duties of women lay in their roles as wives, mothers, and homemakers. At the time, very few middle-class urban women joined the modern workforce.

Women's integration into the formal sector remained minimal up until the deep structural changes implemented by the new regime of 1952. The Free Officers' regime moved gradually toward the deepening of industrialization through the use of the state as the main instrument for capital accumulation. The role of the state grew quickly from the first nationalization measures of 1957 to the full so-called socialist laws of 1961. The steep process of development via import-substitution industrialization required the creation of a well educated and trained labor force. Free education was extended to all, regardless of class or gender. In 1959, Egyptian labor law 91 granted women the right to work and provided them with special social protection, such as a maternity leave of fifty days, fully paid by employers, and requiring establishments that employed more than one hundred women to provide child daycare services. The system also guaranteed employment to all high school and university graduates irrespective of gender. Women's employment in the formal sector of the economy developed rapidly during the period.

The Nasser regime also granted women their full political rights in 1956 (the right to vote and to stand as candidates in elections), a right that women in Egypt had fought for since the establishment of the first nationalist government under the Wafd in 1923.[33] However, Nasser's regime did not attempt to change the personal status laws of 1929. Mervat Hatem argues that state feminism under Nasser led to women's independence, especially in the economic sphere, from their families, but that they became dependent on the state for employment, social services, and political representation. State feminism did not challenge the bases of the patriarchal family, leaving women dependent on men through the unchanged personal status laws, while creating a system of public patriarchy.[34] But the Nasser regime did not extend these rights to women alone but to all members of society, creating a corporate society that extended its patriarchal shadow over the system as a whole. Hazem El-Biblawy, a renowned Egyptian economist, has repeated often enough that the Nasserist state transformed all citizens into the children of the regime. But while he gave women equal rights in the public domain, why did Nasser leave the family code, which belonged, according to his ideology, to the Egyptian feudal system that he so deplored, untouched?

The Nasser regime's reluctance to change the personal status laws can be explained by political considerations. Nasser attempted to marginalize the role of the al-Azhar religious institution by bringing al-Azhar University under state supervision and introducing secular courses into its curricula. He also confiscated al-Azhar's (and the Coptic Church's, for that matter) *awqaf* (charitable endowments) and brought them under state control. More importantly, he abolished shari'a courts that were staffed by religious judges and integrated personal status laws into the state's modern judicial systems. Any attempt to change the personal status laws, which were based fully on Islamic laws and were the sole remaining power lever of al-Azhar and religious conservatives, would have brought dissent with the regime out into the open. Nasser did not want to engage in an open battle with these forces, especially after the open struggle with the Society of the Muslim Brothers and the imprisonment of their leaders' rank and file. Changing the personal status laws at that time would have brought most of what was a very conservative society into open revolt. Taking away men's privileges and their complete control over women would have created a generalized crisis that the regime did not want to confront. In addition, the regime believed that the process of development and the integration of women into the public sphere would empower women to better their position within the family through a process of negotiation, where educated and gainfully employed women would have more power to change their family power relations.

The hypothesis that development influences relations within the family toward more equality was not supported by the experience of Egypt, even during the 1960s and especially for the majority of poor women living in rural or poor urban areas. The rewards of female labor in traditional agriculture were, and still are, appropriated by the family without any compensation. The agricultural sector in Egypt had the largest proportion of women to men in any working sector, yet female labor is categorized as unpaid family help. Valentine Moghadam remarks that while free education encourages female labor participation, access to education and therefore employment is still determined by class.[35] A sizeable proportion of women working in the formal urban sector, and who make up almost one third of all working women, are concentrated in professional, technical, and managerial positions. These women are college graduates and belong mostly to the urban middle and upper-middle classes.[36] Even these highly educated working women were and still are at the mercy of the unequal relations that dominate Egyptian families. For working women this situation results in a high labor bur-den, where women are expected to work full-time in the public sphere in addition to fulfilling their obligations within the household. Women in Egyptian households are completely responsible for childcare, including supervising the children's schoolwork and looking after all their other needs, all household chores, and for serving their husbands. The only duty of husbands is to provide for the household. Even this monetary obligation has eroded through the contribution of working women to household expenditures. The Egyptian Demographic and Health Sur-vey of the year 2000 (EDHS 2000) found that 70 percent of wives contribute to household expenses, in spite of the family status laws. Homa Hoodfar asserts that, contrary to the assumption that the power of the wife increases when she is a wage earner, the power of the wife could in effect decline.[37] When wives have incomes of their own, some husbands keep more of their earnings to themselves, while the wife's income goes toward covering family needs. In this situation working and wage-earning women are subjected to more exploitation and the appropriation of their labor.

The change in Egypt's economic strategy from the mid-1970s and the deepening reliance on the private sector as the main investor, producer, and therefore employer, has undermined the status of women in the labor market. Since the declaration of the *infitah* or 'Open Door' policy in 1974, state commitment to women's integration and equal rights in the labor market has weakened considerably. The new policies canceled the state's commitment to guaranteed employment, which led to the emer-gence of high open unemployment in the system. The private sector, which replaced the public sector in terms of investment and employment

Gender Relations and Development in Egypt   147

generation, has been very hostile to women's employment and most of the labor force engaged in the formal private sector is male. structural adjustment policies have further eroded the capacity of the state to generate new employment opportunities in the government or in state owned enterprises. These policies led to a sharp retreat in women's employment trends, to the extent that some researchers have claimed that the adoption of export-oriented industrialization in Egypt has led to the de-feminization of the labor force, contrary to the process of feminization that occurred in the newly industrialized countries of East Asia.[38]

With the implementation of structural adjustment policies in the 1990s, the situation of working women in Egypt worsened dramatically. During the period 1988–98, the civilian labor force grew by 2.7 percent annually. Male labor force participation declined by 4 percent, while female labor participation increased by 4 percent. These numbers in fact reflect the reduction of the male labor force due to the withdrawal of older, less educated, and self-employed males. The increase in female participation is due to some increase in participation of females in unpaid female labor in agriculture, the high growth of female unemployment,[39] and the delayed withdrawal of older educated females from the labor force.[40]

Wage employment in the government sector continued to grow during 1988–98 at 4.8 percent per annum. Most of that increase was generated by the desire of the government to alleviate the high unemployment that emerged in the context of structural adjustment policies. Women benefited slightly more from this government policy, where the female share increased by 30.8 percent compared to 28.7 percent for males.[41] However, this increase of female employment in the government sector was due less to the government's positive policies toward female employment than to the move of qualified males to the private sector, where wages are much higher. At the same time, female employment in state owned enterprises dropped drastically, from 14 percent to 12 percent for the same period. Although private sector wage employment increased at a relatively healthy pace during the decade under consideration (3.3 percent per year), most of that increase benefited male wageworkers, whose numbers increased at the rate of 3.7 percent per year, compared to a mere 0.5 percent for females. Similar trends prevail for the state owned enterprise sector as well. There is therefore a marked de-feminization of wage employment in the private and the state owned enterprise sectors.[42]

148   Gender and Development: Women's Rights, State, and Society

The trend of defeminization of the wage-earning labor force continues to this day. According to the Labor Force Sample Survey of 2004, the economic participation rates in the labor force for the population aged fifteen to sixty-four years reached 72.5 percent for males and 22.5 percent for females. However, the unemployment rate for the same period reached 10.3 percent, with a rate of only 5.9 percent for males and a staggering 24.3 percent for females. The unemployment rate for urban females was 30.5 percent, while the rate for urban males did not exceed 7 percent.[43]

The highest percentage of female economic participation is in the category of wageworkers, where 62 percent of urban females and 21 percent of rural females are classified as wageworkers. Thirty-eight and a half percent of female rural labor and 3.2 percent of female urban labor are categorized as unpaid family workers. Of all unpaid female family workers, 68 percent are concentrated in rural areas, and the majority work in the informal sector, namely agriculture.[44] Many women who are classified as unpaid family workers do not consider themselves workers because they do not receive wages and because husbands are still considered the breadwinners. Female unpaid family workers consider their work as simply ancillary to that of their husbands or to the family, when they are in fact working and participating in the production process.[45]

The majority of women in Egypt work out of economic necessity, or because they have achieved a high level of education. Forty-one percent of total employed females are illiterate (6.1 percent urban and 60.7 percent rural). Twenty-seven percent of the employed female labor force has an intermediary certificate (39 percent urban and 20 percent rural). At the other extreme, 18.6 percent of women have a college degree or more, that is, a master's degree or doctorate (40 percent urban and 6.5 percent rural). This pattern has not changed much in the last three to four decades. Working women are either illiterate and work mainly in the agricultural sector or the informal urban sector (mostly as home servants), or are highly educated and work in professional occupations, particularly recently in the fields of health and education.[46]

In urban areas, women are concentrated in professional and technical occupations. Sixty-two percent of all urban working women are concentrated in these occupations versus just 29 percent of all working urban males. The highest concentration rates for urban women are in education (32 percent of all working females), followed by defense and administration (22.5 percent), and health and social work (11.3 percent). In rural areas, 70 percent of all working women are concentrated in agricultural occupations versus only 44 percent of rural working males.[47]

The above statistics demonstrate two important facts: First, that educated female workers are concentrated in very few occupations (education, health and social services, and general administration), jobs generally considered better suited to women and are extensions of their caring and nurturing roles within the family. Women in agriculture are mostly illiterate, unpaid family workers, and are not even dignified by a recognition of their contribution as work, but are considered to be performing part of their role as submissive wives. This concentration of females in just a few occupations reinforces the general perception of rigid gender roles, where females specialize in occupations considered feminine. Second, the percentage of females in the category of production workers has declined from 10 percent in 1990 to just 1.1 percent in 2004,[48] an indication of the marginalization of women and of employers' discrimination against them, whether in the private sector or in state owned enterprises, as noted above by Ragui Assaad (see note 38).

The decline of employment opportunities for females, the great increase in their unemployment rates, and the high rate of female-headed households indicate a tendency of feminization of poverty in Egypt.

Gender and Poverty

The 1995 Beijing Conference for women used two indicators to measure the poverty of women: female unemployment rates and the percentage of female-headed households. The World Bank report on engendering development disputes the viability of the female-headed household indicator as a measure of female poverty. The report stresses that many female-headed households can be formed of single career women. In the context of Egypt's social norms and culture, single women, even professional ones, rarely live alone. Cultural sanctions and traditions of the protection of women's morality do not encourage single women to live apart from the family. In addition, the most recent Labor Force Sample Survey (2004) reveals that almost 16 percent of all households are female-headed. The majority of these females are illiterate (around 64 percent) or semi-illiterate (18 percent), a total of 82 percent. Illiteracy is another indicator of poverty. So, the female-headed household indicator might be a more viable measure of female poverty in the context of Egyptian society.

150   Gender and Development: Women's Rights, State, and Society

Another indicator of poverty is the female unemployment rate discussed above. In addition, the lack of access of poor women to resources such as land, credit, and technology indicates that the phenomenon of the feminization of poverty might be more widespread than the World Bank report seems inclined to believe. Nevertheless, the notion that more empirical studies are needed in this area is difficult to dispute.

Heba El-Laithy has attempted to use more sophisticated measures of gender poverty, relying on the Households Income, Expenditure and Consumption Survey (HIECS) of 1999/2000 for the analysis.[49] She finds large variations in poverty according to employment status. The largest segements of the poor are females who are out of the labor force (33 percent of the urban poor and 26 percent of the rural poor). El-Laithy's total findings demonstrate that for females the probability of being poor rises by 2.3 percent in urban areas and by almost 5 percent in rural areas. The probability of poverty for females increases if they are employed in the private sector of the economy. A high percentage of poor females (77 percent) work for the private sector, especially in the private informal sector, while only 23 percent of poor females work for the government and public sector.[50] These results seem to reinforce Assaad's results, referred to above, which indicate that women are more discriminated against in the private sector.

El-Laithy also attempted to measure female poverty using the UNDP measure, the Human Poverty Index. This index is composed of three measures, which try to estimate deprivation of longevity (percentage of people not expected to live beyond the age of forty), deprivation of knowledge (adult illiteracy rate), and deprivation of a decent standard of living (a composite of the percentage of individuals with no access to health services and safe drinking water and the percentage of children under five who are underweight). The Human Poverty Index for Egypt would indicate a much higher incidence of poverty for females (35 percent) than for males (29 percent). The main difference between the two human poverty indices is due to the deprivation of knowledge gap, with female illiteracy being much higher than male illiteracy.[51]

Finally, it is clear, no matter what measure is used, that female poverty is much higher than that of males. Females have less access to economic resources and benefits, education, and employment. The poverty of females is in reality a measure of gender discrimination and reveals unequal power relations between males and females that are perpetuated by societal, cultural, and legal measures borne of a highly patriarchal system that permeates institutions of both society and state.

In the end, unequal gender relations in Egypt are rooted in the personal status laws that codify them. While the state claims that the personal status laws are based on shari'a, they are in fact based on a specific interpretation of the shari'a, which goes back to the thirteenth century, and on custom and tradition. These unequal relations have been strengthened during the last three decades by the mounting religious trend permeating the whole of Egyptian society. Nevertheless, an enlightened interpretation of shari'a can change many of the inequities built into the family code. The passing of new family laws in 2000, giving women the right to unilateral divorce (*khul'a*), the lifting of travel restrictions on married women, and the granting to women of the right to confer their citizenship on their children, demonstrate that many of women's equal rights can be obtained within a modernized interpretation of shari'a. A more radical approach would be to formulate a secular personal status law that would serve as a law for the population as a whole, instead of the multiplicity of personal status laws based on religious interpretations of Islam and different Christian denominations, including Coptic, Greek Orthodox, Evangelical, and others.

As demonstrated above, the family code gives validity to unequal gender relations in all other fields of society, including the public sphere. The state has been unwilling to enact a personal status law based on equality for two main reasons: First, the state does not want to engage in an open battle with conservative and Islamist forces and, second, the state is using women's rights as a bargaining card in situations of political conflict between state elites and Islamist elites. Modernizing or secularizing the personal status law would deprive the state of a major tool of political confrontation and negotiation.

Notes

Notes to Introduction

1. David Hirst, "Egypt Stands on Feet of Clay: A Middle East Indonesia in the Making," *Le Monde Diplomatique*, October 1999.
2. Jon B. Alterman, "Egypt: Stalled But For How Long?," *The Washington Quarterly*, Autumn 2000, 107–18.
3. Ibid.
4. National Democratic Party, *Reform Policy Papers* (Cairo: NDP, September 2004).
5. Nadia Ramsis Farah, *Religious Strife in Egypt: Crisis and Ideological Conflict in the Seventies* (New York and London: Gordon and Breach Publishers, 1986).
6. A faction is a special power group within a social class. While the members of a class as a whole share similar interests, at certain historical junctures that class may become divided into different factions and along opposing political lines.
7. Barry Hindess, *Discourses of Power: From Hobbes to Foucault* (Oxford: Blackwell, 1996).
8. Michel Foucault, "The Subject and Power," in *Power: Essential Works of Michel Foucault 1954–1984*, Vol. 3, edited by J. D. Faubion (London: Penguin Books, 2002).
9. C. Wright Mills, *The Power Elite* (Oxford: Oxford University Press, 1956).
10. Ibid., 3–4.
11. Ibid., 5.
12. Nicos Poulantzas, *Political Power and Social Classes* (London: Verso, 1978).

153

154 Notes

13. Ibid.
14. Periodization is the division or categorization of time into discrete phases.
15. Farah, *Religious Strife*.
16. Peter Evans, "Predatory, Developmental, and Other Apparatuses: A Comparative Political Economy Perspective on Third World States," in A. Douglas Kincaid and Alejandro Portes, eds., *Comparative National Development: Society and Economy in the New Global Order* (Chapel Hill: University of North Carolina Press, 1994).
17. Alice N. Sindzingre, "Bringing the Developmental State Back In: Contrasting Development Trajectories in Sub-Saharan Africa and East Asia," paper presented to the Annual Meeting of the Society for the Advancement of Socio-Economics, Washington D.C., Georges Washington University, July 9–11, 2004.
18. Peter Evans, Dietrich Rueschemeyer, and Theda Skocpol, eds., *Bringing the State Back In* (New York: Cambridge University Press, 1985).
19 Charles Polidano, *Don't Discard State Autonomy: Revisiting the East Asian Experiment of Development* (Manchester: Institute for Development Policy and Management, University of Manchester, 1998).
20. Peter Evans. *Embedded Autonomy: States and Industrial Transformation* (Princeton, NJ: Princeton University Press, 1995).
21. Polidano, *Don't Discard State Autonomy*.
22. Guillermo O'Donnell and Philippe Schmitter, *Transitions from Authoritarian Rule: Tentative Conclusions about Uncertain Democracies* (Baltimore: Johns Hopkins University Press, 1986).
23. Dietrich Rueschemeyer, Evelyne Huber Stephens, and John D. Stephens, *Capitalist Development and Democracy* (Cambridge, UK: Polity Press, 1992).
24. Ibid., 52.
25. Ibid., 57.
26. Stephens, Evelyne Huber, "Capitalist Development and Democracy in South America" (paper prepared for the meetings of the Midwest Political Science Association, Chicago, April 1988).
27. Ibid., 2.
28. Ibid., 2.
29. Ibid.
30. Farah, *Religious Strife*.
31. Ibid., 58.
32. Caroline Moser, *Gender Planning and Development: Theory Practice and Training* (New York: Routledge, 1993).
33. World Bank Report, *Engendering Development Through Gender Equality in Rights, Resources and Voices* (New York: Oxford University Press, 2001).

Notes to Chapter 1

1. Ralph Miliband, *The State in Capitalist Society* (New York: Basic Books, 1969).
2. Nicos Poulantzas, *State, Power, Socialism* (London: Verso, 1980).
3. Ibid.
4. F.A. Hayek, *The Fundamentals of Freedom*, Vol. 2. (Chicago: Chicago University Press, 1979).
5. Chalmers Johnson, *MITI and the Japanese Miracle: The Growth of Industrial Policy, 1925–1975* (California: Stanford University Press, 1982).
6. Alice Amsden, *Asia's Next Giant: South Korea and Late Industrialization* (New York: Oxford University Press, 1989) and Robert Wade, *Governing the Market: Economic Theory and the Role of Government in East Asian Industrialization* (Princeton, NY: Princeton University Press, 1990).
7. Peter Evans, Dietrich Rueschemeyer, and Theda Skocpol, eds., *Bringing the State Back In* (Cambridge: Cambridge University Press, 1985).
8. Alexander Gershenkron, *Economic Backwardness in Historical Perspective* (Cambridge, MA: Harvard University Press, 1962).
9. Yun Tae Kim, "Neoliberalsim and the Decline of the Developmental State," *Journal of Contemporary Asia* 29, no. 4 (1999).
10. David M. Kotz, "The Role of the State in Economic Transformation: Comparing the Transition Experience of Russia and China," Political Economy Research Institute, University of Massachusetts, Amherst, Working Paper No. 95, 2004.
11. Ibid.
12. Ibid.
13. The six ministers are: Mohamed Rashid, minister of trade and industry; Mr. Mohamed Mansour, minister of transportation; Amin Abaza, minister of agriculture; Ahmed ElMaghrabi, minister of housing; Hatem ElGabali, minister of health; and Mr. Aly Moseilhy, minister of social welfare.
14. Nadia Ramsis Farah, "Historical Roots of Contemporary Economic Development in Egypt," in Dan Tschirgi, ed., *Development in the Age of Liberalization: Egypt and Mexico* (Cairo: American University in Cairo Press, 1996).
15. Nadia Ramsis Farah, "The Social Formations Approach and Arab Social Systems," *Arab Studies Quarterly* 10, no. 3 (Summer 1988).
16. "In March 1811 a massacre of the Mamluks rid him [Muhammad 'Ali] of the old elite, when twenty-four beys and an undetermined number of lesser dignitaries lost their lives in a passageway leading from the Citadel, where they had been invited for a ceremony." André Raymond, *Cairo: City of History* (Cairo: American University in Cairo Press, 2001), p. 304.

156   Notes

17. This policy of extracting the agricultural surplus to direct it toward industrialization is exactly what the modernization theory recommended for the
process of industrialization for developing countries after the wave of independence that followed the Second World War.

18. Saad Eddin Ibrahim, "Egypt's Landed Bourgeoisie," in Ayse Oncu, Calgar
Keyder, and Saad Eddin Ibrahim, eds., *Developmentalism and Beyond* (Cairo:
American University in Cairo Press, 1994).

19. Farah, *Religious Strife*.

20. Ibrahim, "Egypt's Landed Bourgeoisie."

21. Murad Magdi Wahba, *The Role of the State in the Egyptian Economy: 1945–1981*
(Reading, UK: Ithaca Press, 1994).

22. Ibrahim, "Egypt's Landed Bourgeoisie."

23. National Center for Criminological and Sociological Research, *Comprehensive
Sociological Survey of Egypt: 1952–1980* (Cairo: NCCSR, 1985).

24. Ibrahim, "Egypt's Landed Bourgeoisie."

25. Nadia Ramsis Farah, "Political Regimes and Social Performance: The Case of
Egypt," in Ibrahim, et al., *Developmentalism and Beyond.*

26. Farah, "Political Regimes and Social Performance."

27. Muhammad Khattab, a member of the Egyptian Senate, advocated a ceiling of 50 feddans in 1944. Merrit Boutros Ghali renewed the call for a
ceiling of 100 feddans in 1945. Ghali was explicit that capital should be
invested in industry. In 1947, the Financial Committee of the Chamber of
Deputies decried the highly unequal distribution of land ownership and
asked for an increase in land taxes on the wealthy while exempting small
owners, that is, those who own 5 feddans or less. See in this context
Wahba, *Role of the State*, and Robert Tignor, *State, Private Enterprise and Economic Change in Egypt: 1918–1952* (Princeton, NJ: Princeton University
Press, 1984).

28. Ibrahim, "Egypt's Landed Bourgeoisie."

29. Farah, "Political Regimes and Social Performance," 144.

30. Wahba, *Role of the State.*

31. Ibid.

32. John Waterbury, *The Egypt of Nasser and Sadat: The Political Economy of Two
Regimes* (Princeton, NJ: Princeton University Press, 1983).

33. Wahba, *Role of the State.*

34. Waterbury, *Egypt of Nasser*, 103.

35. Lobna Abdellatif, "Egypt's Manufacturing Sector: Factor Inputs and TFP
over Half a Century," research paper (Cairo: Economic Research Forum, September 2003).

36. D. Mead, *Growth and Structural Change in the Egyptian Economy* (Homewood: Yale University Press, 1967).
37. Waterbury, *Egypt of Nasser*, 81.
38. Wahba, *Role of the State*, 92.
39. Ibid., 95.
40. Waterbury, *Egypt of Nasser*, 90.
41. Wahba, *Role of the State*, 96.
42. The share of the sale price obtained by the tenants was concluded determined by the parties, not set by the government. But the long and inherited tenure of agricultural land and real estate forced owners to share the sale price with the tenants in exchange for cancellation of tenancy contracts.
43. Farah, "Political Regimes and Social Performance," 144.
44. Nadia Ramsis Farah, "The Crisis of the Public Sector in Egypt," paper presented at the conference on the Public Sector held by al-Wafd Party, Cairo, Egypt, February 9, 1987.
45. Raymond Hinnebush Jr., *Egyptian Politics Under Sadat: The Post-Populist Development of An Authoritarian-Modernizing State* (London, New York: Cambridge University Press, 1985).
46. Wahba, *Role of the State*, 139.
47. Waterbury, *Egypt of Nasser*, 99.
48. Ibid.
49. Wahba, *Role of the State*.
50. Farah, *Religious Strife*, 114.
51. In 2006 American aid stood in 2006 at just US$1.4 billion. Further reductions have occurred annually since.
52. Farah, *Religious Strife*, 114.
53. Waterbury, Egypt of Nasser.
54. Ibid.
55. IMF: International Financial Statistics.
56. Karima Korayem, "Egypt's Economic Reform and Structural Adjustment (ERSAP)," Cairo: The Egyptian Center for Economic Studies, Working Paper No. 19 (October 1997): 6.
57. Wahba, *Role of the State*, 154.
58. World Bank: World Debt Tables. Debt and International Finance Division, Washington D.C., 1993.
59. Ibid.
60. Hanaa Kheir-El-Din and Tarek Abdellatif Moursi, "Sources of Economic Growth and Technical Progress in Egypt: An Aggregate Perspective" (Cairo: Economic Research Forum, September 2003).

158   Notes

61. Abdellatif, "Egypt's Manufacturing Sector," 16.

62. Hadi Salehi Esfahani, *The Experience of Foreign Investment in Egypt under Infitah* (New Jersey: Center for Economic Research in Africa, School of Business, Montclair State University, August 1993).

63. Naglaa El-Ehwany and Heba El-Laithy, *Poverty, Employment and Policy Making in Egypt: A Country Profile* (Cairo: ILO Area Office, 2001).

64. El-Ehwany and El-Laithy, *Poverty*.

65. Esfahani, *Experience of Foreign Investment*.

66. El-Ehwany and El-Laithy, *Poverty*.

67. Kheir El Din and Moursi, "Sources of Economic Growth," 10.

68. Farah, *Religious Strife*, 115.

69. Mohamed Abdel-Wahed Mohamed, "The Impact of Foreign Capital Inflow on Savings, Investment and Economic Growth Rate in Egypt: An Econometric Analysis," *Scientific Journal of King Faisal University* 4, no. 1 (2003).

70. Alia El-Mahdi, "Labor in Egypt," *Global Policy Network*, October 2003.

71. Ministry of Planning statistics: http://www.mop.gov.eg/gdp.htm

72. Economic Intelligence Unit, *Country Report*, February 2006.

73. IMF Country Report No. 06/253, p. 24/

74. Kheir-El-Din and Moursi, "Sources of Economic Growth," 10.

75. Ministry of Planning statistics: http://www.mop.gov.eg/gdp.htm

76. Abdellatif, "Egypt's Manufacturing Sector," 16.

77. Economic Intelligence Unit, *Country Report*, February 2006.

78. USA Embassy in Cairo: *Economic Trends Report, 2006*.

79. Kheir El-Din and Moursi, "Sources of Economic Growth," 10.

80. Ibid.

81. Samiha Fawzy, "Investment Policies and Unemployment in Egypt" (Egyptian Center for Economic Studies, Working Paper No. 68, September 2002).

82. Abdellatif, "Egypt's Manufacturing Sector," 18.

83. Abdellatif, "Egypt's Manufacturing Sector," 24–25.

84. *Ministry of Industry and Trade: Quarterly Report* 1., no. 4 (January–March 2006), Cairo, pp. 30 and pp. 83–85.

85. Ministry of Industry and Trade.

86. Al-Ahram Center for Strategic and Political Studies, *The Strategic Economic Trends Report 2005* (Cairo: al-Ahram, 2005).

87. Ministry of Foreign Trade, Egypt, 2004.

88. Land Center for Human Rights, *Labor Conditions in Egypt* (Economic Social Rights Series, Cairo, Issue 7, 1999).

Notes   159

89. Joel Benin, "Egyptian Textile Workers: From Craft Artisans Facing Euro-
     pean Competition to Proletarians Contending with the State" (paper
     presented to the *Conference on Egypt Textile*, IISH, November 11–13, 2004).

90. The 2006/2007 data is from by the ministry of economic development, the
     ministry of finance, and the Central Bank of Egypt.

91. Mohamed Abdel-Aal, "Agrarian Reform and Tenancy Problems in Upper
     Egypt" (Social Research Center, American University in Cairo, n.d.).

92. Mohamed Atif Kishk, "Mechanisms of Impoverishment of the Rural Poor
     in Contemporary Egypt" (Minia: Minia University, n.d.).

93. Timothy Mitchell, *Rule of Experts: Egypt, Techno-Politics, Modernity* (Berkeley:
     University of California Press, 2002).

94. Ibid., 265.

95. T.N. Srinivasan, "Challenges of Economic Reform in Egypt" (Stanford Uni-
     versity Center for International Development, Working Paper No. 253,
     September 2005).

96. U.S. Embassy in Cairo: *Economic Trends Report 2006*.

97. Nader Fergany, "Unemployment and Poverty in Egypt," in M.A. Kishk ed.
     Poverty of Environment and Environment of Poverty (Cairo: Dar al-Ahmady for
     Publishing, 1988).

98. El-Ehwany and El-Laithy, *Poverty*, 47.

99. World Bank, *World Bank Report*. Statistical Appendix (Washington D.C.:
     World Bank, 2001).

100. Srinivasan, "Challenges of Economic Reform," 2.

101. Egyptian Center for Economic Studies. *Ara' fi-l-siyasa al-iqtisadiya*, no. 19
     (July 2006).

102. Ministry of Investment.

103. IMF, *Arab Republic of Egypt IMF Country Report No. 05/177* (Washington D.C.:
     IMF, July 2005).

104. IMF: *Arab Republic of Egypt IMF Country Report No. 06/253*. Washington
     D.C.: July 2006, 12).

Notes to Chapter 2

1.   John Gerring, Philip Bond, William T. Brandt, and Carola Moreno, "Democ-
     racy and Economic Growth: A Historical Perspective," *World Politics* 57
     (April 2005).

2.   Robert Dahl, *On Democracy* (New Haven: Yale University Press, 1998); Barring-
     ton Moore, *Social Origins of Democracy and Dictatorship: Lord and Peasant in the
     Making of the Modern World* (Boston: Beacon Press, 1966); Joseph Alois Schum-
     peter, *Capitalism, Socialism, and Democracy* (New York: Harper and Bros, 1942).

160   Notes

3. S. Martin Lipset, *Political Man: The Social Bases of Politics* (Baltimore: Johns Hopkins University Press, 1959).
4. Khandakar Elhai and Constantine P. Danopoulos, "Democracy, Capitalism and Development," *Journal of Security Sector Management* 2, no. 2 (June 2004).
5. Torsten Persson, "Forms of Democracy, Policy and Economic Development," (Institute for International Economic Studies, Stockholm University, January 2005, http://www.iies.su.se/-perssont/papers/paper050131.pdf).
6. R. Burkhart and Michael Lewis-Beck, "Comparative Democracy: The Economic Development Thesis," *American Political Science Review* 88 (1994); John Londregan and Keith Poole, "Poverty, the Coup Trap, and the Seizure of Executive Power," *World Politics* 42 (1990); John Londregan and Keith Poole, "Does High Income Promote Democracy?" *World Politics* 49 (1996); Adam Przeworski and Fernando Limongi, "Modernization: Theories and Facts," *World Politics* 49 (1997); Adam Przeworski, Michael E. Alvarez, José Antonio Cheibub, and Fernando Limongi, *Democracy and Development: Political Institutions and Well-being in the World, 1950–1990* (Cambridge: Cambridge University Press, 2001).
7. Amartya Sen, *Development as Freedom* (New York: Albert A. Knopf, 1999).
8. Londregan and Poole, "Does High Income Promote Democracy?"; Przeworski, et al., *Democracy and Development.*
9. Amartya Sen, *Development as Freedom* (New York: Albert A. Knopf, 1999).
10. Rita Abrahamsen, *Disciplining Democracy: Development Discourse and Good Governance* (London, New York: Zed Books, 2000).
11. Ibid.
12. World Bank: *Governance and Development* (Washington, D.C.: World Bank, 1992); Sylvia Chan, *Liberalism, Democracy, and Development* (New York: Cambridge University Press, 2002); Joseph E Stiglitz, *Globalization and its Discontents* (New York: W.W. Norton, 2002); Ronald Inglehart and Christian Welzel, *Modernization, Cultural Change, and Democracy: The Human Development Sequences* (New York: Cambridge University Press, 2005).
13. Hyok Yong Kwon, "Economic Reform and Democratization: Evidence from Latin America and Post-Socialist Countries," *British Journal of Political Science* 34, no. 2 (2004).
14. Jon Elster, "The Necessity and impossibility of Simultaneous Economic and-Political Reform," in Douglas Greenberg, Stanley N. Katz, Melanie Beth Oliviero, and Steven C. Wheatley, eds., *Constitutionalism and Democracy: Transitions in the Contemporary World* (Oxford: Oxford University Press, 1993); Adam Przeworski, "The Neoliberal Fallacy," in Larry Diamond and Marc F. Plattner, eds., *Capitalism, Socialism, and Democracy Revisited* (Baltimore: Johns Hopkins University Press, 1993).

15. Mathurin C. Houngnikpo, " Pax Democratica: The Gospel According to St. Democracy," *Australian Journal of Politics and History* 49, no. 2 (2003).

16. Pranab Bardhan, "Democracy and Development: A Complex Relationship," in I. Shapiro and C. Hacker-Cordon, eds., *Democracy's Value* (Cambridge University Press, Cambridge, 1999).

17. Ibid.

18. Marx J. Gasiorowski, "Democracy and Macroeconomic Performance in Underdeveloped Countries: An Empirical Analysis," *Comparative Political Studies* 33, no. 3 (April 2000).

19. S. Haggard and R. Kaufman, *Politics of Economic Adjustment.* (Princeton, NJ: Princeton University Press, 1992); Mark Gasiorowski, "Economic Crisis and Political Regime Change: An Event History Analysis," *American Political Science Review* 89, no.4 (1995); Hyug Baeg Im, "The Rise of Bureaucratic Authoritarianism in South Korea," *World Politics* 39, no. 2 (1987).

20. Nita Rudra, "Globalization and the Strengthening of Democracy in the Developing World," http://www3.interscience.wiley.com/journal/118692636/abstract?CRETRY=1&SRETRY=0.

21. Syliva Maxfield, "Comparing East Asia and Latin America: Capital Mobility and Democratic Stability," *Journal of Democracy* 11, no. 4 (2000), and Sylvia Maxfield, "Understanding the Political Implications of Financial Internationalization in Emerging Market Countries," *World Development* 26, no. 7 (1998).

22. Leslie E. Armijo, "Mixed Blessing: Expectations About Foreign Capital Flows and Democracy in Emerging Markets," in Leslie E. Armijo, ed., *Financial Globalization and Democracy in Emerging Markets* (New York: St. Martin's Press, 1999).

23. R. Keohane and H. Milner: *Internationalization and Domestic Politics* (Cambridge: Cambridge University Press, 1996).

24. Dani Rodrik, *Has Globalization Gone Too Far?* (Washington, D.C.: Institute for International Economics, 1997, http://www.iie.com/publications/chapters_preview/57/11ie2415.pdf); Stephan Haggard and Sylvia Maxfield, "The Political Economy of Financial Internationalization in the Developing World," *International Organization* 50, no. 1 (1996).

25. Adam Prezeworski, "Democracy and Economic Development," in Edward D. Mansfield and Richard Sisson, eds., *Political Science and the Public Interest.* Columbus: Ohio: State University Press, http://www.nyu.edu/gsas/dept/politics/faculty/przeworski/papers/sisson.pdf.

26. Ibid.

27. Torsten Persson and Guido Tabellini, "Democracy and Development: Devil in the Details." (Institute for International Economic Studies, Stockholm

162   Notes

University, December 2005, http://www.aeaweb.org/annual_mtg_papers/2006/0106_1015_1402.pdf).

28. Torsten Persson and Guido Tabellini, *The Economic Effects of Constitutions* (Cambridge: MIT Press, 2003), and Torsten Persson and Guido Tabellini, "Constitutional Rules and Fiscal Policy Outcomes," *American Economic Review* 94 (2004).

29. Persson, "Forms of Democracy."

30. Svante Ersson and J. Lane, "Democracy and Development: Statistical Exploration" in A. Leftwich, ed., *Democracy and Development* (Cambridge, UK: Polity Press 1996).

31. Michael Ross, "Does Oil Hinder Democracy?" *World Politics* 53, no. 3 (2001), and Gordon O.F. Johnson, "The Oil Peril to Democracy and Development in Muslim Nations: The 'Curse of Oil' – Public Choice Theory at Work – Economic Rent Seeking in Extreme" (paper presented at the Center for The Study of Islam and Democracy Sixth Annual Conference, Washington, D.C., April 22–23, 2005). http://www.islam-democracy.org/documents/pdf/6th_Annual_Conference-GordonJohnson.pdf.

32. Larry Diamond, "Thinking about Hybrid Regimes," *Journal of Democracy* 13, no. 2 (April 2002), and Andreas Schedler, "The Nested Game of Democratization by Elections," *International Political Science Review* 23, no. 1 (2002).

33. Terry Lynn Karl, "The Hybrid Regimes of Central America," *Journal of Democracy* 6, no. 3 (July 1995).

34. Larry Diamond, *Developing Democracy: Toward Consolidation* (Baltimore: The Johns Hopkins University Press, 1999).

35. Fareed Zakaria, "The Rise of Illiberal Democracy," *Foreign Affairs* 76, no. 6 (November–December 1997).

36. Martha Brill Olcott and Marina S. Ottaway, "The Challenge of Semi-Authoritarianism" (Carnegie Endowment for Peace Working Paper No. 7, Washington, D.C., 1999).

37. Paul Brooker, *Non-Democratic Regimes: Theory, Government and Politics* (New York: St. Martin's Press, 2000).

38. Jacob M. Landau, *Parliaments and Parties in Egypt* (New York: Praeger, 1953).

39. Nadia Ramsis Farah, *Religious Strife in Egypt: Crisis and Ideological Conflict in the Seventies* (London and New York: Gordon and Breach, 1986).

40. Landau, *Parliaments and Parties.*

41. Gabriel Baer, *A History of Landownership in Modern Egypt 1800–1950* (London: Oxford University Press, 1962).

42. Landau, *Parliaments and Parties.*

43. Salah Issa, *The Orabi Revolution* (Cairo: The Egyptian Public Organization for Books, 1976).
44. Farah, *Religious Strife*, 88.
45. Ibid.
46. Charles Issawi, *Egypt: An Economic and Social Analysis* (London and New York: Oxford University Press, 1947).
47. Ibid.
48. Robert Tignor, *Modernization and British Colonial Rule in Egypt 1882–1914* (Princeton, NJ: Princeton University Press, 1966).
49. Farah, *Religious Strife*, 90.
50. Farah, *Religious Strife*, 92.
51. Issawi, *Egypt*.
52. A. Crouchley, *The Economic Development of Modern Egypt* (London: Longmans, 1938), and Issawi, *Egypt*.
53. Issawi, *Egypt*.
54. Crouchley, *Economic Development*.
55. Farah, *Religious Strife*.
56. Jean Lacouture and Simonne Lacouture, *Egypt in Transition* (New York: Criterion Books, 1958).
57. Abdo Baaklini, Guilian Denoeux, and Robert Springborg, *Legislative Politics in the Arab World: The Resurgence of Democratic Institutions* (Boulder, CO: Lynne Reinner, 1999).
58. Landau, *Parliaments and Parties*.
59. Lacouture and Lacouture, *Egypt in Transition*.
60. Farah, *Religious Strife*.
61. Don Peretz, *The Middle East Today* (New York: Holt, Reinhart and Winston, 1963).
62. Keith Wheelock, *Nasser's New Egypt: A Critical Analysis* (New York: Praeger, 1960).
63. Wheelock, *Nasser's New Egypt*.
64. Peretz, *Middle East Today*.
65. The ASU was the only legitimate political party, and its members were elected by the public; those elected, in turn, voted for the members of the national assembly.
66. Baaklini, Denoeux, and Springborg, *Legislative Politics*.
67. Nadia Ramsis Farah, "Political Regimes and Social Performance: The Case of Egypt," in Saad Eddin Ibrahim, et al., eds., *Developmentalism and Beyond: Society and Politics in Egypt and Turkey* (Cairo: American University in Cairo Press, 1994).
68. Ibid.

164   Notes

69. Bahgat Korany, "Restricted Democratization from Above," in Rex Brynen, Bahgat Korany, and Paul Noble, *Political Liberalization and Democratization in the Arab World*, Vol.2 (Boulder, CO: Lynne Reinner, 1998).

70. Daniel Brumberg, "Democratization versus Liberalization in the Arab World: Dilemmas and Challenges for U.S. Foreign Policy" (http://www.strategicstudiesinstitute.army.mil/pdffiles/pub620.pdf, July 2005).

71. Farah, *Religious Strife*, 115–16.

72. Farah, *Religious Strife*, 117.

73. Paul M. Lubeck, " Islamist Responses to Globalization: Cultural Conflict in Egypt, Algeria, and Malaysia," http://repositories.cdlib.org/uciaspubs/research/98/9/.

74. Hassanein Tawfiq Ibrahim, *The Political Economy of Economic Reforms* (Cairo: Center for Political and Strategic Studies, 1999).

75. Ahmed El-Najjar, *The Egyptian Economy* (Cairo: Center for Political and Strategic Studies, 2002).

76. Ahmed El-Najjar, *The Egyptian Economy* (Cairo: Center for Political and Strategic Studies, 2002).

77. Stephen King, *Democratic Failure and the New Authoritarianism in the Middle East and North Africa* (Washington D.C.: Georgetown University, 2006).

78. Marsha Pripstein Posusney, *Labor and the State in Egypt: Workers, Unions and Economic Restructuring* (New York: Columbia University Press 1997).

79. King, *Democratic Failure*.

80. Brumberg, "Democratization versus Liberalization."

81. Amr Hamzawy, "Autumn of Polls," *Al-Ahram Weekly*, November 10–16, 2005.

82. The judiciary supervises the legislative elections. Due to the small number of judges, compared to the very high number of poll stations serving a population of 77 million, the legislative elections are held in three rounds to cover all the country's governorates and polling stations.

83. Challiss McDonough, "Vote Buying Rife in Egyptian Politics," November 16, 2005, http://www.voanews.com/english/archive/2005-11/2005-11-16-voa59.cfm.

Notes to Chapter 3

1. M. Weber, *The Protestant Ethic and the Spirit of Capitalism*, translated by Talcott Parsons (London: Allen and Unwin, 1930).

2. S.M. Lipset and G.S. Lenz, "Corruption, Culture, and Markets," in L.E. Harrison and S.P. Huntington, eds., *Culture Matters: How Values Shape Human Progress* (New York: Basic Books, 2000).

3. David Hume, *The Natural History of Religion*, J.C.A. Gaskin, ed. (Oxford: Oxford University Press, 1993).

4. Gerrieter Haar, "Religion: Source of Conflict or Resource for Peace?" in Gerrieter Haar and James J. Busuttil, eds., *Bridge or Barrier: Religion, Violence and Visions for Peace* (Leiden: Brill, 2005).

5. L.R. Iannaccone, R. Stark, and R. Finke, "Rationality and the 'Religious Mind'," *Economic Inquiry*, July 1998.

6. B. Sacerdote and E.L. Glaeser, "Education and Religion," NBER working paper No. 8080, January 2001.

7. E. Glaeser and S. Glendon, "Incentives, Predestination and Free Will," *Economic Inquiry*, July 1998.

8. Adam Smith, *An Inquiry into the Nature and Causes of the Wealth of Nations*, 6th ed. (London: Strahan, 1791).

9. L.R. Iannaccone, "The Consequences of Religious Market Structures: Adam Smith and the Economics of Religion," *Rationality and Society*, April 1991; R. Stark and W.S. Bainbridge, *A Theory of Religion* (New York: P. Lang, 1987); R. Finke and R. Stark, *The Churching of America 1776–1990* (New Brunswick, NJ: Rutgers University Press, 1992).

10. Robert J. Barro and Rachel R. McCleary, "Religion and Economic Growth Across Countries," *American Sociological Review* 68, no. 5 (2003).

11. See for example, Christopher Alexander, "Opportunities, Organizations, and Ideas: Islamists and Workers in Tunisia and Algeria," *International Journal of Middle East Studies* 34, no. 4 (2001); Carrie Rosefsky Wickham, *Mobilizing Islam: Religion, Activism and Political Change in Egypt* (New York: Columbia University Press, 2002); and Mohammed M. Hafez, *Why Muslims Rebel: Repression and Resistance in the Islamic World* (Boulder, CO: Lynne Rienner, 2003).

12. See Charles Tilly, *From Mobilization to Revolution* (Reading, MA: Addison-Wesley, 1978) and Mayer N. Zald and John D. McCarthy, *Social Movements in an Organizational Society* (New Brunswick, NJ: Transaction Books, 1987).

13. Doug McAdam, "Recruitment to High-Risk Activism: The Case of Freedom Summer," *American Journal of Sociology* 92 (1986); Bert Klandermans and Dirk Oegema, "Potentials, Networks, Motivations, and Barriers: Steps toward Participation in Social Movements," *American Sociological Review* 52 (1987).

14. James M. Jasper, *The Art of Moral Protest: Culture, Biography, and Creativity in Social Movements* (Chicago: University of Chicago Press, 1997).

15. David A. Snow, E. Burke Rochford, Jr., Steven K. Wordon, and Robert D. Benford, "Frame Alignment Processes, Micromobilization, and Movement Participation," *American Sociological Review* 51 (1986).

16. Anne Marie Baylouny, "Emotions, Poverty, or Politics: Misconceptions About Islamic Movements," *Strategic Insights* 3, no. 1 (January 2004).

17. Ibid.

166 Notes

18. Bronislaw Misztal and Anson Shupe, "Fundamentalism and Globalization: Fundamentalist Movements at the Twilight of the Twentieth Century," in Anson Shupe and Bronislaw Misztal, eds., *Religion, Mobilization, and Social Action* (Westport, CT: Praeger, 1998).

19. B. Misztal and A. Shupe, *Religion and Politics in Comparative Perspective: Revival of Fundamentalism in East and West* (Westport, CT: Praeger, 1992).

20. Shupe and Bronislaw, *Religion, Mobilization, and Social Action*.

21. Nadia Ramsis Farah, *Religious Strife in Egypt: Crisis and Ideological Conflict in the Seventies* (New York and London: Gordon and Breach Publishers, 1986).

22. Fereydoun Hoveyda, *The Broken Crescent: The Threat of Militant Islamic Fundamentalism* (Westport, CT: Praeger, 1998).

23. Ibid.

24. Michael Hudson, "Islam and Political Development," in John Esposito, ed., *Islam and Development: Religion and Socio-Political Change* (Syracuse: Syracuse University Press, 1980).

25. Samuel P. Huntington, *The Clash of Civilizations: Remaking of World Order* (New York: Simon and Schuster, 1996), 216–18.

26. Bernard Lewis, *Islam and the West* (New York: Oxford University Press, 1993) and Daniel Pipes, *In the Path of God: Islam and Political Power* (New Brunswick, NJ: Transaction Publishers, 2002).

27. Lewis, *Islam and the West*.

28. Ernest Gellner, *Postmodernism, Reason and Religion* (London: Routledge, 1992).

29. Bruce B. Lawrence, *Defenders of God* (New York: Harper and Row, 1989).

30. Hoveyda, *Broken Crescent*.

31. 'Daniel Crecelius, "The Course of Secularization in Modern Egypt," in Esposito, *Islam and Development*.

32. Farah, *Religious Strife*, 88.

33. In 1903 Muhammad 'Abdu published a *fatwa* that drew a distinction between the legitimate and permissible interest obtainable on loans and unreasonably high rates of interest, or *riba* (usury).

34. Ibid., 89–90.

35 Fawzi Najjar, "The Debate on Islam and Secularism," *Arab Studies Quarterly* 18, no. 2 (1996).

36. Ziad Munson, "Islamic Mobilization: Social Movement Theory and the Egyptian Muslim Brotherhood," *Sociological Quarterly* 42, no. 4 (January 2002).

37. Barry Rubin, *Islamic Fundamentalism in Egyptian Politics* (New York: Palgrave McMillan, 2002).

38. Ibid.
39. Richard Mitchell, *The Society of the Muslim Brothers* (Oxford and New York: Oxford University Press, 1969).
40. Najjar, "Debate on Islam."
41. Ibid.
42. Mitchell, *Society of the Muslim Brothers.*
43. Ibid., 112–13.
44. Najjar, "Debate on Islam."
45. Mitchell, *Society of the Muslim Brothers*, 151.
46. Crecelius, "Course of Secularization in Modern Egypt."
47. See for example Yvonne Y. Haddad, "Islamists and the 'Problem of Israel': The 1967 Awakening," *Middle East Journal* 46, no. 2 (1992); Nikki R. Keddie, "The Revolt of Islam, 1700 to 1993: Comparative Considerations and Relations to Imperialism," *Comparative Studies in Society and History* 36, no. 3 (1994); R. Hrair Dekmejian, *Islam in Revolution: Fundamentalism in the Arab World* (Syracuse: Syracuse University Press, 1995); John L. Esposito, *Islam and Politics* (Syracuse: Syracuse University Press, 1998).
48. See Farah, *Religious Strife.*
49. Kirk Beattie, *Egypt During the Sadat Years* (New York: Palgrave, 2000).
40. Ibid.
51. Ibid.
52. Farah, *Religious Strife*, 114.
53. Ibid.
54. Mark Cooper, *The Transformation of Egypt* (London: Croom Helm, 1982), 106–107.
55. Carries Rosefsky Wickham, *Mobilizing Islam: Religion, Activism, and Political Change in Egypt* (New York: Columbia University Press, 2002).
56. Farah, *Religious Strife*, 122–23.
57. Robert Springborg, *Mubarak's Egypt: Fragmentation of the Political Order* (Boulder, CO: Westview Press 1989).
58. Ibid., 217.
59. Gilles Kepel, *Jihad: The Threat of Political Islam* (London: I.B. Taurus, 2002), 284.
60. "Reading Between the 'Red Lines' the Repression of Academic Freedom in Egyptian Universities," *Human Rights Watch* 17, no. 6 (E) (June 2005), p. 77. http://www.hrw.org/en/reports/2005/06/08/reading-between-red-lines-repression-academic-freedom-egyptian-universities-0

Notes to Chapter 4

1. N. Lagerlof, "Gender Inequality, Fertility, and Growth" (Mimeographed. Department of Economics, University of Sydney, 1999).

2. David Dollar and Roberta Gatti, "Gender Inequality, Income, and Growth: Are Good Times Good for Women?" (Policy Research Report on Gender and Development, Working Paper Series No.1. Washington D.C.: World Bank, May 1999).

3. Stephan Klasen, "Does Gender Inequality Reduce Growth and Development? Evidence from Cross Country Regressions" (Policy Research Report on Gender and Development, Working Paper Series, No. 7. Washington D.C.: World Bank, November 1999).

4. Deon Filmer, "The Structure of Social Disparities in Education: Gender and Wealth" (Policy Research Report on Gender and Development, Working Paper Series No. 5. Washington D.C.: World Bank, November 1999).

5. Klasen, "Does Gender Inequality Reduce Growth and Development?"

6. Ibid.

7. Stephanie Seguino, "Export-led Growth and the Persistence of Gender Inequalities in the Newly Industrialized Countries," in Rives and Yousefi, eds., *Economic Dimensions of Gender Inequalities: A Global Perspective* (Westport, CT: Praeger, 1997).

8. See Seguino, "Export-led Growth"; Joyce Jacobson, "Workforce Sex Segregation in Developing Countries," in Rives and Yousefi, *Economic Dimensions of Gender Inequalities*; Stephanie Borass and William Rodgers, "How Does Gender Play a Role in the Earnings Gap? An Update," *Monthly Labor Review* 126, no. 3 (2003).

9. See David Macpherson and Barry Hirsch, "Wages and Gender Composition: Why do Women's Jobs Pay Less?" *Journal of Labor Economics* 13, no. 3 (1995); Elaine Sorensen, "Measuring the Pay Disparity Between Typically Female Occupations and Other Jobs: A Bivariate Selectivity Approach," *Industrial and Labor Relations Review*, July 1989.

10. Elissa Braunstein, "Foreign Direct Investments, Development and Gender Equity: A Review of Research and Policy," *United Nations Research Institute for Social Development*, January 2006.

11. Susan Joekes, "A Gender-analytical perspective on trade and sustainable development." In UNCTAD, *Trade, Sustainable Development and Gender* (New York and Geneva: UNCTAD, 1999).

12. Braunstein, "Foreign Direct Investments."

13. Diane Elson and Ruth Pearson, "Nimble Fingers Make Cheap Workers: An Analysis of Women's Employment in Third World Export Manufacturing," *Feminist Review* 7 (1981).

Notes   169

14. Jane Guyer, "Dynamic Approaches to Domestic Budgeting: Cases and Methods from Africa," in Daisy Dwyer and Judith Bruce, eds., *A Home Divided: Women and Income in the Third World* (Palo Alto: Stanford University Press, 1988); Sudhanshu Handa, "Gender, Headship and Intra Household Resource Allocation," *World Development* 22, no. 10 (1994); and Agnes Quisumbing and John Maluccio, "Intrahousehold Allocation and Gender Relations: New Empirical Evidence," *Policy* Research Report on Gender and Development, Working Paper Series No. 2 (Washington D.C.: World Bank, November 1999).

15. Maria Sagrario Floro and Stephanie Seguino, "Gender Effects on Aggregate Saving," Policy Research Report on Gender and Development, Working Paper Series No. 23 (Washington D.C.: World Bank, September 2002).

16. World Bank Report, *Engendering Development Through Gender Equality in Rights, Resources and Voices* (New York: Oxford University Press, 2001).

17. Geske Dijkstra, "A Larger Pie Through A Fair Share? Gender Equality and Economic Performance," Working Paper No. 315 (The Hague, Netherlands: ORPAS- Institute of Social Studies, April 2000).

18. Swasti Mitter, "On Organizing Women in Casualized Work: A Global Overview," in Sheila Rowbotham and Swasti Mitter, eds., *Dignity and Daily Bread: New Forms of Organizing among Poor Women in the Third World and the First* (London and New York: Routledge, 1994).

19. Charles Hennon and Suzanne Loker, "Gender and Home-Based Employment in a Global Economy" in Charles Hennon, Suzanne Locker, and Rosemary Walker, eds., *Gender and Home-Based Employment* (Westport, CT and London: Auburn House, 2000).

20. World Bank Report, *Engendering Development*.

21. Ibid.

22. Mayra Buvinic and Geeta Rao Gupta, "Female-headed Households and Female-maintained Families: Are They Worth Targeting to Reduce Poverty in Developing Countries?" *Economic Development and Cultural Change* 45, no. 2 (January 1997): 259–80.

23. Ibid.

24. T. Killick, "Structural Adjustment and Poverty Alleviation: An Interpretative Survey," *Development and Change* 26 (1995); and Sally Baden, "Economic Reform and Poverty" (report, Brighton: Institute of Development Studies, 1997).

25. See for example: M. Abramovitz, *Regulating the Lives of Women: Social Welfare Policy from Colonial Times to the Present* (Boston, MA: South End Press, 1988); R. Lister, *Women's Economic Dependency and Social Security* (Manchester, UK: Equal Opportunities Commission, 1992); and L. Gordon, ed., *Women, the*

170   Notes

State and Welfare (Madison, WI: University of Wisconsin Press, 1990); Ann Orloff, "Gender in the Welfare State," *Annual Review of Sociology* 22 (1996).

26. Tanja Van Der Lippe and Liset Van Dijik, "Comparative Research on Women's Employment," *Annual Review of Sociology* 28 (2002): 221–41.

27. Yana van der Meulen Rodgers, "Protecting Women and Promoting Equality in the Labor Market: Theory and Evidence," Policy Research Report on Gender and Development, Working Paper Series No. 6 (Washington D.C.: World Bank, November 1999).

28. Lama Abu Odeh, "Modernizing Muslim Family Law: The Case of Egypt," *Vanderbilt Journal of Transnational Law* 37, no. 4 (2004).

29. Andrea B. Rugh, *Family in Contemporary Egypt* (Cairo: American University in Cairo Press, 1988).

30. Shari'a law allows individuals to leave one third of their assets subject to inheritance any party, by will, in exemption to the inheritance laws. Rarely is this right used for the benefit of women, if at all.

31. In fact, the marriage contract under shari'a allows a woman to set any conditions she requires on condition that it does not fundamentally contradict Islamic laws.

32. Margot Badran, *Feminists, Islam, and Nation: Gender and the Making of Modern Egypt* (Princeton, NJ: Princeton University Press, 1995).

33. See a full explanation of the feminist movement's struggle to obtain women's political rights in Badran, *Feminists, Islam, and Nation*.

34. Mervat Hatem, "Economic and Political Liberation in Egypt and the Demise of State Feminism," *International Journal of Middle East Studies* 24.

35. Valentine Moghadam, "The Political Economy of Female Employment in the Arab Region," in Nabil Khoury and Valentine Moghadam, eds., *Gender and Development in the Arab World* (London: Zed Books, 1995).

36. Sunita Kishor and Katherine Neitzel, *The Status of Women, Indicators for Twenty-Five Countries. DHS Comparative Studies* 21. Calverton, MD: Macro International, Inc., 1996.

37. Homa Hoodfar, "Household Budgeting and Financial Management in a Lower Income Cairo Neighborhood," in Daisy Dwyer and Judith Bruce, eds., *Women and Income in the Third* World (Palo Alto: Stanford University Press, 1988).

38. Ragui Assaad and Melanie Arntz, "Constrained Geographical Mobility and Gendered Labor Market Outcomes Under Structural Adjustment: Evidence from Egypt," *World Development* 33, no. 3 (2005).

39. Labor force participation rates include the participation rates of those who are employed in addition to those who are seeking work but have not found work, that is, the unemployed. So while the overall economic participation

rate may increase, the increase might be attributed to the high unemployment of the first entrants in the labor market.

40. Ragui Assaad, "The Transformation of the Egyptian Labor Market: 1988–1998." In Ragui Assaad, ed., *The Labor Market in a Reforming Economy: Egypt in the 1990s* (Cairo: American University in Cairo Press, 2002).

41. Assaad and Arntz, "Constrained Geographical Mobility."

42. Ibid.

43. Calculated by the author from Labor Force Sample Survey 2004. Cairo: CAPMAS, 2005.

44. Calculated by the author from Labor Force Sample Survey 2004. Cairo: CAPMAS, 2005.

45. Hoodfar, "Household Budgeting."

46. Calculated by the author from Labor Force Sample Survey 2004. Cairo: CAPMAS, 2005.

47. Calculated by the author from Labor Force Sample Survey 2004. Cairo: CAPMAS, 2005.

48. Nadia Ramsis Farah, *al-Mar'a al-'arabiya: al-wad' al-hali wa muqtadayat al-tanmiya* (Amman: ESCWA Research Series on Arab Women in Development No. 18, 1992; and Labor Force Sample Survey 2004 (Cairo: CAPMAS, 2005).

49. Heba El-Laithy, "The Gender Dimensions of Poverty in Egypt" (ERF Working Papers Series No. 127, January, 2001).

50. Ibid.

51. Ibid.

Bibliography

Abdel-Aal, Mohamed. "Agrarian Reform and Tenancy Problems in Upper Egypt." Cairo: Social Research Center, American University in Cairo, n.d.

Abdel-Fadil, Mahmoud. *The Political Economy of Nasserism.* Cambridge: Cambridge University Press, 1980

Abdellatif, Lobna. "Egypt's Manufacturing Sector: Factor Inputs and TFP over half a Century." Research paper. Cairo: Economic Research Forum, September 2003.

Abdel-Malek, Anouar. *Egypt Military Society: The Army Regime, the Left and Social Change under Nasser.* New York: Vintage, 1968.

Abrahamsen, Rita. *Disciplining Democracy: Development Discourse and Good Governance.* London, New York: Zed Books, 2000.

Abramovitz, M. *Regulating the Lives of Women: Social Welfare Policy from Colonial Times to the Present.* Boston, MA: South End Press, 1988.

Abu Odeh, Lama. "Modernizing Muslim Family Law: The Case of Egypt." *Vanderbilt Journal of Transnational Law* 37, no. 4 (2004). http://www.questia.com/Index.jsp.

Adams, Richard. "Self-Targeted Subsidies: The Distributional Impact of the Egyptian Food Subsidy System." World Bank Policy Research Working Paper, No. 2322, April 2000.

Al-Ahram Center for Strategic and Political Studies. *The Strategic Economic Trends Report 2005.* Cairo: Al-Ahram, 2005.

Alexander, Christopher. "Opportunities, Organizations, and Ideas: Islamists and Workers in Tunisia and Algeria." *International Journal of Middle East Studies* 34, no. 4 (2001): 465–90.

174   Bibliography

Alterman, Jon B. "Egypt: Stable But For How Long?" *The Washington Quarterly,* Autumn 2000, 107–18.

Amdsen, Alice. *Asia's Next Giant: South Korea and Late Industrialization.* New York: Oxford University Press, 1989.

Aoude, Ibrahim. "From National Bourgeois Development to Infitah: Egypt 1952–1992." *Arab Studies Quarterly* 16 (1994). http://www.questia.com/Index.jsp.

Armijo, Leslie E. "Mixed Blessing: Expectations About Foreign Capital Flows and Democracy in Emerging Markets," in Leslie E. Armijo, ed., *Financial Globalization and Democracy in Emerging Markets.* New York: St. Martin's Press, 1999.

Assaad, Ragui. "The Transformation of the Egyptian Labor Market: 1988–1998," in Ragui Assaad, ed., *The Labor Market in a Reforming Economy: Egypt in the 1990s.* Cairo: American University in Cairo Press.

Assaad, Ragui and Arntz, Melani. "Constrained Geographical Mobility and Gendered Labor Market Outcomes Under Structural Adjustment: Evidence from Egypt." *World Development* 33, no. 3 (2005): 431–54.

Baaklini, Abdo, Guilian Denoeux, and Robert Springborg. *Legislative Politics in the Arab World: The Resurgence of Democratic Institutions.* Boulder, CO: Lynne Reinner, 1999.

Baden, Sally. "Economic Reform and Poverty: A Gender Analysis." Bridge No. 50 Report, prepared for the Gender Equality Unit, Swedish International Development Cooperation Agency (SIDA). Brighton: Institute of Development Studies, 1997.

Badran, Margot. *Feminists, Islam, and Nation: Gender and the Making of Modern Egypt.* Princeton, NJ: Princeton University Press, 1995.

Baer, Gabriel. *A History of Landownership in Modern Egypt 1800–1950.* London: Oxford University Press, 1962.

Baker, Raymond. "Egypt in Time and Space of Globalism." *Arab Studies Quarterly* 21 (1999): 1–11.

———. *Egypt's Uncertain Revolution under Nasser and Sadat.* Cambridge: Cambridge University Press, 1978.

Bardhan, Pranab. "Democracy and Development: A Complex Relationship," in I. Shapiro and C. Hacker-Cordon, eds., *Democracy's Value.* Cambridge: Cambridge University Press, 1999.

Barro, Robert J. and Rachel R. McCleary. "Religion and Economic Growth Across Countries." *American Sociological Review* 68, no. 5 (2003): 760–81.

Bibliography 175

Baylouny, Anne Marie. "Emotions, Poverty, or Politics: Misconceptions About Islamic Movements." *Strategic Insights* 3, no. 1 (January 2004): 1–4.

Beattie, Kirk. *Egypt During the Sadat Years.* New York: Palgrave, 2000.

Benin, Joel. "Egyptian Textile Workers: From Craft Artisans Facing European Competition to Proletarians Contending with the State." Paper presented to "A Global History of Textile Workers 1600–2000" conference, International Institute of Social History (IISH), Amsterdan, November 11–13, 2004.

Borass, Stephanie and William Rodgers. "How Does Gender Play a Role in the Earnings Gap? An Update." *Monthly Labor Review* 126, no. 3 (2003): 9–15.

Braunstein, Elissa. "Foreign Direct Investments, Development and Gender Equity: A Review of Research and Policy." New York: United Nations Research Institute for Social Development, January 2006.

Brooker, Paul. *Non-Democratic Regimes: Theory, Government and Politics.* New York: St. Martin's, 2000.

Brumberg, Daniel. "Democratization versus Liberalization in the Arab World: Dilemmas and Challenges for U.S. Foreign Policy," July 2005, http://www.strategicstudiesinstitute.army.mil/pdffiles/pub620.pdf

Burkhart, R., and Michael Lewis-Beck. "Comparative Democracy: The Economic Development Thesis." *American Political Science Review* 10 (1994): 903–10.

Bush, Ray. *Economic Crisis and the Political Reform in Egypt.* Boulder, CO: Westview Press, 1999.

Buvinic, Mayra and Geeta Rao Gupta. "Female-Headed Households and Female-Maintained Families: Are They Worth Targeting to Reduce Poverty in Developing Countries?" *Economic Development and Cultural Change* 45, no. 2 (1997): 259–80.

Chan, Sylvia. *Liberalism, Democracy, and Development.* Cambridge: Cambridge University Press, 2002

Crecelius, Daniel. "The Course of Secularization in Modern Egypt," in John Esposito, ed., *Islam and Development: Religion and Sociopolitical Change.* Syracuse, NY: Syracuse University Press, 1980.

Crouchley, A. *The Economic Development of Modern Egypt.* London: Longmans, 1938.

Dahl, Robert. *On Democracy.* New Haven: Yale University Press, 1998.

Diamond, Larry. "Thinking about Hybrid Regimes." *Journal of Democracy* 13, no. 2 (April 2002): 21–35.

176   Bibliography

_____. *Developing Democracy: Toward Consolidation*. Baltimore: Johns
Hopkins University Press, 1999.

Dijkstra, Geske. "A Larger Pie Through A Fair Share? Gender Equality
and Economic Performance." Working Paper 315. The Hague, Netherlands: ORPAS-Institute of Social Studies, April 2000.

Dollar, David and Gatti, Roberta. "Gender Inequality, Income, and
Growth: Are God Times Good for Women." Policy Research Report
on Gender and Development, Working Paper Series No.1., Washington D.C. World Bank, May 1999.

Economic Intelligence Unit. *Egypt Country Report*, February 2006.

El-Ehwany, Naglaa and Heba Nassar. *Poverty Employment and Policy Making in Egypt: A Country Profile*. Cairo: ILO Area Office, 2001.

Elhai, Khandakar and Constantine P. Danopoulos. "Democracy, Capitalism and Development." *Journal of Security Sector Management* 2, no.2
(June 2004): 1–11.

Elson, Diane and Ruth Pearson. "Nimble Fingers Make Cheap Workers:
An Analysis of Women's Employment in Third World Export Manufacturing." *Feminist Review* 1, no. 7 (1981): 87–107.

Elster, Jon. "The Necessity and Impossibility of Simultaneous Economic
and Political Reform," in Douglas Greenberg, Stanley N. Katz,
Melanie Beth Oliviero, and Steven C. Wheatley, eds., *Constitutionalism
and Democracy: Transitions in the Contemporary World*. Oxford: Oxford
University Press, 1993.

Ersson, Svante and J. Lane. "Democracy and Development: Statistical
Exploration," in Adrian Leftwich, ed., *Democracy and Development, Theory and Practice*. Cambridge, MA: Polity, 1996.

Esfahani, Hadi Salehi. *The Experience of Foreign Investment in Egypt under
Infitah*. Research publication. New Jersey: Center for Economic
Research on Africa, Department of Economics and Finance, School
of Business, Montclair State University, August 1993.

Evans, Peter. "Predatory, Developmental, and Other Apparatuses: A
Comparative Political Economy Perspective on Third World States,"
in A. Douglas Kincaid and Alejandro Portes, eds., *Comparative
National Development: Society and Economy in the New Global Order.*
Chapel Hill: University of North Carolina Press, 1994.

_____. *Embedded Autonomy: States and Industrial Transformation*. Princeton,
NJ: Princeton University Press, 1995.

Evans, Peter, Dietrich Rueschemeyer, and Theda Skocpol, eds. *Bringing
the State Back In*. Cambridge: Cambridge University Press, 1985.

Farah, Nadia Ramsis. *Religious Strife in Egypt: Crisis and Ideological Conflict in the Seventies.* London and New York: Gordon and Breach, 1986.

_____. "The Crisis of the Public Sector in Egypt." Paper presented at the Conference on the Public Sector held by al-Wafd Party, Cairo, February 9, 1987.

_____. "The Social Formations Approach and Arab Social Systems." *Arab Studies Quarterly* 10, no. 3 (Summer 1988).

_____. "Science, Ideology and Authoritarianism in Middle East Economics," in Earl Sullivan and Jacqueline Ismail, eds., *The Contemporary Study of the Arab World.* Alberta: University of Alberta Press, 1991.

_____. *Arab Women and Employment: Current Status and Development Requirements.* ESCWA Research Series on Arab Women in Development, No. 18, 1992.

_____. "Political Regimes and Social Performance: The Case of Egypt," in Saad Eddin Ibrahim, Caglar Keyder, Ayse Oncu, and Abdel Monem Said Aly, eds. *Developmentalism and Beyond: Society and Politics in Egypt and Turkey.* Cairo: American University in Cairo Press, 1994.

_____. "Historical Roots of Contemporary Economic Development in Egypt," in Dan Tschirgi, ed., *Development in the Age of Liberalization: Egypt and Mexico.* Cairo: American University in Cairo Press, 1996.

_____. *Egypt Gender Indicators.* Cairo: National Council for Women, 2002.

Fawzy, Samiha. "The Business Environment in Egypt: Constraints to Private Sector Development." Paper presented to the Conference on the Public Private Partnerships in the MENA Region, The Mediterranean Development Forum, Marrakesh, September 3–6, 1998.

_____. "Investment Policies and Unemployment in Egypt." Cairo: Egyptian Center for Economic Studies, Working Paper No. 68, September 2002.

Fergany, Nader. "Unemployment and Poverty in Egypt," in M.A. Kishk ed., *Poverty of Environment and Environment of Poverty.* Cairo: Dar al-Ahmady for Publishing, 1988.

Filmer, Deon. "The Structure of Social Disparities in Education: Gender and Wealth." Policy Research Report on Gender and Development, Working Paper Series, No. 5. Washington D.C.: World Bank, November 1999.

Finke, R. and R. Stark. *The Churching of America 1776–1990.* New Brunswick, NJ: Rutgers University Press, 1992.

178   Bibliography

Floro, Maria Sagrario and Seguino, Stephanie. "Gender Effects on Aggregate Saving." Policy Research Report on Gender and Development, Working Paper Series, No. 23. Washington D.C.: World Bank, September 2002.

Foucault, Michel. "The Subject and Power," in J.D. Faubion, ed., *Power: Essential Works of Michel Foucault 1954–1984*, vol. 3. London: Penguin Books, 2002.

El-Garph, Mona. "Role of the State and Deregulation." ECES Working Papers 104, August 2005.

Gasiorowski, Mark J. "Economic Crisis and Political Regime Change: An Event History Analysis." *American Political Science Review* 89, no. 4 (1995): 882–97.

_____."Democracy and Macroeconomic Performance in Underdeveloped Countries: An Empirical Analysis." *Comparative Political Studies* 33, no. 3 (April 2000): 319–49.

Gellner, Ernest. *Postmodernism, Reason and Religion*. London: Routledge, 1992.

Gerring, John, Philip Bond, William T. Brandt, and Carola Moreno: "Democracy and Economic Growth: A Historical Perspective." *World Politics* 57 (April 2005): 323–64.

El-Ghonemy, M. Riad. *Egypt in the Twenty First Century*. Gainsville, FL.: University Press of Florida, 2003.

Glaeser, E. and S. Glendon. "Incentives, Predestination and Free Will." *Economic Inquiry*, July 1998, 429–43.

Goldberg, Ellis. Review of *Egypt During the Sadat Years*, by Kirk J. Beattie. *Political Science Quarterly* 17 (2002): 517–19.

Gordon L., ed. *Women, the State and Welfare*. Madison, WI: University of Wisconsin Press, 1990.

Gutner, Tammi. "The Political Economy of Food Subsidy Reform in Egypt." Food Consumption and Nutrition Division (FCND) discussion paper. International Food Research Institute, November 1999.

Guyer, Jane. "Dynamic Approaches to Domestic Budgeting: Cases and Methods from Africa," in Daisy Dwyer and Judith Bruce, eds., *A Home Divided: Women and Income in the Third World*. Palo Alto: Stanford University Press, 1988.

Haar, Gerrieter. "Religion: Source of Conflict or Resource for Peace?" in Gerrieter Haar and James J. Busuttil, eds., *Bridge or Barrier: Religion, Violence and Visions for Peace*. Leiden: Brill, 2005.

Hafez, Mohammed M. *Why Muslims Rebel: Repression and Resistance in the Islamic World*. Boulder, Colorado: Lynne Rienner, 2003.

Haggard, S. and R. Kaufman. *Politics of Economic Adjustment*. Princeton, New Jersey: Princeton University Press, 1992.

Haggard, Stephan and Sylvia Maxfield. "The Political Economy of Financial Internationalization in the Developing World." *International Organization* 50, no. 1 (1996): 35–68.

Hamzawy, Amr. "Autumn of Polls," *Al-Ahram Weekly*, November 10–16, 2005.

Handa, Sudhanshu. "Gender, Headship and Intra Household Resource Allocation." *World Development* 22, no. 10 (1994): 1535–47.

Harik, Illya. *Economic Policy Reform in Egypt*. Gainsville, FL.: University Press of Florida, 1997.

Hassan, S.S. *Christians Versus Muslims in Modern Egypt: The Century-Long Struggle for Coptic Equality*. Oxford: Oxford University Press, 2003.

Hatem, Mervat. "Economic and Political Liberation in Egypt and the Demise of State Feminism." *International Journal of Middle East Studies* 24:231–51.

Hayek, F.A. *The Fundamentals of Freedom*, vol. 2. Chicago: Chicago University Press, 1979.

Hennon, Charles and Suzanne Loker. "Gender and Home-Based Employment in a Global Economy," in Charles Hennon, Suzanne Locker, and Rosemary Walker, eds., *Gender and Home-Based Employment*. Westport, CT and London: Auburn House, 2000.

Hindess, Barry. *Discourses of Power: From Hobbes to Foucault*. Oxford: Blackwell, 1996.

Hinnebush Jr., Raymond. *Egyptian Politics Under Sadat: The Post-Populist Development of An Authoritarian-Modernizing State*. London, New York: Cambridge University Press, 1985.

Hirst, David. "Egypt Stands on Feet of Clay: A Middle East Indonesia in the Making." *Le Monde Diplomatique,* October 1999.

Hoodfar, Homa. "Household Budgeting and Financial Management in a Lower Income Cairo Neighborhood," in Daisy Dwyer and Judith Bruce, eds., *Women and Income in the Third World*. Stanford, California: Stanford University Press, 1988.

Houngnikpo, Mathurin C.: "Pax Democratica: The Gospel According to St. Democracy." *The Australian Journal of Politics and History* 49, no. 2 (2003): 197–210.

Hoveyda, Fereydoun. *The Broken Crescent: The Threat of Militant Islamic Fundamentalism*. Westport, CT: Praeger, 1998.

180   Bibliography

Hudson, Michael. "Islam and Political Development," in John Esposito, ed., *Islam and Development: Religion and Socio-Political Change.* Syracuse: Syracuse University Press, 1980.

Hume, David. *The Natural History of Religion*, J.C.A. Gaskin, ed. Oxford: Oxford University Press, 1993.

Huntington, Samuel P. *The Clash of Civilizations: Remaking of World Order.* New York: Simon and Schuster, 1996.

Ianchovichina, Elena and Pooja Kacker. "Growth Trends in the Developing World: Country Forecasts and Determinants." World Bank Policy Research Working Paper 3775, November 2005.

Iannaccone, L.R. "The Consequences of Religious Market Structures: Adam Smith and the Economics of Religion." *Rationality and Society*, April 1991, 117–56.

Iannaccone, L.R., R. Stark, and R. Finke. "Rationality and the Religious Mind." *Economic Inquiry*, July 1998, 373–89.

Ibrahim, Saad Eddin. "Egypt's Landed Bourgeoisie," in Ayse Oncu, Calgar Keyder, and Saad Eddin Ibrahim, eds., *Developmentalism and Beyond: Society and Politics in Egypt and Turkey.* Cairo: American University in Cairo Press, 1994.

Im, Hyug Baeg: "The Rise of Bureaucratic Authoritarianism in South Korea." *World Politics* 39, no. 2 (1987): 231–57.

IMF. IMF Country Report No. 05/776. Arab Republic of Egypt. Washington D.C.: IMF, July 2005.

IMF. IMF Country Report No. 06/253. Arab Repblic of Egypt. Washington D.C.: IMF, July 2006.

Inglehart, Ronald and Christian Welzel. *Modernization, Cultural Change, and Democracy: The Human Development Sequences.* New York: Cambridge University Press, 2005.

Issa, Salah. *The 'Urabi Revolution.* Cairo: The Egyptian Public Organization for Books, 1976.

Issawi, Charles. *Egypt: An Economic and Social Analysis.* London and New York: Oxford University Press, 1947.

Jasper, James M. *The Art of Moral Protest: Culture, Biography, and Creativity in Social Movements.* Chicago: University of Chicago Press, 1997.

Joekes, Susan. "A Gender-analytical Perspective on Trade and Sustainable Development," in United Nations Conference on Trade and Development (UNCTAD), *Trade, Sustainable Development and Gender.* New York and Geneva: UNCTAD, 1999.

Johnson, Gordon O.F. "The Oil Peril to Democracy and Development in Muslim Nations: The Curse of Oil, Public Choice Theory at Work, Economic Rent Seeking in Extreme." Paper presented at the Center for The Study of Islam and Democracy 2005 Annual Conference, Washington, D.C., April 23, 2005.

Karl, Terry Lynn. "The Hybrid Regimes of Central America." *Journal of Democracy* 6, no.3 (July 1995): 72–86.

Keohane, R. and H. Milner. *Internationalization and Domestic Politics.* Cambridge: Cambridge University Press, 1996.

Kepel, Gilles. *Muslim Extremism in Egypt: The Prophet and The Pharaoh.* Berkeley, CA: Berkeley University Press, 1993.

Kheir-El-Din, Hanaa and Tarek Abdellatif Moursi. "Sources of Economic Growth and Technical Progress in Egypt: An Aggregate Perspective." ERF Papers. Cairo: Economic Research Forum, September 2003.

Killick, T. "Structural Adjustment and Poverty Alleviation: An Interpretative Survey." *Development and Change* 26 (1995): 305–31.

King, Stephen. *Democratic Failure and the New Authoritarianism in the Middle East and North Africa.* Washington D.C.: Georgetown University, January 2006.

Kishk, Mohamed Atif. "Mechanisms of Impoverishment of the Rural Poor in Contemporary Egypt." Unpublished paper, Minya University, Minya, Egypt.

Kishor, Sunita and Neitzel, Katherine: "The Status of Women, Indicators for Twenty-Five Countries." Democratic and Health Surveys Comparative Studies 21. Calverton, MD: Macro International, Inc., 1996.

Klandermans, Bert, and Dirk Oegema. "Potentials, Networks, Motivations, and Barriers: Steps toward Participation in Social Movements." *American Sociological Review* 52 (1987): 519–31.

Klasen, Stephan. "Does Gender Inequality Reduce Growth and Development? Evidence from Cross Country Regressions." Policy Research Report on Gender and Development, Working Paper Series, No. 7. Washington D.C., World Bank, November 1999.

Korany, Bahgat. "Restricted Democratization from Above," in Rex Brynen, Bahgat Korany, and Paul Noble, eds., *Political Liberalization and Democratization in the Arab World*, Vol. 2. Boulder, CO: Lynne Reinner, 1998.

Korayem, Karima. "Egypt's Economic Reform and Structural Adjustment (ERSAP)." Working Paper No. 19. Cairo: The Egyptian Center for Economic Studies, October 1997.

182   Bibliography

Kotz, David M. "The Role of the State in Economic Transformation: Comparing the Transition Experience of Russia and China." Working Paper No. 95, Political Economy Research Institute, University of Massachusetts, Amherst, 2004.

Kwon, Hyok Yong. "Economic Reform and Democratization: Evidence from Latin America and Post-Socialist Countries." *British Journal of Political Science* 34, no. 2 (2004): 357–68.

Lagerlof, N. "Gender Inequality, Fertility, and Growth," Mimeographed. Department of Economics, University of Sydney, 1999.

El-Laithy, Heba. "The Gender Dimensions of Poverty in Egypt." ERF Working Papers Series No. 127, January 2001.

El-Laithy, Heba, Michael Lockshin, and Arup Banerjie. "Poverty and Economic Growth in Egypt." World Bank Research Working Paper, June 2003.

Land Center for Human Rights: "Labor Conditions in Egypt." Economic Social Rights Series, Issue 7, Cairo, 1999.

Landau, Jacob M. *Parliaments and Parties in Egypt.* New York: Praeger, 1953.

Lawrence, Bruce B. *Defenders of God.* New York: Harper & Row, 1989.

Lewis, Bernard. *Islam and the West.* New York: Oxford University Press, 1993.

Lippman, Thomas. *Egypt After Nasser: Sadat, Peace and the Mirage of Prosperity.* New York: Paragon House, 1989.

Lipset, S. Martin. *Political Man: The Social Bases of Politics.* Baltimore: Johns Hopkins University Press, 1959.

Lipset, S.M. and G.S. Lenz: "Corruption, Culture, and Markets," in L.E. Harrison and S.P. Huntington, eds., *Culture Matters: How Values Shape Human Progress.* New York: Basic Books, 2000.

Lister R. *Women's Economic Dependency and Social Security*. Manchester, UK: Equal Opportunities Commission, 1992.

Londregan, John, and Keith Poole. "Poverty, the Coup Trap, and the Seizure of Executive Power." *World Politics* 42 (1990): 151–83.

Londregan, John, and Keith Poole. "Does High Income Promote Democracy?" *World Politics* 49 (1996): 1–30.

Lubeck, Paul M. "Islamist Responses to Globalization: Cultural Conflict in Egypt, Algeria, and Malaysia," http://repositories.cdlib.org/uci-aspubs/research/98/9/ (accessed November 14, 2008).

Mabro, Robert and Samir Radwan. *The Industrializtion of Egypt 1939–1973: Policy and Performance.* Oxford: Clarendon Press, 1976.

Macpherson, David and Barry Hirsch. "Wages and Gender Composition: Why do Women's Jobs Pay Less?" *Journal of Labor Economics* 13, no. 3 (1995): 426–71.

El-Mahdi, Alia. "Labor in Egypt." Global Policy Network, October 2003. http://www.gpn.org/

Maxfield, Sylvia. "Understanding the Political Implications of Financial Internationalization in Emerging Market Countries." *World Development* 26, no.7 (1998): 1201–19.

_____. "Comparing East Asia and Latin America: Capital Mobility and Democratic Stability." *Journal of Democracy* 11, no. 4 (2000): 95–106.

McAdam, Doug. "Recruitment to High-Risk Activism: The Case of Freedom." *American Journal of Sociology* 92 (Summer 1986): 64–90.

McDonough, Challiss. "Vote Buying Rife in Egyptian Politics," November 16, 2005, http://www.voanews.com/english/archive/2005-11/2005-11-16-voa59.cfm (accessed November 14, 2008).

Mead, D. *Growth and Structural Change in the Egyptian Economy.* Yale University: Economic Growth Center, 1967.

Miliband, Ralph. *The State in Capitalist Society.* New York: Basic Books, 1969.

Mills, C. Wright. *The Power Elite.* Oxford: Oxford University Press, 1956.

Misztal B. and A. Shupe. *Religion and Politics in Comparative Perspective: Revival of Fundamentalism in East and West.* Westport, CT: Praeger, 1992.

Misztal, Bronislaw and Anson Shupe. "Fundamentalism and Globalization: Fundamentalist Movements at the Twilight of the Twentieth Century," in Anson Shupe and Bronislaw Misztal, eds., *Religion, Mobilization, and Social Action.* Westport, CT: Praeger, 1998.

Mitchell, Timothy. *Rule of Experts: Egypt, Techno-Politics, Modernity.* Berkeley: University of California Press, 2002.

Mitter, Swasti. "On Organizing Women in Casualized Work: A Global Overview," in Sheila Rowbotham and Swasti Mitter, eds., *Dignity and Daily Bread: New Forms of Organizing among Poor Women in the Third World and the First.* London and New York: Routledge, 1994.

Moghadam, Valentine. "The Political Economy of Female Employment in the Arab Region," in Nabil Khoury and Valentine Moghadam, eds., *Gender and Development in the Arab World.* London: Zed Books, 1995.

Mohamed, Mohamed Abdel-Wahed. "The Impact of Foreign Capital Inflow on Savings, Investment and Economic Growth Rate in Egypt: An Econometric Analysis." *Scientific Journal of King Faisal University* 4, no. 1 (2003).

184   Bibliography

Momani, Bessma. "IMF-Egyptian Debt Negotiations." *Cairo Papers in Social Science* 26, no. 3 (Fall 2003).

Moore, Barrington. *Social Origins of Democracy and Dictatorship: Lord and Peasant in the Making of the Modern World*. Boston: Beacon Press, 1966.

Moser, Caroline. *Gender Planning and Development: Theory Practice and Training*. New York: Routledge, 1993.

Munson, Ziad. "Islamic Mobilization: Social Movement Theory and the Egyptian Muslim Brotherhood." *Sociological Quarterly* 42, no. 4 (January 2002): 487–510.

El-Najjar, Ahmed. *The Egyptian Economy*. Cairo: Center for Political and Strategic Studies, 2002.

Najjar, Fawzi. "The Debate on Islam and Secularism." *Arab Studies Quarterly* 18, no. 2 (1996): 13–19.

National Center for Criminological and Sociological Research (NCCSR). *Comprehensive Sociological Survey of Egypt: 1952–1980*. Cairo: NCCSR, 1985.

National Democratic Party (NDP). *Reform Policy Papers*. Cairo: NDP, September 2004.

O'Donnell, Guillermo and Philippe Schmitter. *Transitions from Authoritarian Rule: Tentative Conclusions about Uncertain Democracies*. Baltimore: Johns Hopkins University Press, 1986.

Olcott, Martha Brill and Marina S. Ottaway. "The Challenge of Semi-Authoritarianism." Carnegie Endowment for Peace Working Paper No. 7. Washington, D.C., 1999.

Orloff, Ann. "Gender in the Welfare State." *Annual Review of Sociology* 22 (1996). http://www.questia.com

Panizza, Ugo. "Macroeconomic Policies in Egypt: An Interpretation of the Past and Options for the Future." ECES Working Paper No. 61, 2001.

Peretz, Don. *The Middle East Today*. New York: Holt, Reinhart, and Winston, 1963.

Persson, Torsten. "Forms of Democracy, Policy and Economic Development." (Institute for International Economic Studies, Stockholm University, January 2005). http://www.iies.su.se/~perssont/papers/paper050131.pdf (accessed July 21, 2008).

———. "Forms of Democracy, Policy and Economic Development." National Bureau of Economic Research Working Paper No. 11171, 2005.

Persson, Torsten and Guido Tabellini. *The Economic Effects of Constitutions*. Cambridge: MIT Press, 2003.

_____. "Constitutional Rules and Fiscal Policy Outcomes." *American Economic Review* 94 (2004): 25–46.

_____. "Democracy and Development: Devil in the Details." Institute for International Economic Studies, Stockholm University, December 2005. http://www.aeaweb.org/annual_mtg_papers/2006/0106_1015_1402.pdf (accessed July 21, 2008).

Pipes, Daniel. *In the Path of God: Islam and Political Power*. New Brunswick, NJ: Transaction Publishers, 2002.

Polidano, Charles. *Don't Discard State Autonomy: Revisiting the East Asian Experiment of Development*. Manchester: Institute for Development Policy and Management, University of Manchester, 1998.

Posusney, Marsha Pripstein. *Labor and the State in Egypt: Workers, Unions and Economic Restructuring*. New York: Columbia University Press, 1997.

Poulantzas, Nicos. *Political Power and Social Classes*. London: Verso, 1978.

_____. *State, Power, Socialism*. London: Verso, 1980.

Przeworski, Adam. "The Neoliberal Fallacy," in Larry Diamond and Marc F. Plattner, eds., *Capitalism, Socialism, and Democracy Revisited*. Baltimore: Johns Hopkins University Press, 1993.

_____. "Democracy and Economic Development," in Edward D. Mansfield and Richard Sisson, eds., *Political Science and the Public Interest*. Columbus: Ohio: State University Press. http://politics.as.nyu.edu/docs/IO/2800/sisson.pdf.

Przeworski, Adam, Michael E. Alvarez, Jos Antonio Cheibub, and Fernando Limongi. *Democracy and Development: Political Institutions and Well-Being in the World, 1950–1990*. Cambridge: Cambridge University Press, 2001.

Przeworski, Adam and Fernando Limongi. "Modernization: Theories and Facts." *World Politics* 49 (1997): 155–83.

Rodrik, Dani. *Has Globalization Gone Too Far?* Washington, D.C.: Institute for International Economics, 1997.

Ross, Michael. "Does Oil Hinder Democracy?" *World Politics* 53, no. 3 (2001): 325–61.

Rubin, Barry. *Islamic Fundamentalism in Egyptian Politics*. New York: Palgrave Macmillan, 2002.

Rudra, Nita. "Globalization and the Strengthening of Democracy in the Developing World." *American Journal of Political Science* 49, no. 4:704–30, http://www.blackwell-synergy.com/doi/pdf/10.1111/j.1540-5907.2005.00150.x (accessed July 21, 2008).

186   Bibliography

Rueschemeyer, Dietrich, Evelyne Huber Stephens, and John D. Stephens. *Capitalist Development and Democracy*. Cambridge: Polity Press, 1992.

Schedler, Andreas: "The Nested Game of Democratization by Elections." *International Political Science Review* 23, no. 1 (2002): 103–22.

Schumpeter, Joseph Alois. *Capitalism, Socialism, and Democracy*. New York: Harper and Bros, 1942.

Seguino, Stephanie. "Export-Led Growth and the Persistence of Gender Inequalities in the Newly Industrialized Countries," in Janet Rives and Mahooud Yousefi, eds., *Economic Dimensions of Gender Inequalities: A Global Perspective*. Westport, CT: Praeger, 1997.

Sen, Amartya. *Development as Freedom*. New York: Albert A. Knopf, 1999.

Sindzingre, Alice N. "Bringing the Developmental State Back In: Contrasting Development Trajectories in Sub-Saharan Africa and East Asia." Paper presented to the Annual Meeting of the Society for the Advancement of Socio-Economics, Washington D. C., Georges Washington University, July 9–11, 2004.

Skocpol, Ruschemeyer, and Alexander Gershenkron. *Economic Backwardness in Historical Perspective*. Cambridge, MA: Harvard University Press, 1962.

Smith, Adam. *An Inquiry into the Nature and Causes of the Wealth of Nations*, 6th ed. London: Strahan, 1791.

Snow, David A., E. Burke Rochford, Jr., Steven K. Wordon, and Robert D. Benford. "Frame Alignment Processes, Micromobilization, and Movement Participation." *American Sociological Review* 51 (1986): 464–81.

Sorensen, Elaine. "Measuring the Pay Disparity Between Typically Female Occupations and Other Jobs: A Bivariate Selectivity Approach." *Industrial and Labor Relations Review* 42 (July 1989): 624–39.

Springborg, Robert. *Mubarak's Egypt: Fragmentation of the Political Order.* Boulder, CO: Westview Press, 1989.

Srinivasan, T.N. "Challenges of Economic Reform in Egypt." Stanford University Center for International Development, Working Paper No. 253, September 2005.

Stark, R. and W.S. Bainbridge. *A Theory of Religion*. New York: P. Lang, 1987.

Stiglitz, Joseph E. *Globalization and its Discontents*. New York: W.W. Norton, 2002.

Sullivan, Dennis and Sana Abdel-Kotob. *Islam in Contemporary Egypt: Civil Society vs. the State*. Boulder, CO: Lynne Reinner Publishers, 1999.

Bibliography 187

Tae Kim, Yun. "Neoliberalsim and the Decline of the Developmental State." *Journal of Contemporary Asia* 29, no. 44 (1999): 441–61.

Tawfiq Ibrahim, Hassanein. *The Political Economy of Economic Reforms.* Cairo: Center for Political and Strategic Studies, 1999.

Tignor, Robert. *Modernization and British Colonial Rule in Egypt 1882–1914.* Princeton, NJ: Princeton University Press, 1966.

_____. *State, Private Enterprise and Economic Change in Egypt: 1918–1952.* Princeton, NJ: Princeton University Press, 1984.

Tilly, Charles. *From Mobilization to Revolution.* Reading, MA: Addison-Wesley, 1978.

UNDP. *Egypt Human Development Report: Choosing our Future: Toward a New Social Contract.* Cairo: UNDP, 2005.

USA Embassy in Cairo. *Economic Trends Report.* Cairo: Embassy of the United States of America, 2006.

Van Der Lippe, Tanja and Liset Van Dijik."Comparative Research on Women's Employment." *Annual Review of Sociology* 28 (2002): 221–41.

Vatikiotis, P.J. *The History of Modern Egypt: From Muhamed Ali to Mubarak.* Baltimore: John Hopkins University Press, 1991.

Wade, Robert. *Governing the Market: Economic Theory and the Role of Government in East Asian Industrialization.* Princeton, NY: Princeton University Press, 1990.

Wahba, Murad Magdi. *The Role of the State in the Egyptian Economy: 1945–1981.* Reading, UK: Ithaca Press, 1994.

Walsh, John. "Egypt's Muslim Brotherhood: Understanding Centrist Islam." *Harvard International Review* 24, no. 4 (2004): 32–35.

Waterbury, John. *The Egypt of Nasser and Sadat: The Political Economy of Two Regimes.* Princeton, NJ: Princeton University Press, 1983.

Weber, M. *The Protestant Ethic and the Spirit of Capitalism,* translated by Talcott Parsons, London: Allen & Unwin, 1930.

Wheelock, Keith. *Nasser's New Egypt: A Critical Analysis.* New York: Praeger, 1960.

Wickham, Carrie Rosefsky. *Mobilizing Islam: Religion, Activism and Political Change in Egypt.* New York: Columbia University Press, 2002.

World Bank. *Governance and Development.* Washington, D.C.: World Bank, 1992.

World Bank. *Engendering Development through Gender Equality in Rights, Resources and Voices.* New York: Oxford University Press, 2001.

World Bank. *World Bank Report 2001.* Statistical Appendix, Washington D.C.: World Bank, 2001.

188   Bibliography

World Bank: World Debt Tables. Debt and International Finance Division, Washington D.C., 1993.

Zakaria, Fareed. "The Rise of Illiberal Democracy." *Foreign Affairs* 76, no. 6 (November–December 1997), http://www.foreignaffairs.org/19971101faessay3809/fareed-zakaria/the-rise-of-illiberal-democracy.html (accessed 16 November 2008).

Zald, Mayer N. and John D. McCarthy. *Social Movements in an Organizational Society.* New Brunswick: Transaction Books, 1987.

Index

1919 Revolution, 105
1952 Revolution, 71, 83
'Abbas, Khedive, 66
Abd al-Nasser, Gamal, 19, 23, 37, 71;
    assassination attempt, 73
'Abd al-Ra'uf, 'Abd al-Mun'im, 108
'Abd al-Raziq, Sheikh Ali, 106
al-Afghani, Jamal al-Din, 102
agriculture, 9, 26; exports, 27
al-Ahram Beverages, 81
al-Ahram Center for Political and
    Strategic Studies, 45
Alexandria Stock Exchange, 49
Alexandria Tire Company (Trenco),
    50
allies, 38
Amin, Qasim, 102, 143
Ammoun Hotel, 50
Anglo-Ottoman Convention (1838),
    27
Arab–Israeli War: 1948, 70, 107; 1967,
    37, 76, 112; 1973, 20. *See also* Israel
Arab nationalism and independent
    development, 108–11
Arab Socialist Union, 37, 75, 77,
    78, 112
arrests of Muslim Brothers, 73
Asia, 17
Asian financial crises (1997, 1998), 43
assassination of Anwar Sadat, 77

Assembly of Delegates, 14, 63
Asyut, 48
Asyut Cement, 81
authoritarianism: regimes, 9
authoritarianism (1952–76), 71–77
autonomy: of social forces, 18; state, 7,
    14, 24, 71–77
Axis powers, 32
al-Azhar *ulama* (religious clergy), 25
al-Azhar University, 111, 145

Badrawi, Husam, 84
Bangladesh, 90
bankruptcy, 28, 64
al-Banna, Hasan, 108
Banque Misr, 29
Basha, Hasan Abu, 118
Beni-Suef, 48
El-Biblawy, Hazem, 145
Bible, 88
Bonaparte, Napoleon, 61, 98
border wars, 26
bourgeoisie, 54
BrettonWoods Institutions, 19
bribery, 36
British Camel and Labor Corps, 67
British Commissioner, 65
British Embassy Oriental Counselor,
    110

189

190   Index

British High Commissioner, 32
British invasion of Egypt, 61–65
British rule of Egypt, 28
budget deficits, 41
bureaucratic elite, 76
Bush, George W., 83
business elite, power of, 1

Cairo Stock Exchange, 49
Calvinist doctrines, 88
Camp David Accords, 79
capital growth, 41
capitalism, 54; return to, 76
capitalist class, emergence of
    (1976–91), 77–80
Capital Market Authority, 49
capital markets, 21; development of,
    58
cement, 81
Central Security Forces, 117
childcare services, 134
Children of the Alley, 120
China, 19, 90; role of state, 22; Transi-
    tion Crisis theory, 95
Christian countries, 90
civil society organizations, 60
Civil War (United States), 62
Clash of Civilizations, The, 96
classes, working, 9
colonial economic structures, gender,
    131
Colonial period, Transition Crisis the-
    ory, 95
commercial navy, 27
commodity boards, 26
compensation, gender inequalities,
    125
conflicts, 6, 83
consequences for democracy, 9
Constantinople, 61
constitution: 1956, 74; 1964, 75
Constitutional Court, 141
Constitutionalist Party, 66
Constitutional Reform Party, 66, 104
consumer price index (CPI), 47

consumption, demand for, 57
Cooper, Mark, 115
Copts, 118
corporate taxes, 49
Corrective Revolution (1971), 77
corruption, 36
cotton, 27; crisis of (1906-1907),
    103–108; demand for during U.S.
    Civil War, 62; production (1913),
    65; reduced demand for, 28; Sudan,
    67; women's involvement in pro-
    duction of, 143
coup (1952), 31
Credit Agricole, 29
crises: primary-product export
    strategies, 103–108; Transition cri-
    sis, Islam as state ideology, 112–121
Crisis Explanation, religion and the,
    92–94
Cromer, Lord, 65
crops, export, 27. *See also*
    agriculture
cruise ships, attacks on, 119

Damietta, 48
dams, 62
debt, 28, 40; foreign, 63, 80
deficits, budgets, 41
demand: for consumption, 57; for
    products, 128
democracy: classification of, 59; con-
    sequences for, 9; development,
    53–54, 80–85; power relations,
    8–10; promotion of, 9; relation-
    ship between development and,
    54–61; Relative Class Power
    Model of Democratization, 8;
    religion and the Crisis Explana-
    tion, 93; requirements of, 55;
    survival of, 58
demonstrations, 46
deposits, 40
depressions, 28
development: of capital markets, 58;
    of democracy, 53–54, 80–85;

economic, 90; gender and, 123. *See also* gender; intervention of the state, 6; and nationalism, 108–11; power relations in, 5–6; relationship between democracy and, 54–61; relationship between religion and, 10–11; religion's impact on, 88–90; role of the state in, 17–58; state and, 19–25; state-led Nasserist experiments (1952–70), 30–37; strategies and gender inequalities, 130–33; theoretical approaches, 88–95

al-Din, Khalid Muhi, 72

discrimination, gender, 150. *See also* gender

disobedient *(nashiz),* 139

dissolution of the Egyptian–Syrian Union (1961), 35

distribution, land, 81

divorces, 139, 140; gender. *See* gender; unilateral divorce *(khula),* 151

downsizing, labor, 45

earnings, gender inequalities, 125

East Asia, 17; Transition Crisis theory, 95

Economic Commission of Latin America, 20

economic development, 90; gender inequalities, 127

economic liberalization, 115; 1974–91, 37–41

Economic Organization, 34

Economic Reform and Structural Adjustment Program (ERSAP), 42, 48

economic reform policies (1991–2005), 41–48

economy: crises (1960s), 36; liberalization process, 1, 2; power, 3; relations and, 6–8

education, 51, 91; affect of religion on, 89; occupations, women in, 148; public, 76;

traditional primary level school *(kuttab),* 98; women, 143

Egypt: British invasion of, 61–65; as a developmental state, 52; gender relations and development in, 135–58; as a hybrid regime, 85

Egyptian Demographic and Health Survey of the year 2000 (EDHS 2000), 146

Egyptian Embassy, terrorist attacks on, 119

Egyptian Family Code, 139

Egyptian Feminist Union (EFU), 138

Egyptianization Law (1947), 29

Egyptian Pepsi Cola Company, 81

Egypt Socialist Party, 77

elections, 70, 83; 1981, 117

elite, 2, 3. *See also* power; bureaucratic, 76; industrial elite, emergence of (1923–52), 65–71; landowners, 29; Turkish-Circassian, 101

El-Laithy, Heba, 150

El Najjar, 81

empirical evidence, religion's affect on development, 90–94

employment, 36

Ersson, Svante, 59

Ethiopia, 119

Evans, Peter, 6

Executive Committee, 73

exports: agriculture, 27; cotton, 65; growth phases, 5; petroleum, 40; restrictions on, 67

failure of the developmental state, 27

Family Budget Survey (1996), 44

family laws, 135–41

Faruk, King, 68, 108

fascist parties, 31

Federation of Egyptian Industries, 29, 34

female. *See* gender

fertility: affect of religion on, 89; rates, 123, 124

feudalism, 32, 71, 145

192　Index

First World War, 28, 61, 65, 104, 105
Five Year Plan, 34
food riots (1977), 115
foreign aid, 43
foreign debt, 63, 80
foreign direct investment, 43
foreign investment, attracting, 38
freedom of speech, 60
free markets, reliance on, 27–28
Free Officers, 31, 71, 108; industrial-
　ization, 144
free trade rules, 31
free zone investments, 39
Fu'ad, King, 68, 106
Fuda, Farag, 118
fundamentalism, religious, 97

gender, 123; development in Egypt,
　135–58; inequalities, 123–30; and
　poverty, 149–52; power, 12–16; role
　of state, 130–35
General Authority for Investment,
　49
General Authority for Real Estate
　Finance, 49
globalization, 57, 58; religion's affect
　on, 93
governance, 56
grants, 40
Gross Domestic Output, 44
Gross Domestic Product (GDP), 30,
　35, 39; growth, 44
groups, Islamist, 87
growth, 17; capital, 41; Gross Domes-
　tic Product (GDP), 44; high rates
　of (1975–85), 39; role of state and,
　24; in the 1960s, 36
Gulf War (1991), 41

Haykal, Muhammad Hasanayn, 116
health insurance system, 51
hegemony, 8; economic, 75; power of
　groups, 18

High Dam, 34
higher education ministry, 51
Hindess, Barry, 4
history: of liberalism, 61–65; relation-
　ship between capitalism and
　democracy, 56; review of the role
　of state (1805–1952), 25–30
Hong Kong, 90; Transition Crisis
　theory, 95
Hoodfar, Homa, 146
Households Expenditures Survey
　(1999–2000), 48
Households Income, Expenditure
　and Consumption Survey
　(HIECS) of 1999/2000, 150
al-Hudaybi, Hasan, 109
Human Poverty Index, 150
human rights, 56
Husayn, 'Adil, 118

ideologies, 3; power, 4, 10–11; reli-
　gions, 15; Transition crisis, Islam as
　state, 112–21
imperialism, 71
imports: import-substitution indus-
　trialization, 21; of luxury goods,
　40; during the Second World War,
　29
income, gender inequalities, 123–30
India, Transition Crisis theory, 95
industrial elite, emergence of
　(1923–52), 65–71
industrialization, 5; attempts at,
　28–30; Free Officers, 144; import-
　substitution, 21; intervention, 22;
　in South America, 10; success of,
　17
inequalities: development in Egypt,
　135–58; gender, 12, 123–30; role of
　state, 130–35
inflation, 20, 47
infrastructure, investment in, 127
inheritance: gender inequalities, 136;
　of rent contracts, 35

International Monetary Fund (IMF),
1, 19, 42; liberalization programs,
80; reforms under the Nazif cabinet, 50
intervention: industrialization, 22;
state, 14
investments, 7, 57; attracting foreign,
38; incentives, 33; infrastructure,
127; restrictions on foreign direct,
21
iron, 34, 81
irrigation, 26; canals, 62
Islam, 2. *See also* religion; nationalism
and, 95–111; and the role of the
state, 87–88; as state religion, 68;
Transition crisis, Islam as state
ideology, 112–21
al-Islam wa usul al-hukm, 107
Islamic Conference Organization, 97
Islamic Development Bank, 97
Islamic *fiqh* (legal) schools, 12
Islamic law (shari'a), 95, 97
Islamic Republic of Imbaba, 119
Islamic Social Movements (ISMs), 95
Islamism (political Islam), resurgence
of, 95
Islamist extremists (al-Gihad group),
79
Islamist groups, 87
Isma'il, Khedive, 14, 27, 62; exile of,
64
Isma'il, Muhammad Othman, 114
Israel, peace with, 76
Issawi, Charles, 67

Japan, 90
Jehan's Laws, 139
Johnson, Chalmers, 22
joint ventures, 38
judges, female, 141

Kafr al-Dawwar Spinning and Weaving Company, 46
Kamalists, 104

Kamel, Mustafa, 66, 103
Kepel, Gilles, 96
Keynesian policies, 20

labor: downsizing, 45; laws, 38; in
manufacturing sectors, 44
Labor Corps Battalions, 104
Labor Party, 118
Labor Sample Survey (1998), 44
La Caisse de la Dette Publique, 63
land: distribution, 81; Muqabla law
(1871), 62; property rights, 55;
reform, 74, 75
landowners, 9, 29
land reform laws (1952), 33
Lane, Jan-Erik, 59
Latin America, 9, 19; Economic
Commission of, 20; financial
crises (1997, 1998), 43
Law 43 (1974), 38–41
Law 44 (1979), 139
Law 91 (2005), 49
Lawrence, Bruce, 97
laws, 111; divorces, 139; family, 135–41;
gender-related, 134; investment,
43; labor, 38; land reform (1952), 33;
Muqabla (1871), 62; personal status, 135–41; reform, 32;
secularization of personal status,
13; women's rights, 140
layoffs, 46
leftists, 2
legal opinions *(fatawa),* 99
Lewis, Bernard, 96
Liberal Constitutionalists, 106
liberalism: history of, 61–65;
restricted (1923–52), 65–71;
restricted political liberalization
(1976–91), 77–80
liberalization: democracy, 60; economic, 37–41, 115; policies, 23
liberal nationalism, export strategies,
103–108
Liberation Rally, 72, 109
loans, 40

Lower Egypt, 48
Lutheran doctrines, 88
Luxor massacre, 120

Mahalla al-Kubra textile factory
    strikes, 79
Mahfouz, Naguib, 120
al-Mahgub, Rif'at, 118
Malaysia, 90; female workforce, 126;
    Transition Crisis theory, 95
male. *See* gender
Mamluks, 25, 99, 135
manufacturing sectors, labor in, 44
marital rights, 136; divorces, 139
markets: approach to religious plural-
    ism, 90; development of, 58;
    reliance on free markets, 27–28;
    systems, 21
Marxist theories, 53, 88, 89
men, 12–16. *See also* gender
Meridien Hotel, 81
Michelin, 50
middle class, formation of, 36
Middle East, women's roles in, 12
military: annual aid from United
    States, 43; building, 71; history of,
    26
Mills, C. Wright, 4
Milner Commission, 68
Minister of Charitable Endowments,
    116
Misr Group, 34
modernization, 3, 53, 87, 88, 89,
    98–103; integration of women,
    142; theories, 20, 54
Moghadam, Valentine, 146
monopolies, 62, 81; eradication of, 71;
    religious pluralism and, 90; state,
    26
mortality rates, 67
Moser, Caroline, 13, 133
Mubarak, Gamal, 2, 48, 84
Mubarak, Hosni, 1, 2, 116–121; assassi-
    nation attempts on, 119
Muhammad 'Ali, 1, 19, 23, 25; Anglo-

Ottoman Convention (1838), 27;
    control of religious institutions,
    136; liberalism and, 61; moderniza-
    tion and, 98
Muqabla law (1871), 62
murshid (leader), 108
Muslim Brothers. *See* Society of the
    Muslim Brothers
Muslim countries, 90

Naguib, Muhammad, 72, 110
al-Nasr Boilers, 81
Nasser, Gamal Abd al-. *See* Abd al-
    Nasser, Gamal
Nasserists, 2, 15; nationalism and
    independent development,
    108–11; state-led development
    (1952–70), 30–37
National Congress of Popular Forces,
    75
National Council for Motherhood
    and Childhood, 140
National Democratic Party (NDP), 1,
    2, 48, 77; policies, 24
nationalism, 64, 102; 1952–76, 71–77;
    and independent development,
    108–11; and Islam, 95–111
Nationalist Party, 66, 103
nationalization, 33
National Union, 74
navy, commercial, 27
Nazif, Ahmed, 2, 48–51
neoliberalism, 20; emergence of, 55;
    reform agenda of, 48–52; theory,
    18
Non-Aligned Movement, 111
non-governmental organizations
    (NGOs), 83, 140
non-Muslims (the *jizya*), 100
North Sinai, 48
al-Nuqrashi, Mahmud Fahmi, 108

Open Door (liberalization) economic
    policy, 38–40

opposition, restriction of political, 3
Othman, Othman Ahmad, 114
Ottoman army, 25
Ottoman Empire, 61

Pakistan, 90
Palace, 66; liberal and parliamentary system, 70
Pasha, Sa'd Zaghlul, 67, 105
passports, 141
peasants' protests, 47
People's Assembly, 78
People's Party, 66, 104
Permanent Council for the Development of National Production, 32
personal status laws, 135–41; secularization of, 13
personal taxes, 49
petroleum exports, 40
Philippines, female workforce, 126
Pipes, Daniel, 96
pluralism, religion, 90
policies: economic reform policies (1991–2005), 41–48; International Monetary Fund (IMF), 19; Keynesian, 20; National Democratic Party (NDP), 24; neoliberalism, 20; protectionist, 20; redistribution, 21; reform policy papers, 2; state, on gender inequalities, 133–35; welfare, 83; World Bank Policy Research Paper, 19
Policies Committee, 84
Policy Unit, 48
political conflict, 6
political mobilization, use of Islam for, 87
political parties, 60; emergence of (1907–14), 66; formation of, 78
political power, 4
political repression, 57
politicization of religion, 11
polygamy, 138
populist system (1960s), 75

ports, 27
Port Said, 37, 48
post-developmental state, 7
poverty, 1, 36, 44, 47, 48; gender and, 149–52; gender inequalities, 129
power: of business elite, 1; of classes, 18; definition of, 3; democracy, 8–10; gender, 12–16; ideologies, 10–11; regimes, 10; relations, 4–5. *See also* relations; religion, 10–11; state and the economy, 6–8; struggles between classes of elite, 54; theories, 5–6
Prebish, Raoul, 20
pre-colonial economic structures, gender, 131
prices: controls, 42; cotton, 67; deregulation, 47
primary-product export strategies, crisis of, 103–108
principal source *("masdarun ra'isiyun"),* 114
Private Gross Investments, 33
privatization, 1, 20, 80; forcing, 49; of state owned enterprises, 45
production, 36; cotton (1913), 65
professional occupations, women in, 148
Progressive Unionist Party (Tagammu'), 72, 83
proletariat, 54
promotion of democracy, 9
property rights, 55. *See also* land
protectionist policies, 20
Protestant Ethic and the Spirit of Capitalism, The, 88
Protestant ethics, 88
protests, 46, 63; peasants', 47; religion's effect on, 93
Public Debt Fund, 63
public education programs, 76
Public Enterprise Office, 49
public health programs, 35–36
public investment, decline in, 43
public sector, emergence of, 36
public sphere, women in the, 141–49

al-Qa'ida, 98
Qalyub Spinning Factory, 50
Qena, 48
Qur'an, 110

radicalization, 92
railways, 27
real estate, 35, 75
redistribution policies, 21
reform: agenda of neoliberals, 48–52;
    economic reform policies
    (1991–2005), 41–48; land, 74, 75;
    land reform laws (1952), 33; laws,
    32; policy papers, 2
regimes: power relations and, 8–10;
    stability, 7; totalitarian, 56; types
    of, 60
reinternalization phases, 5
relations: of classes, 18; democracy,
    8–10; gender, 12–16; power, 4–5;
    regimes, 10; religion, 10–11; state
    and the economy, 6–8; theories,
    5–6
Relative Class Power Model of
    Democratization, 8
religion: and the Crisis Explanation,
    92–94; development, theoretical
    approaches, 88–95; fundamental-
    ism, 97; ideologies, 15; impact of
    on development, 88–90; Islam as
    state, 68; pluralism, 90; politiciza-
    tion of, 11; power, 10–11;
    Transition Crisis theory, 94–95
religious endowments (awqaf), 99
rent: controls, 75, 82; inheritance of
    contracts, 35
Rentier economy, emergence of
    (1974–91), 37–41
representative (wali), 98
repression, political, 57
resolution of political conflict, 6
restrictions: on cotton exports, 28,
    67; on foreign direct investments,
    21; liberalism (1923–52), 65–71;

political liberalization (1976–91),
    77–80
Revolutionary Command Council
    (RCC), 72, 109
revolutions, 9
rights, women's, 132. See also gender
riots, 42
roles: gender, 12, 137; historical review
    of the role of state (1805–1952),
    25–30; of state in development,
    17–58
Russia, role of state, 22

Sabri, Ali, 113
Sadat, Anwar, 2, 15, 38, 77, 79, 108;
    assassination of, 77, 116–17; Transi-
    tion crisis (1970s), 112–16
Sadat, Jehan, 139
Said, Khedives, 62, 100
Salafiya (fundamentalist) school of
    Islamic modernism, 102
Salama, Ghassan, 96
sanctions, cultural, 149
savings, 7, 57
scientific reasoning, 89
Second World War, 22, 29; export
    crises during, 107; gender inequali-
    ties, 131; hardships because of, 30;
    Transition Crisis theory, 95; Wafd
    Party allies during, 32; Wafd Party
    reaction to, 70
Secret Order, 73
secularism, 97
secularization, 87; of al-Azhar Uni-
    versity, 111; of personal status laws,
    13
September 11, 2001, 43, 98
al-Sharif, Safwat, 119
Sha'rawi, Huda, 138
Sharqiya, 48
Singapore, 90; Transition Crisis the-
    ory, 95
Six Day War (1967), 38
Six Points Program, 31

Smith, Adam, 90, 91
Social Movement Theory, 92
Society of the Muslim Brothers, 71, 72–73, 107; alliance with RCC, 109; personal status laws, 145
socioeconomic strategies, 113
Sohag Governorate, 48, 119
South America, 9; industrialization in, 10
South Asia, 17; Transition Crisis theory, 95
South Korea, 90; female workforce, 126; terrorist attacks on tourists, 119; Transition Crisis theory, 95
South Sinai, 48
Soviet–American détente (1972), 38
Soviet Union, collapse of (1990s), 17
speech, freedom of, 60
stability, 58; regime, 7
state: autonomy, 7, 14, 24, 71–77; councils (shura), 99; and development, 19–25; gender and power relations, 12–16; gender inequalities, role of, 130–135; gender relations, 13; historical review of the role of (1805–1952), 25–30; intervention, 23; Islam, 87–88; monopolies, 26; power relations and, 6–8; role of development in, 17–58; state-led Nasserist experiment (1952–70), 30–37; Transition crisis, Islam as state ideology, 112–21; violence against the, 120; withdrawal of, 27–28
steel, 34, 81
Stephens, Huber, 9, 10
Strategic Economic Trends Report, 45
strikes, 46; Mahalla al-Kubra textile factory, 79
structural adjustment policies, 19; 1991–2005, 41–48
subsidies, elimination of, 51
subsidized fixed-price goods, 47
Sudan, 26; cotton production, 67
Suez, 48; conflict (1956), 111
Suez Canal, 32, 34; reopening of, 114

suicide bombings, 119
supply side approach to religious pluralism, 90
Supreme Guide of the Muslim Brothers, 109
Syria, 26

Tahrir al-mar'a (The Liberation of Women), 143
Taiwan, 90; Transition Crisis theory, 95
Taliban, 119
taxes, 42, 119; corporate, 49; cuts, 49; Muqabla law (1871), 62; personal, 49
technology, 128; occupations, women in, 148
terrorism, 83, 98; radical Islamist groups responsible for, 119
textiles, 65. *See also* cotton; industry, 26; Mahalla al-Kubra factory strikes, 79
Thailand, 90
theories: Marxist, 53, 88; Marxist t, 89; modernization, 20, 54, 88; neoliberal, 18; power relations, 5–6; religion and development, 88–95; Social Movement Theory, 92; Transition Crisis theory, 94–95
third world development, 5–6
Three Year Plan, 34
totalitarian regimes, 56
tourism, 39
tourists, terrorist attacks on, 119
trade rules, 31
traditional primary level school (kuttab), 98
transition crisis theory, 94–95; Islam as state ideology, 112–121
transportation ministry, 51
travel rights, 141
Turkey, 90
Turkish-Circassian elite, 64, 101
types of regimes, 8–10, 60

198　Index

umma (nation), 3, 98
UN Convention on the Elimination
　of All Forms of Discrimination
　Against Women, 133
UNDP Human Development
　Report, 127
unemployment, 20, 45, 104
UNFPA, 140
UNICEF, 140
unilateral divorce *(khul'a)*, 151
United Nations (UN), 13; UN Popula-
　tion Conference (1994), 140; UN
　Women's Conference, 140
United States: Civil War, 62; eco-
　nomic aid to Egypt, 43
Upper Egypt, 48
'Urabi revolt, 15, 28, 64, 65, 101, 104
urbanization, 91
urban renewal, 27

Versailles Peace Conference, 67, 105
violence against the state, 120
Wafd Party, 31, 32, 68, 69, 106; affect
　of rent controls, 82; reaction to
　Second World War, 70
wages, 36

wali (governor), 1
Washington Consensus, The, 17, 47
Waterbury, John, 39
welfare policies, 83
westernization, 96
Wilson, Woodrow, 67
Wilsonian doctrine, 105
women, 12–16. *See also* gender; in the
　public sphere, 141–49; in the work-
　force, 148
working class, 9
World Average Annual Per Capita
　Gross Domestic Product, 19
World Bank, 1, 15; financing the High
　Dam, 34; gender and poverty, 149;
　liberalization programs, 80; poli-
　cies, 19; Policy Research Paper, 19;
　survey (1995), 48
world *(umma)*, 3, 98
Yemen War (1963–67), 37
Young Egypt, 31
Youth Organization, 114

zakat (alms), 107
Zeid, Nasr Abu, 120